Other Titles in the Psychology of Series

THE
PSYCHOLOGY
OF DEXTER

EDITED BY BELLA DePAULO, PhD

WITH LEAH WILSON

AN IMPRINT OF BENBELLA BOOKS, INC.

Dallas, TX

Smart Pop is an Imprint of BenBella Books, Inc.
10300 N. Central Expy., Suite 530
Dallas, TX 75231
www.benbellabooks.com
www.smartpopbooks.com
Send feedback to feedback@benbellabooks.com

Printed in the United States of America
10 9 8 7 6 5 4 3

Library of Congress Cataloging-in-Publication Data is available for this title.
ISBN 978-1-935251-97-2

Copyediting by Erica Lovett and Stephanie Fingleton
Proofreading by Gregory Teague and Stacia Seaman
Cover design by Sammy Yuen, Jr.
Text design and composition by PerfecType, Nashville, TN
Printed by Lake Book Manufacturing

Distributed by Perseus Distribution
http://www.perseusdistribution.com/

To place orders through Perseus Distribution:
Tel: (800) 343-4499
Fax: (800) 351-5073
E-mail: orderentry@perseusbooks.com

Significant discounts for bulk sales are available. Please contact Glenn Yeffeth at glenn@benbellabooks.com or (214) 750-3628.

TABLE OF CONTENTS

INTRODUCTION:

FOR THE LOVE

OF DEXTER

BELLA DePAULO

*D*exter may well be one of the most psychologically delicious treats in television history. We love Dexter. We root for him, season after season.

But he's a *killer*—a *serial* killer! Why do we relish Dexter so much? And why don't we at least feel guilty about our love? Is it because Dex is so unlike us that we don't worry others might misinterpret our interest in him as a sign of our own darkness? Or is the dynamic something much different—that we all have a wisp of Dex's Dark Passenger within us? As fans who identify with our twisted hero, do we get to let our own demons out to play an hour a week, knowing that it's not for real and no one will actually get hurt?

1

I've tried to talk about *Dexter* to all sorts of people. Some I just know will be interested. They are the people who read true crime books and watch other murder-filled movies and TV shows. What stuns me, though, is when I discover, time and again, that *Dexter* has resonated with people who simply don't fit that mold. What is it about the hero and the show that is so powerful?

Dexter is a feast for the psychologically-minded. Watching him, we realize—maybe in a way we never have before—what makes us human. We all feel things. We read other people effortlessly and intuitively. We reach out to fellow humans. We *want* to connect to them and to nurture those connections. That's so obviously what we do that we don't need to think about it.

But what if none of that came naturally? That's one of the most tantalizing questions posed by *Dexter*. Sure, it's fun to think about murderers and psychopaths and what makes them tick. But we've probably all pondered that at times. In your life before Dexter, though, did you ever consider what it would take to pass as an ordinary human if you didn't have the same feelings and needs and desires as everyone around you?

The show is seeded with tiny bursts of surprise and delight, as Dexter fumbles the most ordinary human reactions and mangles routine social interactions. Then we're charmed in an entirely different way when Dexter says or does exactly the right thing, even when we know he's just faking it or mimicking someone else.

Season after season, the writers of *Dexter* address some of the most profound questions about human behavior. For example: What determines who we are and who we become? We are all products of genetic roulette, but no self-respecting scientist believes in genetic determinism. We inherit tendencies, but our environments, including the important people in our lives, shape those inclinations.

Some of the most pessimistic predictions in the writings of psychologists are about psychopaths. For a long time, the prevailing view was that little could be done to set them on a constructive life path. More recently, though, that perspective has been challenged, including by a number of the contributors to this book.

You will find among these chapters the argument that Harry really blew it with Dexter. He thought Dex was doomed to a lifetime of irresistible impulses to kill—but he was wrong. He could have guided Dex in an entirely different direction. Maybe Dex is not a full-blown psychopath after all but merely has psychopathic tendencies.

Harry had the opportunity to shepherd his foster son while Dexter was still young. To many psychologists, those early years are the crucial ones, especially for children whose little lives have already been so sodden with trauma. The Dexter we fans see is an adult. Is there still hope for him at this (psychologically) late date? That's another question addressed in this book.

Dexter has had his angels. Camilla and Rita were there for him in seasons past, and Deb has been there all along. From psychological research and theory we know what these people could do in order to draw Dexter away from his homicidal urges. Eventually we will see if Deb, building on the work that Camilla and Rita have already done, will succeed.

Another fundamental question addressed by the writers of *Dexter* concerns the nature of evil. Should we think of Dexter as evil because he kills people, or is he redeemed by his choice of victims? There are so many nefarious characters on the show: the criminals Dexter targets; the murderers without a code who are hunted down by the justice-seekers of Miami Metro; the men such as Miguel who tread on one side of the legal line in their public life but descend into atrocity in private; the crazed characters such as Lila; and the despicable ones, like Paul. We can rank order the wickedness of their demonic deeds, can't we?

Maybe. But some of the contributors to this collection will shake your assumptions. Do you think Dexter is way better than Paul? That Paul was abusive but Dex was not? Gong! Maybe you're wrong. Do you think that the certifiable psychopaths are the scariest of criminals? You will find within these pages an argument that it is the most ordinary among us who have the potential to inflict the greatest harm.

Even before I read all of the other chapters in this book, I found myself questioning my initial impressions of Dexter as I wrote my chapter on his deceptions. Dexter, I would begin to say, doesn't worry much about getting caught, the way other humans do. But then I'd remember instances in which Dexter did seem apprehensive. Same for his emotions. I'd start out thinking he has no real feelings for other people, only to recognize that he did develop what looked like genuine caring for Deb and Camilla and Rita and the kids. Dexter, it turns out, has evolved over the course of the series. That's not just good television—that's damned good psychology.

The other contributors concur. One after another noted that the portrayal of Dexter and the people around him is right on target—it's psychologically real.

That left me reminding myself that Dexter is a creation. He came out of the mind of Jeff Lindsay, author of *Darkly Dreaming Dexter,* and the minds of all of the subsequent writers who shaped Dexter into the lovable murderer, colleague, partner, friend, brother, and father that we see on screen. And what a set of minds that is! Together, they've crafted one of the most psychologically rich heroes on television, and the essays you're about to read will help you appreciate just how complex and well-written Dexter and *Dexter* really are.

After watching just the first few episodes, I thought I had a pretty good sense of what this Dexter character was all about. Not too interested in sex. Not very emotional. Eerily dispassionate about blood. None of those infamous delusions of grandeur we expect serial killers to have. He's a killer, sure. But he's a killer with a cause. Dexter snuffs out human lives, but it's not for his own satisfaction, sexual or otherwise. He's making the world a safer place. He's doing it for us. I don't usually like to be wrong, but reading Jared DeFife's essay and having my initial assumptions pulled apart, limb by limb, was a delight.

PREDATOR ON THE PROWL

Is Dexter a Psychopathic, Organized Sexual Sadist?

JARED A. DeFIFE

D exter Morgan. America's favorite serial killer. We're charmed by the man in the emotional mask and even more curious to find out what's underneath it. How do we get inside his head (without using a sixteen-inch carbon steel bone saw)? While Dexter's ever-present voiceover is an excellent entrée to his inner thoughts, even Dexter isn't always quite sure what makes Dexter tick.

Behavioral scientists and law enforcement officials have spent decades attempting to understand and classify serial killers: their motivations, their methods, their personalities. But no two serial killers are exactly alike. They run the gamut from the psychotically disorganized—such as David Berkowitz, who claimed that his involvement with a Satanic cult and orders from a demon-possessed neighbor's dog led him to terrorize

New York City through a series of impulsive fatal shootings—
to the cold and calculating—such as Theodore Kaczynski, who
resigned from a prominent university position and sent bombs
to academics and airlines.

Despite the range of ritual and motivation among serial killers, the work of mental health professionals and criminologists
investigating serial homicides can still help shed some light on
Dexter and his dark secrets. Unlike the delusional visionary
killer acting on orders from a hallucination, or the mission-oriented killer seeking to change society through flagrant displays
of violence, Dexter would be classified as a particularly rare and
exceptionally dangerous type of serial killer known as a "lethal
predator." Like a predator on the prowl, these killers are efficient and organized:

> They are deliberate, sadistic, and often highly intelligent.
> Their crimes tend to be carried out in a ritualistic manner,
> have a strong sexual component, and often involve rape or
> torture. They are hunters. They plan, then pursue, charm,
> capture, torture, and kill their prey . . . They lack feelings of
> guilt or remorse. Their violence and cruelty typically escalate
> over time, driven by fantasies that feed their predatory nature
> and lead them to compete with themselves in a twisted game
> of "practice makes perfect."[1]

It's fitting that our first introduction to Dexter had him prowling
the streets of Miami, telling us, "Tonight's the night. And it's going
to happen. Again and again it has to happen" ("Dexter," 1-1).

A lethal predator has the callous remove of a psychopath and
is meticulously efficient in committing multiple acts of sexual or

---

[1] Ochberg, F. M., A. C. Brantley, R. D. Hare, P. D. Houk, R. Ianni, E. James,
M. E. O'Toole, and G. Saathoff, "Lethal Predators: Psychopathic, Sadistic, and
Sane" in *Profilers: Leading Investigators Take You inside the Criminal Mind*, 2004.

sexually symbolic violence. But is that really our Dexter? We'll look at each of these qualities and see how Dexter fits the mold of a psychopathic, organized, and sexually sadistic serial killer.

Psychopathy: Dexter's Disconnect

The term "psychopath" is used rather frequently. On the one hand, we jump to using it for just about anyone who has committed some heinously violent crime; on the other, we might use it to describe some jerk who cuts us off in traffic, a boss who has slighted us, or an ex-lover who has jilted us. The term conjures images of some deranged nutcase busted out of his loony-bin straitjacket and on the run from the law.

Psychopathy, however, is not just about the bad things people do (which is an aspect of psychopathy known as *antisocial behavior*), but is also about a particular set of personality traits that includes emotional shallowness, superficial charm, impulsivity with poor judgment, deceitfulness, unreliability, manipulation, and disregard for the feelings of others. Psychopathy is frequently, but not always, associated with criminal behavior. Not all criminals, not even all murderers, are psychopaths. The man who murders his wife in a crime of jealous passion is generally without the remorselessness and emotional emptiness seen in psychopaths. Furthermore, these same psychopathic traits can sometimes even be used in healthy and adaptive ways. A car salesman, for example, offers a valuable product, but he might need to rely on natural charm and manipulation skills to be successful on the job and wouldn't get by very well if he lost sleep every time he bilked an unassertive customer out of a few extra bucks.

Dexter's most prominent psychopathic features are his impoverished emotional life, his lack of remorse or guilt, and the way he masks that through deception and superficial charm. From the very beginning of the series, Dexter has told us that he doesn't have feelings about anything at all and is a well-studied faker of human interactions. He doesn't understand or experience conventional expressions of love, sexuality, comfort, grief, humor, or remorse.

At the same time, Dexter is exceptionally charming. He brings donuts, is quick with a compliment, and lends a (seemingly) sympathetic ear to others. He's a model coworker. Dexter has pulled a fast one on the Miami homicide department, but he isn't the only psychopath to get one over on coworkers involved with law enforcement. In the 1970s, crime writer Ann Rule began work with the police department on a series of then-unsolved murders of young women in Washington state. Rule was later shocked to learn that the man arrested in 1975 and convicted of those crimes was Ted Bundy, someone she had befriended while working alongside him for years on the same crisis counseling hotline.[2] More recently, Eric Harris happily charmed workers in his juvenile justice rehabilitation program into believing he was repentant for a minor theft and a "very bright young man . . . likely to succeed in life," while at the same time compiling bombs and guns for a planned murder spree at Columbine High School.[3]

Like many psychopaths, Dexter not only justifies his crimes as necessary but can also play upon them in such a way as to elicit sympathy for his own victimization. Serial killer John Wayne Gacy described himself as a victim, cheated out of a childhood and left to wonder if "there would be someone, somewhere who would understand how badly it hurt to be John Wayne Gacy."[4] When Dexter confessed to the group at Narcotics Anonymous about the pain and confusion from his Dark Passenger, was it genuine revelation, or a great performance? When

---

[2] Rule, A., *The Stranger Beside Me*, 2000.
[3] Cullen, D., *Columbine*, 2010.
[4] Hare, R. D., *Without Conscience: The Disturbing World of the Psychopaths among Us*, 1999.

dealing with the lies and mask of a psychopath, Dexter told us, "otherwise right-thinking people don't stand a chance" ("Popping Cherry," 1-3). Dexter's charms also work on us, as viewers. He's not only a likable character, but one we feel sympathy for and even cheer on to evade capture.

Dexter can often fake a feeling without actually experiencing it. When it comes to emotions, a psychopath "knows the words, but not the music,"[5] a sentiment that Dexter shared with Lila before killing her. It would be oversimplification, however, to say that psychopaths experience *no* emotions whatsoever. Rather, their emotional reactions are typically more limited and shallow than those of others. Dexter does experience bursts of anger, anxiety about getting caught, curiosity, and even excitement over his kills.

Because their emotional states are so shallow, many psychopaths are driven by short-term rewards and engage in thrill-seeking behavior such as gambling, theft, or physical risk-taking without fear of the consequences. However, the emotional rush that comes from these thrills is limited and rarely lasts long, resulting in increasingly risky behavior to regain that fleeting excitement. The rush that Dexter gets from killing and evading capture is one of his few genuinely emotional experiences, meaning that like a drug addict seeking a fix, he is unlikely to stop for too long. Like other lethal predators, Dexter is able to cover his tracks and even contain his killing impulses when the risks appear to be too great (such as when Sergeant James Doakes was on his tail), but too much restraint leaves him impatient and edgy.

However, Dexter doesn't perfectly match all the traits of psychopathy. For example, he doesn't show the kind of grandiosity

---

[5] Johns, J. H. and H. C. Quay, "The Effect of Social Reward on Verbal Conditioning in Psychopathic and Neurotic Military Offenders," *Journal of Consulting Psychology*, Vol. 26, No. 3 (1962): 217–220.

typically seen in psychopathic individuals. Sure, he's had fantasies of parades being held in his honor, heralding him as a hero, but he is rarely boastful and would much rather blend into the crowd than stick out as the center of attention. He often refers to himself as a monster and seems acutely aware of his human defects and shortcomings. If anything, Dexter could even be seen as somewhat lacking in the self-esteem department. On the other hand, he does show moral grandiosity over his victims, imbuing himself with god-like control over who deserves to live or die, and you can't help but feel he takes pride in the elaborate mask he's constructed to fool everyone.

Also, Dexter is much more reliable than most psychopaths. Psychopathic individuals often wander through life aimlessly, hopping from job to job and relationship to relationship. They will typically bolt at the first sign of conflict or of getting caught in their lies and petty cons. Psychopathic individuals have even been known to have multiple marriages and families *at the same time* in different cities. Their unreliability and willingness to skip town often leave behind a trail of broken hearts and empty bank accounts. But not everyone fits cleanly into distinct psychiatric categories, especially when talking about personality. Dexter holds a steady job that he performs well, and although he has alluded to some quickly abandoned romantic relationships, he maintains relatively stable work and family relationships. So isn't the fact that Dexter is able to maintain these relationships and show caring or even fiercely protective behaviors toward his family and coworkers evidence that he's not a detached and uncaring psychopath? Not entirely. A notable real-life example is Dennis Rader, known as the BTK (Bind-Torture-Kill) killer, who was responsible for systematically stalking and remorselessly slaying ten people. Rader was faithfully married for thirty-three years, raised two children, and held a respectable position in his Lutheran church.

"True enough, psychopaths are sometimes skillful in pretending love for a woman or simulating parental devotion to their children," Dr. Hervey Cleckley wrote in *The Mask of Sanity*, his classic 1941 work on the psychopathic personality. Even if the psychopath is not entirely aware of the shallowness of his or her attachment, Cleckley wrote that this "pseudolove . . . consists in concern for the other person only (or primarily) insofar as it enhances or seems to enhance the self." Dexter's involvement with Rita and her kids fits Cleckley's concept and was initially only a way of keeping up appearances: "I became a husband, a father," he said. "I had to evolve; it was the only way to survive" ("If I Had a Hammer," 4-6).

The world sees dearly devoted Dexter: charming, reliable, calm, and caring. But underneath the emotional mask is still the mind of a detached, deceptive, and deadly psychopath—albeit one who fits somewhat uncomfortably within the traditional mold.

Pass the Shrink Wrap, Please: The Organized Homicidal Offender

Killing people and keeping your day job is no easy task. These things take forethought, planning, and organization. As a forensic expert, Dexter knows that it's all about the details. Serial homicide offenders are commonly distinguished into the categories of disorganized and organized. Disorganized offenders lack discipline and planning, often striking their victims in sudden blitz attacks. They are not smooth operators; they depersonalize their victims, don't talk much, and leave behind messy crime scenes. The attacks of a disorganized offender bear hallmark characteristics of rage and fury, often showing escalating brutality with each kill. Despite a common fantasy of Jack the Ripper as a polished elite London aristocrat, the Whitechapel murders were actually very, very messy, reflecting the characteristics of a disorganized offender. The Ripper's victims were targets of relative convenience, prostitutes vulnerable to sudden attacks in the night. He took no particular care at selecting victims, killed in the open, made no efforts to hide the bodies, and left behind weapons at the crime scene. The Ripper murders were particularly grisly, characterized by evisceration, facial/genital mutilation, and removal of organs. The emotional ups and downs of mood disorders and psychosis are more prominent in disorganized offenders than the even-keeled emotional detachment of a psychopath.

Dexter, on the other hand, is an organized offender who can appreciate a clean crime scene. Organized offenders are typically knowledgeable about law enforcement procedures and actively follow or try to become involved with police investigations. This allows them not only to become more efficient in evading capture but also gives the satisfaction of outwitting their potential captors. Trained by a respected cop, Dexter takes this one step further by actually working for law enforcement.

Even outside of his crimes as a serial killer, Dexter likes to keep his personal and professional lives almost obsessively tidy. He pays attention to the details and puts a premium on cleanliness. So how could someone so neat and clean be so fascinated with something as dirty as blood? Dexter's obsession with and aversion to blood fits within a pattern known as *reaction formation*, a pattern commonly seen in overly organized people. Individuals showing exaggerated reactions of disinterest, disgust, or moral indignation with taboo or forbidden things are often implicitly fascinated or excited by the objects of their conscious disaffection. A young boy who is nervous and embarrassed about a girl he likes creates a reaction formation by instead being extra mean to her at school. Men with exaggerated fears of homosexuality actually tend to show increased physical signs of sexual arousal when shown video of homosexual intercourse, despite expressing negative views about it. And how many times has a preacher or politician with a reputation for vocal and repeated condemnations of the sins of sex and pornography been exposed as a pedophile or been caught with a prostitute? Born in blood, Dexter is both fascinated with and repulsed by the stuff. He studies blood, samples it, has pictures of it on his office wall, and even collects it. On the other hand, he fetishistically admired the Ice Truck Killer's ability to remove all the blood from his victims and fell into a nauseous panic when confronted with a hotel room full of it.

Dexter's killing methods reflect his high levels of organization. Like many organized serial homicide offenders, Dexter's methods are planned in advance. He identifies a targeted victim, collects information about the victim, prepares or transports his victim to an isolated and controlled crime scene, subdues his victim, and takes pains to avoid detection. He dresses in black, wears gloves, uses a chemical injection, and brings his own prepared kit of tools. His use of shrink wrap is extensive (highlighting his thorough nature) but practical. Other than the cut on the cheek and the killing blow, the mutilation of the bodies of his victims is also more about the business of disposal than it is about pleasure. With meticulous attention to detail, Dexter carefully works to improve his methods for avoiding detection with each kill. Practice makes perfect.

Dex, Sex, and Sadism

Dexter has the callous remove of a psychopath and the clean efficiency of an organized homicide offender. But how does the satisfaction of the kill come into play? To match the profile of a lethal predator, an offender must commit multiple acts of sexual violence. Lethal predators are sexual sadists who achieve emotional and/or physical arousal and release through inflicting pain and degradation on others. Surely this can't be Dexter, right? He doesn't even like sex. Well, not conventionally, at least. Dexter's sexual impulses are connected to violence and satisfied through the act of killing.

Dexter doesn't seem to have much use for sex, but he's not completely uninterested or impotent. His sexual arousal pops up at unusual times, however, and hints of sadism appear in those rare moments when sex does come into the picture. Dexter's first sexual moment with Rita came when he was talking about his admiration for the Ice Truck Killer's methods. As he demonstrated the killer's characteristic cuts and dismemberments, he got swept up and caressed Rita's leg. When she recoiled, he was left wondering about the advance. Their first time having sex happened when Dexter rushed to her following a therapy session during which he uncovered suppressed memories of his mother's brutal murder. Doakes suspected Dexter of getting a hard-on when demonstrating at a crime scene how Jeremy Downs slashed a major artery on his victim with every cut. And later, Lila discovered some of Dexter's taste for aggressive sex.

While only hints of violent tendencies come to the surface in Dexter's sex life, his killing ritual has numerous similarities with homicides committed by sexually sadistic killers. As opposed to other homicide offenders, sexually sadistic killers incorporate rigidly scripted rituals in their crimes. The emotionally charged thrill of the kill comes from completing these rituals (also known as a "signature"), which they will work to recreate and perfect over time. Dexter tells us that his "ritual is intoxicating" ("Dexter," 1-1), and his kills are thoroughly infused with sexual symbolism and physical excitement even without any obvious sexual enactment on his victims.

"In analyzing sexual motivation," Ochberg et al. wrote, "it should be noted that predators may find sexual gratification in activities that most people would find nonsexual, such as the infliction of pain, mutilation, or postmortem display of the body and collection of trophies." Sexual sadism is about gaining satisfaction through the exertion of power or control over another. Restraint, humiliation, dominance, and intimidation are the weapons of a sexual sadist. Killers seeking political or ideological justice tend to gravitate toward impersonal methods such as bombs (for example, the Oklahoma City bomber Timothy McVeigh, or George "the Mad Bomber" Metesky, who took to bombing Con Edison and New York City after he lost his job in an industrial accident) or execution-style shootings. Dexter's methods, however, are more up close and personal. If he were simply trying to bring justice to wrongdoers or clean up the streets, he is very capable of both subduing his victims and quickly dispatching them. But he doesn't. After capturing his victims, Dexter strips them naked, binds them, waits for them to awaken, confronts them with evidence of their crimes, and kills them while they remain conscious.

The thrill of the kill doesn't end for Dexter when the blood stops shedding, but continues past the last drop. Like many organized sexual homicide offenders, Dexter collects trophies from his victims. A killer's trophies, like Dexter's box of slides, are typically kept in the killer's home or in an accessible place where the killer can revisit them to relive the excitement of their crimes. Sexual offenders often maintain close physical proximity with their victims' remains, either through cannibalistically consuming their flesh, keeping bodies in their homes, or by revisiting their body dump sites. Jeffrey Dahmer's apartment contained a nightmarish collection of body parts at the time of his arrest, and Ted Bundy kept the heads of several of his victims in his home before burying them at Taylor Mountain, a site he would revisit for hours at a time. Similarly, Dexter revisits his victims in calm spans of slack tide aboard his boat, the *Slice of Life*.

Harry taught Dexter to channel his sadistic impulses toward inflicting pain only on those who inflict pain on others. In reality, the Code of Harry is simply window dressing on darkly driven impulses. Dexter's true killing motivation is satisfaction, a satisfaction that comes from subjugation, humiliation, and torture of his victims: the hallmarks of a sexual sadist.

———

Dexter Morgan. Family man. Forensic specialist. Psychopathic, organized, sexual sadist. It's complicated. Under the bright light of the Miami sun, everything seems so festive and safe. But there's a lethal predator on the prowl out there, and the night is coming. And it's going to happen. Again and again, it has to happen . . .

Jared DeFife, PhD, is a clinical psychology research scientist at Emory University and associate director of the Laboratory of Personality and Psychopathology (www.psychsystems.net). A former clinical fellow at Harvard Medical School, he earned his master's and doctoral degrees in clinical psychology from Adelphi University.

Dr. DeFife specializes in the study of personality, mood disorders, and psychotherapy. He also frequently publishes and teaches on psychodynamic therapy, research methods, media, politics, film, and literature. He serves on the editorial board of the American Psychological Association journal *Psychotherapy: Theory, Research, Practice, Training* and contributes a regular blog to *Psychology Today*. He is currently working on a National Institute of Mental Health–funded investigation of alternative approaches to personality disorder diagnosis for ICD-11 and DSM-V.

What if Harry was all wrong about Dexter? What if Dexter actually wasn't the psychopath that Harry thought he was? And even if Dexter did fit the psychopath description, what if the conventional wisdom about those people is wrong, and they actually can be treated effectively? That's what Lisa Firestone argues in this provocative chapter. Of course, Dexter was seared by his childhood experience of watching his mother get murdered and dismembered, then sitting in a pool of her blood for days. The result, though, was not psychopathy but something else. Other contributors to this anthology make a compelling case for the development of Dexter's humanity over the course of the show. Dr. Firestone notices ways in which it was there even when he was very young. If only someone had noticed. (But then what fun would that be for us fans?)

RETHINKING

DEXTER

LISA FIRESTONE

I n season one, Dexter entered therapy with the purpose of getting close to a homicidal psychologist. When a fellow patient asked him how he liked therapy, Dexter candidly replied, "I'm a sociopath; there's not much he can do for me" ("Shrink Wrap," 1-8). Although he was half kidding, the statement is indicative of what Dexter truly believes about himself. He is convinced that there is no way he can stop his violent urges, and why shouldn't he be? However, there are two problems with Dexter's assumption that he is an incurable psychopath. First, while he exhibits certain destructive characteristics in line with psychopathology, Dexter also exhibits traits that argue strongly against a psychopathic diagnosis. Second, even if

Dexter is a psychopath, it is a common misconception that this diagnosis is untreatable. Despite his insistence that "there's not much he can do for me," I believe Dexter Morgan has been far too hasty in diagnosing himself as a lost cause.

The Misdiagnosis

At first glance many of Dexter's personality traits could be interpreted to be in keeping with a diagnosis of psychopathy. Psychopathic traits are evident in his lack of empathy, his glib and superficial charm, and his emotional disregard for his victims. However, Dexter's other diagnosable symptoms, such as social awkwardness in intimate relationships and a lack of sex drive, diverge from the picture of a classic psychopath who is casual and calloused in personal and romantic relationships and quite often promiscuous. Where the typical psychopath enjoys excessive flirtation, Dexter avoids flirtatious encounters, as they make him extremely uncomfortable. In the pilot episode, when a policewoman flirted with Dexter by putting her hand on his leg, he was noticeably unnerved and moved away from her. While psychopaths engage in dishonesty and duplicity and are often compulsive liars, Dexter is honest and forthcoming and only lies when it is necessary to keep from getting caught. Psychopaths are generally irresponsible in their lives but Dexter is highly organized and responsible in his actions.

Perhaps the most telling sign that Dexter is not a classically incurable psychopath is the fact that he was able to develop an attachment to his adoptive father, Harry, at a young age. In seeking Harry's approval by dutifully following his code and directing his violence toward only killing evil people, Dexter is honoring Harry. When Harry asked young Dexter why he hadn't acted on his urges to kill a person, Dexter answered, "I thought you and Mom wouldn't like it." At that point in Dexter's childhood, his desire to remain in the good graces of his adoptive father outweighed his urge to commit murder. Even Dexter's reason for killing the neighbor's dog was couched in the interest of his family's happiness: the dog was keeping his sick mother awake. Despite Dexter's insistence that he cannot genuinely feel for people, he does everything in his power to keep the people that he *should* care about safe and content.

As an adult, Dexter's growing attachment to Rita and her children over the course of the show has provided further evidence that he is not truly a psychopath. The development of these relationships is a deviation from the typical mold of a psychopath and indicates a trait that most psychopaths cannot possess: an element of caring. While the thoughts of Dexter's Dark Passenger may suggest that he is vacant of such feeling, Dexter's actions show otherwise. For example, the only times Dexter acted violently on impulse, against the Code of Harry, were in instances where he was trying to protect or defend Rita. When her ex-husband became verbally threatening toward Rita in "Seeing Red" (1-10), Dexter responded by hitting him on the head with a frying pan. Dexter surprised himself with this outburst of aggression; it was a behavioral manifestation of the very care that he claims he is unable feel. His actions throughout each season have demonstrated a deepening emotional investment not only in Rita, but also in her children and his sister, Deb. His ability to develop these attachments, even if they lack serious emotional depth, is a sign that Dexter himself is neither a psychopath nor a lost cause.

The Trouble with the Psychopathic Label

When Dexter first began to indulge in violent, destructive behaviors as a child (i.e., killing animals), Harry, a veteran detective, assumed that his son was revealing the early stages of psychopathy. Psychologist David Farrington argues that there is danger in labeling someone as a psychopath at a young age, in large part because research shows that people who exhibit psychopathic traits in childhood tend to gravitate toward the mean later in life. According to studies done by J. F. Edens and M. Cahill, "some transient developmental characteristics that are relatively common to adolescents can be mistaken for long standing adult psychopathy traits." Additionally, there is limited data on whether or not juveniles who demonstrate psychopathic traits will continue to possess these traits in adulthood. For example, it is common for children to experiment with animal cruelty at a young age, but for most this will never extend past sprinkling salt on a snail or putting ants under a magnifying glass; not every child who kills animals will turn into a serial killer.

Children are not born with a sense of right and wrong; however, they arrive in this world with the innate ability to develop the neural circuitry for empathy. Given the proper attachment experiences as they grow up, humans develop empathy. Research shows that a child's cruelty toward animals almost always arises out of an abusive violent family environment. Although Dexter's early years were shaped by such an environment, his adoptive family provided a potentially reparative experience. Research has also demonstrated that interventions such as humane education that focuses on developing empathy toward animals generalizes to empathy for human beings. The National District Attorneys Association suggests, "If we pay attention to children and youth who perform acts of cruelty on animals and take immediate action to stop their behavior, future crimes can be prevented and lives can be saved." Unfortunately, Harry did not stress the inherent wrongness of killing animals, nor did he take action to stop Dexter from acting sadistically toward them. Instead he assumed that Dexter was on an inevitable course of destruction and encouraged him to commit these "small" acts of murder in the hope that it would keep him from harming people, when a more appropriate response would have been to get Dexter psychological help.

The mistake Harry made with Dexter is the same mistake the criminal justice system often makes with psychopathically labeled juveniles. Studies find that juvenile offenders who are categorized as psychopaths receive less therapeutic attention due to the misconception that they are lost causes. However, the MacArthur Violence Risk Assessment study of adults found that "psychopathic patients appear as likely as nonpsychopathic patients to benefit from adequate doses of treatment in violence reduction." Such studies indicate that society is wrong in its view that all that can be done with these people is to lock them up and throw away the keys; research suggests that psychopaths almost always are treatable if they receive intensive therapy for a proper duration of time.

Dr. Randy Borum's research has shown that intensive intervention, with an emphasis on improved interpersonal relationships and increased self-control, reduced the number of additional offenses in juveniles. This treatment helped young people form essential attachments that cut the risk to reoffend in half. Attachments such as these could have ultimately saved Dexter from his fate as a violent criminal. Had he received a proper psychological evaluation and subsequent therapy, Dexter might have been able to overcome the violent tendencies of his youth.

Childhood Trauma and Post-Traumatic Stress Disorder (PTSD)

I propose that the show's implication that Dexter is a psychopath is a misdiagnosis and that, in fact, Dexter is a victim of childhood post-traumatic stress. At the age of five, Dexter experienced the most horrendous type of trauma imaginable. He watched as his mother was brutally murdered and dismembered before his eyes. He was then trapped in a storage container with her corpse for three days, confined to complete darkness and imprisoned in a two-inch thick pool of blood. In the field of trauma, this combination of witnessing a violent murder, losing a primary caretaker, and subsequently being entrapped would be categorized as the worst type of trauma ("big 'T' trauma") and would certainly lead to PTSD. Studies have shown that almost 100 percent of children who witness parental homicide develop PTSD because of the severity of the traumatic event. Research also shows that 80 percent of children who have been imprisoned or rendered immobile in some way, such as being buried alive, tied up, or tortured, develop PTSD. The factors that tend to indicate whether or not a child will develop PTSD after a traumatic event include "the severity of the traumatic event" and "the physical proximity to the traumatic event." Both of these factors were extreme in the case of Dexter. Another factor is the parental reaction to the traumatic event. Harry was greatly impacted by the death of Dexter's mother through his romantic attachment with her and his partial guilt for her death.

In instances of severe trauma, the child disassociates from him/herself and the memory of the event is suppressed. When Dexter first becomes aware in a therapy session of the circumstances surrounding his mother's death, he thinks, "No wonder I felt so disconnected my entire life. If I did have emotions, I'd have to feel this" ("Truth Be Told," 1-11). Although Dexter is supposedly cut off from all human emotions, empathy is the emotion that he seems to most lack and long for. This lack of empathy, which is often cited as evidence of his psychopathy, can be a direct result of childhood PTSD. Childhood trauma has an impact on actual brain development: it can cause serious structural abnormalities in the frontal lobe, known as "the seat of emotion." Brain researchers have found that these abnormalities often result in deep-seated personality deficits such as an inability to be empathetic.

Another characteristic of individuals suffering from PTSD is that they may be prone to aggression and dehumanization in the service of a cause that they find noble. The Code of Harry, which dictates that "killing should serve a purpose, otherwise it's just murder," provides Dexter with the moral justification and righteousness to see his acts of aggression and dehumanization as upholding a noble cause. Therefore, the code had an effect opposite to the one that Harry intended; rather than control Dexter's violence, it may well have perpetuated it.

An additional common symptom of early childhood PTSD is post-traumatic play, in which children repeat themes or aspects of the trauma they experienced. For Dexter, this post-traumatic play was evident at a young age in his killing and dismembering animals. According to the Department of Veteran Affairs, this (or any) type of post-traumatic play does not relieve anxiety. By encouraging Dexter's post-traumatic play with animals in the hope that it would curb his appetite to murder people, Harry only pushed Dexter further down the path toward homicidal violence. Had Harry sought psychological help for Dexter to deal with the underlying trauma instead of allowing him to continually recreate it in his play, he would have provided his son with more constructive guidance.

The Anti-Self: Identifying with the Aggressor

A few important questions remain unanswered: in suffering from PTSD, what exactly happened to turn Dexter into a killer? Where did his Dark Passenger come from? When childhood events are traumatic enough to cause PTSD, children dissociate from themselves as the helpless victim and identify instead with the aggressor. They identify with the very person who is hurting them, who they see as strong and not vulnerable to the type of pain they are experiencing. This is the only survival strategy available to the child. In Dexter's case, he identified with his mother's murderer. This is evident in his homicidal desires and in his literal reenactment of his mother's murder by dismembering each of his own victims. For Dexter, dismemberment likely has significant meaning and is not simply a practical means of disposing of a body. Interestingly enough, Dexter's brother, who also witnessed their mother's murder and became a serial killer, beheads his victims.

From taking on the aggressor's point of view, Dexter is plagued by destructive thoughts telling him to act out violent and sadistic urges. He calls this point of view his Dark Passenger; clinical psychologist and theorist/author Dr. Robert Firestone calls it the "anti-self." Dr. Firestone has identified a division that exists within all of us between our "real self" and the "anti-self." The nature and degree of this division depends a great deal on early life experiences. Most of us are not as destructive as Dexter, but we do engage in behavior that is both self-destructive and other-destructive on a less extreme level. The anti-self is the incorporation of the negative side of the parenting we received: the emotional neglect or abuse, and any other traumatic treatment that we may have experienced. In situations where a parent "loses it" with the child, the child ceases to identify with him/herself as the helpless victim and instead identifies with the all-powerful parent. In this manner, we "take in" our parents during those extremely stressful incidents when they are at their worst. This identification exists as an anti-self that cannot be fully integrated into the personality. As an adult, when we are under pressure or stress, our unintegrated anti-self manifests itself. Then we act out either on ourselves or on others in ways similar to what was done to us.

The core aspect of the anti-self is a "self-parenting" process in which we treat ourselves as we were treated early on, both soothing ourselves and punishing ourselves. Self-parenting, as it is referred to here, is not self-love; rather, it is the self-infliction of the misattunement and mistreatment the child experienced from its early caregiver. The self-soothing behaviors are strategies we employ to relieve anxiety, such as being self-protective or self-indulgent (as in addiction and substance abuse) or having an inflated sense of self-importance. The self-soothing part of Dexter can be seen in his self-sufficiency and the emotional distance he keeps from people, as well as in his self-aggrandizing belief that he should be acknowledged as a hero. It is the most extreme when his Dark Passenger counsels him that he needs the release that committing murder will bring him. In general, the self-punishing behaviors people engage in are more obvious: they take the form of self-attacks, self-denial, and self-harming actions. The self-hating side of Dexter is revealed in his negative internal dialogue and his thoughts that other people would never accept him if they knew the truth about him.

Although we mature into adults and are no longer threatened by the traumatic or painful situations of childhood, we still carry our alien point of view with us. Dexter's reference to his own anti-self as a Dark Passenger is an apt description of how his destructive thought processes act as a companion, traveling beside him and keeping him company, much as they do in all of us to some extent. Although most of us have not undergone the level of trauma that Dexter has and are not as destructive in our behavior as he is, we all experience negative thought processes that direct and control our lives more than we are aware of.

The Critical Inner Voice

Even though Dexter's innermost thoughts are often excessively violent and unfeeling, his inner struggle is an extreme representation of the "anti-self" and a destructive thought process we all have within us, the "critical inner voice." This critical inner voice operates as a dialogue that advises us and defines us in a negative way.

The critical inner voice is a manifestation of the anti-self and develops when the child first identifies with the adult who is frightening him or her. The critical inner voice is defined as a well-integrated pattern of negative thoughts toward self and others that is at the root of an individual's maladaptive behavior. Critical attitudes toward self and others predispose alienation in personal relationships. Our research shows that these negative thoughts, which we refer to as voice attacks, are directly connected to self-destructive acts and acts of violence toward others. From the time Dexter identified with his mother's murderer, he was plagued by destructive thoughts telling him to act out violent and sadistic urges. Dr. Firestone and I contend that persons who dissociate, which Dexter clearly did as a result of his early childhood trauma, are more prone to experience voice attacks that distort their perceptions. Because the voice is not only antithetical to the self but is also hostile and suspicious toward others, these voice attacks can lead individuals to act on wildly sadistic impulses.

Projection of a Parent's Negative Traits

Dexter was raised from a young age by an adoptive father who saw his son's bouts of rage and violent tendencies as a clear indication that Dexter was a psychopath on an inevitable course toward destruction. Because Harry was convinced that Dexter's dark urges would not go away, he decided to "make the best of it" and provided young Dexter with a moral code through which his son could filter his homicidal impulses. However, it is reasonable to wonder whether Harry could have capitalized on Dexter's respect for him and have developed a different moral code, one that didn't allow for murder at all. How much was this code a projection by Harry of his own "vigilante" side, the part of him that acted out revenge and punishment and wanted to be the hero? Harry's drive to be a hero was so strong that it directly contributed to Dexter's mother's murder.

The "dark side" of Harry, his anti-self, prevented him from providing Dexter with the guidance the boy needed. We know from the views that Harry voiced that he had vigilante feelings that justice should be done to violent criminals who had gone unpunished by the legal system. He could not accept this part of himself that longed for vigilante justice, and tried to rid himself of it by sublimating it in his police work and projecting it onto Dexter. He disowned the unacceptable elements of his own character and saw them instead in his adopted son, believing him to be an untreatable monster. The veteran detective even went so far as to use Dexter to act on his behalf to right the wrongs that he identified in the criminal justice system.

This father/son relationship is unusual in that the life lessons Harry provided Dexter with center around homicide; however, an adult offering misguided and destructive advice to a child in the name of parenting can be found in much less extreme examples in everyday life. It is common for parents to project their negative thoughts and desires onto their children. For instance, a mother who still carries feelings of being a "dirty little girl" will punish her child for making messes and label her a "slob." Or a father with deep-seated feelings that his desire for attention is unacceptable will see his affectionate child as needy and demanding. Harry desperately wanted to see revenge enacted upon criminals, and he projected these murderous fixations onto Dexter. We all have internalized elements of our parents that they did not accept in themselves and instead projected onto us.

When Dexter integrated the negative aspects of Harry, he added to and reinforced the development of his already very destructive anti-self. Harry's view of Dexter as an incurable psychopath supported the voice attacks that define Dexter as a murderer and instruct him to commit violent acts. Therefore, Dexter's loyalty to his destructive voices is not only a result of his identification with his mother's murderer but also of Harry's encouragement of Dexter's violent tendencies. After all, it was Harry who gave Dexter the moral code that provided him with the rationalization that "killing should serve a purpose," trained him to become a successful serial killer by teaching him to murder without getting caught, and even dictated his first victim: a nurse who was poisoning her patients and had tried to kill Harry when he was in the hospital because of a heart attack.

Intergenerational Trauma

One of the most powerful and destructive functions of the critical inner voice is to pass on the "Dark Passengers" from one generation to the next. We have seen how this is done when children integrate their parents' aggression toward them during times of great stress, and the anti-self and the critical inner voice are formed. We then see how it is further transferred when parents project their own negative voices and traits onto their children.

In season two, Dexter discovered that Harry had, in large part, been responsible for the murder of his mother. His adoptive father's insistence on following his own moral code and bringing a criminal to justice had led him to be negligent in relation to Dexter's mother and her children. Dexter struggled to forgive the man whose selfishness resulted in the horrifying and bloody scene that traumatized him as a young boy. The last episode of season four was chillingly familiar, as Dexter's selfish desire to be the one to bring the Trinity Killer to justice resulted in the death of his own wife, Rita. The final scene was a recreation of Dexter's childhood: we saw his son, Harrison, on the bathroom floor crying, sitting in a pool of his mother's blood. This is a graphic illustration of a basic psychological reality: if people do not deal with their own inner demons and distinguish their real selves from their anti-selves, they leave their children with a horrifying legacy.

Effective Therapies

Even though the dramatic childhood trauma and psychological stress associated with PTSD can certainly cause irreversible emotional and psychological damage, with the proper therapy model even the most severe trauma can be treated with good results. Research has now established that psychotherapy can change the brain and increase a person's ability to experience empathy, insight, morality, and emotional balance. Unfortunately, Dexter did not get the treatment as a young child that could have effectively changed the course of his life. Even as an adult, Dexter is responsive to psychotherapy, as indicated by his reaction to his brief encounter with therapy. A sustained, trauma-focused treatment where he would be able to form a positive secure attachment to his therapist could allow him to change himself, his brain, and his life.

Recent research has demonstrated that the specific psychological treatments for the disorders of obsessive-compulsive disorder, major depression, social phobias, and post-traumatic stress disorder actually alter the brain. The treatment process emphasizes resisting acting out symptom behavior, enacting new positive behavior, and engaging in mass practice in these positive behaviors. There are many effective therapies for treating trauma disorders in children. Dyadic development psychotherapy is an evidence-based treatment for children with complex trauma and attachment disorders. The therapy is based on the findings from attachment research. Evidence-based treatments—treatments that integrate behavioral management strategies and cognitive behavioral therapy, which makes repressed traumatic memories explicit in order to integrate them and thus form a coherent narrative of one's life—can effectively manage the behavioral regulation problems that occur in traumatized children. Had Dexter received this type of therapy as a young child, he would have been encouraged to make sense of the traumatic circumstances involving his mother's death. He would have been taught relaxation techniques and learned to correct thoughts that were inaccurate or distorted as a result of his trauma. His acting-out behaviors would have been controlled and modified by both his therapist and his parents. In the process, he would have re-wired his brain so that he could more fully experience a sense of connection to others and develop empathy.

The fact that Dexter, as an adult, was able to benefit from even three short therapy sessions with Dr. Meridian in season one suggests that Dexter would have been a good candidate for therapy. When Meridian asked Dexter to imagine a time when he felt powerless, Dexter experienced an onslaught of previously untapped childhood memories and first glimpses his initial childhood trauma. This is evidence that Dexter had implicit repressed memories of the event that had never been integrated into his conscious awareness. After the session, Dexter had a self-described "breakthrough" and was able to be intimate with Rita for the first time. If one session could have such a profound effect on Dexter as an adult, imagine how intensive therapy as a child could have altered the course of his life. If Dexter had been given assistance to access and explore his implicit memories and make sense of his trauma by integrating these memories into his understanding of himself, he could have begun to change his brain in ways that would have altered his life course.

Because of his concern with the "Dark Passenger" in all of us, Dr. Firestone developed "voice therapy," a process for bringing out into the open the critical inner voice and its destructive thoughts, then understanding where they come from, developing compassion for ourselves, and changing our behavior, thereby breaking destructive patterns that limit or destroy our lives. People can overcome this destructive thought process and free themselves from their "Dark Passengers" through voice therapy. The five steps of voice therapy include: (a) eliciting and identifying negative thought patterns and releasing the associated effect, (b) discussing insights about where these voices come from (to gain compassion for oneself), (c) verbally responding to the voice, both emotionally and rationally, (d) developing insight into how the voice influences specific destructive behaviors that the individual engages in, and (e) resisting destructive behaviors regulated by the voice and increasing constructive behavior that is in line with the individual's own self-interest (which the voices are discouraging).

Patients who participate in this type of therapy are able to distinguish their "real selves" from their "anti-selves" and are subsequently able to reduce their tendency to act on the negative thoughts, decreasing their risk of being violent against themselves or others. As a result, they are free to develop into goal-oriented, life-affirming individuals. They are able to stop reliving their destructive past and to begin fully living their own lives.

Our fascination with Dexter—a character who manages to intrigue and attract us, even as his primary preoccupation centers on remorseless murder week after week—presents an enticing case in and of itself. Could it be that because we also have a dark side, we get some vicarious pleasure from Dexter's acting on these urges? I believe we do. We all have a "Dark Passenger" who all too often is directing our behavior. We have integrated the negative aspects of our early childhood attachment figures in a manner that is hurtful to ourselves and to others. Part of Dexter's appeal to a mass audience is that his character provides a dramatic example of destructive impulses and thought processes that everyone struggles with.

One reason we are drawn to watching Dexter act out his dark side on "evil people" who deserve to be punished is that we would rather see evil out there in the world than to see it in ourselves or in our loved ones. To defend against seeing ourselves as having been hurt as children by aspects of our parents' dark sides that were acted out on us, we displace their malevolent traits by projecting them onto the world. We focus our fear and anger on the types of "monstrous" people Dexter kills and see them as evil, thus protecting our parents and ourselves from the much lesser evils we are guilty of. We feel justified and get pleasure from Dexter's behavior.

Dexter does have a lovable side that draws us in and makes him a sympathetic character, as well. However, I believe what makes Dexter's character redeeming to a wide audience is not just his lovability or his maintaining a fierce moral code even in his dissociative violent state, but also the fact that through Dexter's inner dialogue we are able to see him as a deeply conflicted and divided character. In this, we are able to identify with him and are made aware that the difference between Dexter and us is only in the degree and character of these negative thoughts.

Lisa Firestone, PhD, is a clinical psychologist in private practice and the Director of Research and Education at the Glendon Association. She conducts clinical training and research on suicide and violence, including developing *The Firestone Assessment of Self-destructive Thoughts* (FAST) and *The Firestone Assessment of Violent Thoughts* (FAVT). Dr. Firestone is the coauthor with her father, Dr. Robert Firestone, of *Conquer Your Critical Inner Voice.*

Was Dexter born bad, or was he shaped into a killer? The nature versus nurture issue is one that has been debated for decades. In biological families in which the parents and children live together, heredity and environment can get hopelessly entangled. If a child is like his father, is it because he emulates his dad's behavior, or because he inherited his genes? With Dexter, though, those two strands are separate—he is raised by Harry, his foster father, and not by his biological father. When siblings are similar to one another, it could be because they were raised by the same parents under the same roof, or because they have inherited some of the same tendencies. Dexter and Deb, however, were raised together but have no biological parents in common. Genetically, they are strangers. The reverse is true for Dexter and Brian; they share heredity, but differ dramatically in their upbringing. So what does it all mean? Follow along as Joshua L. Gowin draws from a long history of thinking and research to show how "even a truly sinister individual can be molded into a heroic, if twisted, adult."

NAUGHTY BY NATURE,

DEXTER BY DESIGN

JOSHUA L. GOWIN

It's unprecedented that a television series can cast a serial killer as the protagonist and still attract 2.6 million viewers as it heads into its fifth season. Most of us shudder at the thought of murderers, psychopaths, and evil-doers. We don't want to get to know them—we want to see them come to a well-deserved bitter end. Not so with Dexter. We're drawn in by his glibness, but also by his humanity, even as he professes to not really experience human emotions. The fact that Dexter can stay up all night dismembering a murder victim and then turn up to work chipper the next morning fills our minds with curiosity. We want to know how he became a cold-blooded antihero with a warm personality and a wry sense of humor, and this is the crux of what makes his character compelling. Was Dexter born bad, or is he just the product of his environment? By nature, Dexter is a merciless killer, cut from the same cloth as Jack the Ripper. By nurture, however, Dexter becomes someone we can relate to; by following the Code of Harry he's courteous, amicable, and comprehensible.

Dexter's two most distinguishing characteristics are his extreme urges for violence and his strict moral policy. Although his violent streak epitomizes his atypical nature, psychopathy, his ethics reflect his even rarer nurture, the Code of Harry. The result is a truly singular personality: a psychopath with a social conscience. *Dexter* is rife with clues to both Dexter's nature and his nurture. Flashbacks to Dexter's childhood and the lessons Harry taught him are a recurring motif, and we watch Dexter restrain his violent urges as often as he adds another blood sample to his collection of victims. In consequence, we're presented with a rare opportunity to objectively observe the development of a psychopath, from troubled youth to nefarious adulthood. The picture we're left with is the darker, less explored side of human nature and the uplifting vision that even a truly sinister individual can be molded into a heroic, if twisted, adult.

Nature and Nurture

The debate about nature and nurture is entirely modern. Throughout most of Judeo-Christian history, a person's character was largely understood to be the result of divine nature. Following the Renaissance, the movement toward empiricism brought us philosophers such as John Locke and René Descartes, who proposed that our ideas come to us through experience.

Thus, the concept of nurture began. The pendulum of scientific thought swung so far in this direction that psychologists of the late nineteenth and early twentieth centuries claimed that a person's behavior could be entirely explained by environmental influences. Like Pavlovian dogs trained to salivate at the sound of a bell, personality was considered to be solely a person's conditioned response to their unique environment. Around the same time, modern understanding of Mendelian genetics provided empirical evidence for the heritability of traits, invigorating the argument that our identity is predetermined—the exclusive product of nature. Since then, there has been continual debate about which is more important in explaining who we become—nature or nurture? These days, the accepted wisdom holds that any understanding of human behavior should account for the influence of both: nature and nurture are not mutually exclusive explanations, but are two coinciding factors that interact to influence our development.

Ultimately, who we become reflects the sum of genetic and environmental influences, even though individual traits may result directly from one or the other. Nature is solely at play in determining our blood type, whereas nurture almost exclusively determines which language we speak. However, the majority of traits fall somewhere in between. For example, we have genes that influence our height, but environmental factors control how those genes will be expressed. The average person is now several inches taller today than a century ago. Even though our genes are not drastically different from our ancestors', improved safety, health care, and diet have enabled increased growth in modern humans. This succinctly reflects the current understanding of how we become who we are: nature via nurture. We inherit a set of traits, but our environment determines how those traits are expressed. Although alcoholism runs in families, not all children of alcoholics will grow up to be drinkers. However, when exposed to the same environment, alcoholics' children are at a greater risk of alcohol dependence compared to a child without a family history of alcoholism.

The primary method used to understand the relative role of nature and nurture is twin studies. Identical twins share all their genes, whereas fraternal twins share roughly half of them. If the trait you are studying is hair color, you would expect all identical twins, but only about half of fraternal twins, to have the same hair color. Hair color is highly heritable: sharing the same genes means you always have the same hair color. This logic applies equally for personality traits as it does for physical characteristics. If fraternal twins share a personality trait only half as often as identical twins, it indicates that the trait is highly influenced by nature and minimally influenced by nurture. However, if both fraternal and identical twins share the trait 70 percent of the time, it indicates that the trait must be highly influenced by nurture and minimally influenced by nature.

Creating a Monster

What does this tell us about Dexter? Are psychopaths born or made? Research has consistently confirmed that nature and nurture each account for about 50 percent of the risk for developing antisocial behavior.[1] However, certain genetically inherited traits, such as callousness, are closely linked with antisocial behavior and can augment the risk of developing conduct problems. Using knowledge of behavioral genetics and antisocial behavior, we can try to dissect Dexter's character to determine what nature and nurture contribute individually and how the two interact to create his persona.

One of the inherent problems with most nature/nurture case studies is that the people who give children their genes,

---

[1] Viding et al., "Quantitative genetic studies of antisocial behavior," *Philosophical Transactions of the Royal Society*, 2008.

the parents, are usually the same people who give children their environment. Does a boy grow up to be confident because his dad taught him to hold his head high or because confidence is a genetic heirloom? Luckily, we avoid this logical hitch because Dexter was raised by an adoptive father, Harry. Any influence Harry has on Dexter is strictly the result of nurture. Dexter has a brother, Brian, who should share half of Dexter's genes, but who did not grow up with Harry's nurture. Some of their shared traits are likely the result of genetics, inherited from their biological parents. Where they differ may be the result of their different upbringings. As further comparison, Dexter's foster sister Deb grew up in the same home as Dexter, but they are no more genetically related to each other than either would be to a random stranger off the street. Accordingly, Brian and Deb provide reference points for Dexter's nature and his nurture.

All in the Family

Let's start with Dexter's nature. Antisocial behavior is heritable, and it seems likely that the Mosers, Dexter's biological family, possessed some antisocial genes: His father spent time in prison and his mother was addicted to drugs. His biological brother Brian is a serial killer who spent time in psychiatric institutions with a diagnosis of antisocial personality disorder. After the age of three Dexter lost contact with his biological family, so the similarities they share with Dexter are presumably the result of nature rather than nurture. However, although Dexter was separated from the Mosers at a young age, he did spend crucial early years of his life with them, which likely affected his development.

Dexter and his brother are both psychopaths, an extreme form of antisocial behavior. Though they kill for different reasons, each of them seems to possess an irrepressible urge to commit violence. They engage in aberrant behaviors and do not display typical emotional responses. When Dexter found a dismembered Barbie doll in his refrigerator that was identical to a sawed-up body from a crime scene, he barely batted an eye. Most of us, alarmed and frightened by the Ice Truck Killer's crimes, would not be able to sleep until he was behind bars and the key had been thrown deep into a volcano. Dexter, on the other hand, casually commented, "I think this is a friendly message, kind of like, 'Hey, wanna play?' And yes, I wanna play. I really, really do" ("Dexter," 1-1).

How can anyone be composed, much less sanguine, when they are the inexplicable target of a serial killer's game? The reason comes from Dexter's, and most psychopaths', nature. Two inherited personality traits (distinguishing features of a person's character, often evident at a young age, that tend to be relatively stable over time regardless of environmental influences) are strongly associated with psychopathy: callous-unemotional and fearlessness. Callous-unemotional describes the degree to which a person possesses a callous disposition—one in which he or she does not respond to the distress of others and displays little emotion. Fearlessness is a lack of anxiety, especially in risky situations.

Callousness can be detected at an early age. When most children hear another child crying, they respond to try and soothe it. For instance, most children will stop biting another child when they see it causes the other child to cry out in pain. Callous children are insensitive to this clear sign of distress. Inheriting a callous-unemotional disposition is a significant risk factor in developing antisocial behavior and psychopathy. In most circumstances, antisocial behavior is equally the product of nature and nurture, but inheriting a callous disposition shifts the balance in favor of nature: antisocial behavior in callous children reflects a genetic influence of roughly 80 percent, according to Viding et al.'s research. Because Dexter and Brian are both callous-unemotional, they were both disposed to developing aggressive behavior regardless of their environment.

Part of Dexter's *modus operandi* is to knock his victims unconscious and immobilize them so they awake naked and lying flat on their back. When the victims realize Dexter's lethal intent, they plead with him not to take their life, claiming they will change their evil ways if they're spared. Such a repentant display would pull at the heartstrings of a typical person, giving them pause, but Dexter is unmoved. His rules are unsympathetic, and they don't account for human emotion, only human deed. As he commented in "Shrink Wrap" (1-8), "All actions have their consequences, and this is yours." Once Dexter snuffs out his prey, he disposes of the body without a trace of guilt. He is an executioner.

Brian was similarly indifferent to human suffering. He hacked off part of Tony Tucci's legs with no signs of remorse and then played doctor and attached prosthetics. His demeanor by the patient's bedside was more reminiscent of a mechanic who had just installed a car engine than a butcher who had recently honed his knife skills on another human being. This callousness Dexter and Brian share is what allows them to engage in their psychopathic killing. It's part of their nature.

Debra, on the other hand, is not genetically related to Dexter, so she is not expected to share heritable traits like callous-unemotional with him. Quite the contrary, Deb openly expresses pain, joy, anger, fear, loneliness, jealousy, and sadness. In many ways she served as a point of contrast in season one to both Brian's heartlessness and Dexter's detached stoicism. Brian expressed no compassion while mutilating Tony Tucci, but Deb empathized with his tragedy. When Tony worried that he would no longer be able to attract girls, Deb arranged for one of her prostitute friends to pay him a visit. Deb seeks to alleviate others' pain. Her nature is distinct from Dexter and Brian's.

Another trait that we see in Dexter, fearlessness, is similarly heritable and evident in infancy. Fearless children are not deterred by danger. Whereas a callous child does not regret mischief, a fearless child engages in mischief even in the face of a penalty. Children with normal levels of fear may hesitate before doing something that could result in punishment, but fearless children are not deterred by negative consequences.

Biologically, more aggressive children tend to have a lower than average resting heart rate. Fearless and callous children's heart rates remain low even in risky or terrifying situations. In "It's Alive!" (2-1), when Dexter nearly shot Harry, he was amazed to learn that Harry's heart began pounding. Dexter had never experienced exhilaration. Seeking this sensation, Dexter stood precariously at the edge of a rooftop in an attempt to get his pulse to race but to no avail. Dexter is unflappable. On several occasions when spying on a prospective victim, Dexter has been caught trespassing. Rather than become flustered, Dexter offered a plausible, poised explanation for his presence. At a killer's junkyard, Dexter was just looking for a headlight for an old car he was fixing up. When caught stealing the ashes of his dead father from a morgue, Dexter deftly escaped and seemed unfazed by this near miss when Brian drove up beside him and offered him a ride.

Like Dexter, Brian easily carried out actions that would cause most of us great fear or anxiety. At the height of the police search for the Ice Truck Killer, he walked right into the lion's den, appearing in the police station with a dozen white roses for Deb, the very person trying to track him down.

As a contrast, Deb reflects typical levels of anxiety in appropriate circumstances. She trips over words when addressing the entire police department, indicating ordinary fear of public speaking. At a crime scene where a woman was murdered in front of her young daughter, a shaken Deb asked Dexter how he could remain so composed. Genetically unrelated to Dexter, she does not possess a fearless temperament, and she expresses normal levels of compassion, fear, and displeasure.

Beyond Nature

Although psychopaths often inherit several traits that predispose them toward antisocial behavior, possessing these traits alone does not predict psychopathy with certainty. "Nature via nurture" suggests that hereditary traits only increase an individual's vulnerability toward conduct problems if they are exposed to enabling circumstances, such as childhood abuse or neglect. One aspect of nurture that both Dexter and Brian share is a traumatic event in their early childhood: they witnessed their mother's death, along with the slaughter of several other individuals, and spent two days in a cargo container with the bodies. Distressing experiences during childhood can dispose individuals to a lifetime of behavioral problems. A recent study of prisoners found that inmates with a history of childhood trauma had a more extensive history of aggressive behavior, began engaging in violence at an earlier age, and continued to engage in more violent behavior when incarcerated.[2] Witnessing their mother's death in a violent massacre surely didn't contribute to a happy childhood for either Dexter or Brian and both appear genuinely traumatized by it. Such a formative experience likely interacted with their genetic predisposition to antisocial behavior and exacerbated their callousness, tipping the scales toward violence. The product of nature and nurture working together can often be greater than the sum of the individual parts.

In discussing the problem of violence, especially in light of nature and nurture, it is important to remember that aggression

---

[2] Sarchiapone et al., "Association between childhood trauma and aggression in male prisoners," *Psychiatry Research*, 2009.

is a normal, adaptive behavior common to all species. From male lions defending their territory to mother hens protecting their chicks from predators, aggression is essential for survival. Even for modern-day humans, some aggressive behavior can be advantageous; getting ahead sometimes requires stepping on a few toes. Aggression becomes problematic when it is excessive in frequency or intensity. Society is primarily concerned with crime and antisocial behavior committed by men, and to a lesser extent women, between the ages of fifteen and thirty because this group causes the most damage. Their aggression can cause loss of life or costly damage to property. However, the most violent age for humans is not young adulthood, but toddlerhood. Aggression is a natural part of human nature and development. In a study observing toddlers' social behavior, almost half the boys around the age of two kicked, bit, or hit their peers. Luckily for our safety's sake, those behaviors diminish as children grow into adolescents and adults, and social instruction likely directs that change.

The Importance of Harry

> "Babies do not kill each other because we do not give them access to knives and guns. The question we've been trying to answer for the past thirty years is how do children learn to aggress. That's the wrong question. The right question is how do they learn not to aggress."
>
> —Richard Tremblay, from "The Violence of the Lambs" in *Science* (2000)

This is the value that nurture holds. Even among identical twins, if one child receives more negativity and less warmth from their parents, that child is more likely to develop antisocial behavior, highlighting the importance nurture plays in development.[3] Estimates of the population hold that roughly one in ten children inherits callous-unemotional traits, putting him or her at risk for developing antisocial behavior.[4] However, even most individuals with an inherited susceptibility for violence do not grow up to become criminals because nurture plays an equally important role in development. This provides insight into the divergence between Dexter and Brian. Even as an adolescent, Dexter managed to avoid trouble while Brian spent his youth in detention. As an adult Brian has difficulty forming meaningful relationships, whereas Dexter not only makes an effort to get along with his colleagues, he also retains a close bond with Deb and strove to be a family man and loving (if awkward) boyfriend and eventually husband to Rita.

Although Dexter's penchant for violence never fades, he learns to harness it and use it only in prescribed circumstances. Ultimately, he develops a unique pathology where he only kills for justice:[5] He kills only those who he believes will continue to kill others if they are left alone. He takes out the trash.

It could be said with little contention that among serial killers, Dexter is an exception. For a callous, unemotional, cold-blooded killer who is unbridled by society's code of conduct, Dexter has a scrupulous capacity for fairness. Referred to as the Code of Harry, this is the clear result of nurture. Harry's rules not only dictate who he can harm, but also how he can harm them. The underlying principles are that no innocent person

---

[3] Caspi et al., "Physical maltreatment victim to antisocial child: evidence of an environmentally mediated process," *Journal of Abnormal Psychology*, 2004.

[4] Moran et al., "Predictive value of callous-unemotional traits in a large community sample," *Journal of the American Academy of Child and Adolescent Psychiatry*, 2009.

[5] Surely the justice of his deeds could be debated, but that is beyond the scope of this essay.

should be hurt, but if someone is corrupt and must be killed, no evidence should be left behind.

The Code of Harry serves several functions. It protects the innocent and gives Dexter a sense of morality; he knows right from wrong intellectually, even if he cannot feel it emotionally. It also offers Dexter a target for the release of his compulsive violence. Beyond these essential functions, the Code of Harry also teaches Dexter how to appear normal. He brings in donuts to colleagues, smiles in pictures, and volunteers to help out if someone needs assistance. Although he may not experience normal feelings, the set of principles Harry taught him helps him appear normal. As Dexter said, "People fake a lot of human interactions, but I feel like I fake them all, and I fake them very well" ("Dexter," 1-1).

Part of the challenge in socializing children who inherit a callous temperament—in teaching them proper behavior—lies in their inherent difficulty with developing a conscience, a crucial personality component for engaging in typical pro-social behavior. Unlike most children, callous-unemotional children are unaffected by the distress of others. Because they do not experience the displeasure other children do when watching someone else suffer, it takes more effort for parents to help them learn socially appropriate behavior. Research has suggested that helping these children develop a conscience requires a positive relationship with their parents, one that involves mutual cooperation.[6] Harry and Dexter exemplify this, as they worked together to help Dexter come to terms with his violent impulses and blend in with society.

A study of intervention techniques for antisocial behavior found that children who were callous-unemotional did not respond to punishment. To help them improve their conduct,

---

[6] Kochanska, "Multiple pathways to conscience with different temperaments: from toddlerhood to age 5," *Developmental Psychology*, 1997.

the most effective treatment was to provide positive reinforcement for pro-social behavior. Because these children also tend to be fearless, punishment does not deter them, but they are as sensitive to rewards as other children.[7]

In school, when Dexter bullied another student, Harry stopped him. Rather than admonishing Dexter for poor behavior, Harry reminded Dexter of the reward for using aggression discreetly. "People remember bullies" ("Let's Give the Boy a Hand," 1-4). If Dexter hoped to hide his sinister temperament, he could not torment his peers. Harry acknowledged Dexter's nature while simultaneously teaching him a more appropriate behavior. This is how Dexter managed to keep his record clean.

While Dexter's piety to the Code of Harry steers him to pro-social behavior, Brian, who did not receive such tender rearing, unleashed his violence without prudence. He had no guiding figure in his life who took interest in developing his conscience. By the age of eighteen, he had already gotten into trouble, whereas Dexter was becoming increasingly efficient at staying out of trouble. To Brian, all that mattered was following his nature, and any steps he took to stay out of trouble as an adult were because he learned that was the only way he could continue to kill. When Dexter did not want to kill Deb, Brian bellowed at him, "You can't be a killer and a hero, it doesn't work that way!" ("Born Free," 1-12). Brian could not comprehend Dexter's character because it reflects a nurture he never knew.

Rather than receive positive reinforcement for his good behavior, Brian was punished for his misdeeds and placed in an institution. He never had a constructive outlet for his antisocial behavior. Most important, he never developed a sense of right

---

[7] Hawes and Dadds, "The treatment of conduct problems in children with callous-unemotional traits," *Journal of Clinical Child and Adolescent Psychology*, 2005.

and wrong. His victims were the innocent and the defenseless. He used people as a means to an end. He charmed Deb as a tool to get closer to Dexter, intending eventually to kill her as an act of solidarity with his biological brother. Dexter does not exhibit similar behavior; it doesn't abide by the Code of Harry.

Research suggests that there is no cookie-cutter strategy for setting a callous-unemotional child right. Effective handling should focus on as many of the problems the child exhibits as possible, which means that treatment needs to be individualized for each particular case.[8] The Code of Harry was highly individualized for Dexter's unique disposition, and while it worked for him, it might have different effects on another child. Nonetheless, the result is clear: Dexter developed a sense of morality, whereas Brian did not.

Ultimately, these moral values led Dexter to a rejection of his blood-brother Brian in favor of his adoptive sister Deb, who shares his sense of morality. He learned from proper parenting and though it pained him to kill his biological brother and condemn his own nature along with Brian's, he saw value in this decision. He couldn't stand to see Deb harmed. Not only was she innocent, but he also admitted he was fond of her. Dexter has a conscience.

The Butterfly Effect

People aren't born psychopaths. They may have inherited traits that dispose them to psychopathy, such as callous-unemotional affect, but that alone does not set a course for problem behavior. In fact, most callous-unemotional children grow up to be productive members of society rather than psychopaths. It requires nurture, or the lack thereof, for those traits to develop unfettered and unbalanced by a sense of morality. A stressful, traumatic,

---

[8] Conduct Problems Prevention Research Group, 2004.

or neglectful childhood is the wind that propels a ship toward mental illness. Brian may have been caught in a trap due to his genetic propensity for trouble coupled with a traumatic and neglected youth. He had no guardian to help him develop a conscience; after his mother's death, he was left behind. Though Dexter inherited the same traits, he received loving support from an understanding foster parent. With proper parenting and a high-quality environment, even children who inherit a fearless temperament and callous-unemotional affect may develop into (seemingly) normal, moral adults and people we can relate to.

After all, we like Dexter—in spite of his penchant for murder.

Joshua L. Gowin was born in Fort Collins, Colorado, on May 3, 1983, the son of Sheila and Frank Gowin. In 2004, he received his BA, with distinction, from the University of Colorado with a major in psychology and a minor in mathematics. For the next year, he worked as an English teacher in France and Russia. In 2006, he entered the University of Texas Health in Houston, Texas, where he received a master's in neuroscience. In the spring of 2009 he worked as an editorial intern for *Psychology Today* in New York City. He is currently finishing up his PhD.

Even if you watch Dexter *just for entertainment, you can see the commonalities in Dexter's kills. There is a characteristic way that he chooses his victims, stalks them, nicks their cheek and collects a smudge of the blood, has a little conversation with them, then murders them. To the trained forensic scientist, though, that's not just one seamless routine, but three separate parts—the modus operandi, the signature or calling card, and the victimology. The different parts matter, and in catching a killer like Dexter, the signature may matter most of all. Clinical psychologist Marisa Mauro, who has worked with all manner of miscreants, believes that she can discern Dexter's fantasies from his calling card. I think her speculations are, well, fantastic!*

THE PSYCHOLOGY OF DEXTER'S KILLS

An Investigation of Modus Operandi, Signature, and Victimology

MARISA MAURO

There is an old police adage that every crime scene tells a story. We all know, thanks to the multitude of television shows depicting police and crime themes, that it is up to the detectives, investigators, and various forensic experts to decipher these sometimes convoluted tales. But armchair analysts are finally getting their turn in the hit television series *Dexter*. Main character Dexter Morgan, Miami City Police Department blood spatter analyst and part-time serial killer, has had a lot of close calls over four fantastic seasons, but has yet to be apprehended for his dark nighttime deeds. This has left viewers with a great deal of time to think about Dexter's story—what makes their unlikely hero tick, his murders, how he accomplishes them, and even why he does it.

Police departments, federal agencies, and criminal researchers have invested substantial resources in uncovering answers to questions just like these in pursuit of real serial killers. Why? Because answering questions that help investigators understand the method and motivation behind killings facilitates the apprehension and conviction of murderers. Clearly *Dexter* fans are not out to catch their serial killer. They are, however, out to understand the whole story behind the Dark Passenger, much of which is yet unanswered by the show. Why does Dexter use particular strategies and tools for his kills? What motivates him to kill? And certainly, what is with that cut he makes on his victims' cheeks?

Some conclusions to these and other questions can be drawn using the same techniques used by recognized experts in criminal investigation. Authors, and authorities on the topic, John Douglas, Ann Burgess, Allen Burgess, and Robert Ressler, in their text *Crime Classification Manual: A Standard System for Investigating and Classifying Violent Crimes*, and Robert D. Keppel in his, *Signature Killers*, discuss several aspects of crime scene investigation that we can apply to help understand the psychological underpinnings of Dexter the serial killer: modus operandi, signature, and victimology.

Modus Operandi

The modus operandi, often referred to as MO, are specific actions taken by a perpetrator in order to complete a crime. To be considered part of an MO, an action must be necessary and not superfluous to carrying out the crime. As a whole, the MO is a set of learned behaviors that are used because they work. An example of an MO for a rapist might be to hang out in shopping mall parking lots at night, force an unaccompanied woman into her car at gunpoint, and rape her. The MO may evolve over time as the criminal gets better and more efficient or suffers setbacks because of a particular method. The evolution of an MO is text-book operant conditioning, a form of learning. It describes a set of voluntarily learned behaviors that are modified as a result of the consequences created by the behaviors in the environment. Thus, as most criminals attempt to improve, we can expect to see their MO change gradually over time. All *Dexter* fans can describe their hero's MO. But let's learn more by taking a look back and identifying Dexter's original MO, its evolution, and, finally, his current strategies.

We saw Dexter's first kill in "Popping Cherry" (1-3). The victim, Mary, a.k.a., The Angel of Death, was a murderous nurse attending to Dexter's foster father, Harry, in the hospital. Harry encouraged Dexter to commit the murder and Dexter did so in the victim's own apartment home, while her cat looked on apathetically. Of his first kill, Dexter stated, "Things were a little messy in the beginning. Hey, perfecting a new craft takes time." We saw that the entire room was covered in plastic, as was Dexter himself. Wearing what appeared to be a plastic hoodie and pants, Dexter waited for the nurse. When she arrived home, Mary walked into the prepared kill room calling for her cat. She was clearly bewildered by all the plastic, but alert; Mary spotted Dexter well in advance as he lunged toward her with a syringe of M-99, and foiled his initial attack. A physical struggle ensued. The two wrestled until Dexter got the upper hand and pinned Mary to the ground. She was finally subdued by a punch to the face. Unconscious for a time, she eventually awoke and found herself gagged and naked in the plastic-wrapped kill room, bound to a table. Fearful, she looked around. Dexter was sitting on the couch leafing through a scrapbook that contained mementos of her victims. Spotting him, she let out a muffled yell. Dexter leapt from the couch and grabbed a knife. Walking toward his helpless victim, he ordered her at knifepoint not to scream, stating that if she did, she would "lose a tongue." Having gained compliance, Dexter removed the gag and allowed Mary a brief explanation for her crimes. Hearing it, he re-inserted the gag and began to stab her repeatedly in the side.

As compared to his slip-ups with Mary, Dexter's future murders were more sophisticated. Re-watching the very first episode, "Dexter" (1-1), it is clear that he had come a long way since that first kill. Dexter's victim, Mike Donovan, was a forty-something boys' choir director who had murdered at least three children. On the night of the kill, Dexter stalked his victim at an outdoor concert. He lay in wait, unseen in the dark night, for the choir director in the backseat of his vehicle. The concert ended and Mike walked down the road to his car. He settled into the driver's seat, plainly oblivious to the danger that was awaiting his return. Dexter swiftly and expertly popped up and choked him into submission with wire. Dexter directed the bound and gagging but still conscious victim to drive to a remote cabin in the woods. As the car came to a stop, three empty graves were visible in the light of the headlamps. Enraged, Dexter violently dragged Mike from the car and into the cabin where the remains of three young boys were displayed on plastic wrap. He forced the terrified man to look at the decaying bodies and admonished him for what he had done to the boys. Standing against the cabin wall crying, Mike admitted, "I couldn't help myself." Dexter, facing him, listened and responded to his pleas and justifications, then stepped forward and abruptly sedated him via injection. Conscious again, Mike found himself gagged, nude, and tied to a table with plastic wrap. Dexter was clad in what we would later learn was his traditional kill suit, an apron, and a welding mask. Seeing that Mike was awake, he quickly went to task. Grabbing a scalpel, he moved to his victim and made a small incision on right side of his face. He took a blood sample from the bleeding wound, encasing a droplet of blood between glass slides. This completed, Dexter chose a tool—a saw—and killed the man by sawing his neck. In the process Dexter stated, "Soon, you'll be packed into a few neatly wrapped Heftys and my own small corner of the world will be a neater, happier place." The show cut immediately to Dexter in his boat, and viewers were left to presume that Dexter chopped up Mike's body, loaded it into garbage bags, and dumped it in the ocean.

By comparing the case of Mike to that of Mary, we can see that Dexter had made a few noteworthy changes to his MO to lessen the risk of being caught. First, he learned that it was easier to subdue his victim from behind. Caught from behind, the choir director was unable to see the attack coming, unlike nurse Mary, who did and had opportunity to prepare and fight back. Second, Dexter learned that it was safer to make the initial attack in a less-populated location. Although Mike was apprehended after a well-attended concert, his car was parked on the side of a dark road. This was in contrast to Mary, who was assaulted in what appeared to be an apartment building, most likely populated with close-by neighbors. This led to the third change, a more remote kill room. As compared to Mary's apartment, Dexter dramatically decreased his chances of getting caught at Mike's remote cabin. Fourth, Dexter had perfected a quick kill. Mike was presumably killed and therefore silenced after the first cut to his neck, while Mary yelled, albeit muffled by the gag, with each stab to her side. Finally, we know that Dexter had mastered the prep required for both himself and the kill room. With the more sophisticated kill suit and kill room in Mike's case, it was likely that Dexter dramatically reduced his prep time and risk from that in Mary's.

Considering the facts of the two cases, we can ascertain that generally, Dexter's MO has evolved with experience. Learning from each kill, he added improved techniques, thereby working toward perfecting his craft. This is consistent with research on serial offenders, which suggests that learning occurs from challenges faced during the commission of crimes, as well as slip-ups that lead to arrests. In this way their MOs, like Dexter's, are dynamic. As the show enters its fifth season, *Dexter* fans know their conscientious and morally minded serial killer's current MO. Barring unusual circumstance, Dexter researches his victims and then completes a stakeout of their typical haunts. He learns their behavioral patterns and then plans the kill, finding an appropriate kill room. The victims are stalked and subdued, usually with M-99 or wire, and brought unconscious to the pre-prepared and plastic-covered kill room, where they are secured to a table and killed. Did I leave out some details? The nudity, the cut on the cheek, the blood slide, the little talk Dexter has with each victim? No. These are not part of Dexter's MO. This is because they go beyond the acts necessary for him to carry out the murders. They are much too personal. As such, they can be considered part of his "signature."

The Signature

The signature, sometimes referred to as a "calling card," is another element of criminal behavior that occurs during the commission of a crime and entails all the aspects of criminal behavior that go beyond those necessary for the completion of a crime (the MO). A signature is most likely to be used by serial offenders like Dexter and is more unique to them than their MO. A comprehensive analysis of a serial killer's signature may reveal his psychological traits, needs, and deviancy. This is because it involves the parts of the crime that are not necessary for its completion and may in fact point toward the personality and unique desires of the perpetrator. In *Signature Killers*, Dr. Keppel states further that the signature is something that the serial killer is "psychologically compelled to leave to satisfy himself sexually." Surviving victims and crime scenes can provide behavioral information that lead to clues about an offender's signature. Examples may include exceptionally detailed, abusive, or vulgar language, excessive use of force, scripted conversations or behavioral patterns, and actions taken to produce certain psychological trauma such as domination or humiliation.

Dexter has a clear signature. Viewers may see the clues that point to his identity in the signature left during the commission of many of his crimes, but Miami Metro has yet to be tipped off. In the great majority of Dexter's murders, the trained killer and police employee does not leave a crime scene or a body behind. Like his MO, Dexter's signature is still safe with his viewers. Let's take a look at it now and all that it reveals about his fantasies, or, in other words, Dexter's deep psychological needs.

To begin, we must revisit Dexter's crimes and take note of each behavior completed in excess of that needed to kill the victim. Dexter's signature involves all of the elements of the crime not identified above, using the cases of Mary and Mike, as part of his MO. These elements include a conversational component, psychological trauma to the victim, a particular, almost scripted time sequence or order of events, and excessive use of force postmortem.

Perhaps one of the most noteworthy aspects of our hero's signature is the fact that he engages each of his victims in some type of conversation about their own victims. These conversations tend to occur at a particular time in the sequence of events leading up to the kill (i.e., once the victim awakens secured to the table) and are prompted by the setup of each kill room. In the case of Mary, Dexter was able to prompt a conversation when he located a scrapbook the nurse kept with information about each of her victims. When she awoke, Dexter stated, "I've just been looking through your photo album . . . hope you don't mind. (Showing her the album) Are all your victims in here?" ("Popping Cherry"). He walked over to her and removed the gag for her to respond. "I helped them, all of them. I took their pain away," she pleaded in her defense. "I understand," said Dexter calmly, adding, "Now it's time to take away your pain," and commenced to stab her in the side. Years later, Dexter prompted a similar conversation with victim Mike by forcing him to look at the decaying bodies of his three young victims. In this case, Dexter uncharacteristically prompted the conversation earlier in the sequence of events—prior to the injection and securing the victim to the kill table. The effect, nevertheless, was the same. Seeing the bodies, the choir director begged for his life, and Dexter directed the conversation toward Mike's victims, asking if they also begged.

"I couldn't help myself," cried Mike in his defense. "I couldn't, I . . . please, you have to understand."

With initial understanding, Dexter replied, "Trust me, I definitely understand. See, I can't help myself either." Then, his tone swinging toward anger, said, "But children, I could never do that, not like you. Never, ever kids."

Interested, Mike whispered, "Why?"

"I have standards," replied Dexter as he stepped forward to inject the child killer with M-99.

Neither this conversation, nor that with Mary, was necessary for the completion of their murderers. As such, it follows that a conversational component is one piece of Dexter's signature. So what might a thorough analysis of his pre-murder conversations reveal about our serial killer's psychological traits, needs, and deviancy? First, it seems safe to conclude that Dexter derives some sort of personal satisfaction from hearing the victims admit to their own crimes. This might fulfill a need for vigilante justice or righteousness. Alternatively, the conversation may simply fulfill Dexter's need to adhere to Harry's Code: hearing the victim's admission of guilt assures that Dexter has a viable victim on his kill table. The conversations also tend to cause the victims some sort of psychological distress, often leading to tears, justification, and/or begging for their own lives. They may be meant to invoke fear, guilt, or remorse. In any case, the nature and setup of the conversations seem to point toward such psychological traits as grandiosity and desire to dominate. This is in stark contrast to Dexter's usual presentation in his daily life as a considerate, agreeable people pleaser. So which version of Dexter is the real Dexter? Criminal investigators may say the former. Experts believe that the signature aspects are repressed fantasies that the serial killer holds on to and daydreams about until he is compelled to act. Viewers may say the latter. Privy to Dexter's internal monologue, we know that there is more to Dexter than his Dark Passenger.

Another element of Dexter's signature is that the victims are stripped nude prior to their murder. Oftentimes they are also nude during the conversation. The nudity, like the conversational component, suggests the intentional infliction of psychological trauma on the victims. Psychologically speaking, the nudity points toward traits of aggression and domination. It may also signify Dexter's need to shame or humiliate his victims.

A third integral signature piece is the small cut Dexter makes on most of his victims' cheeks. When this occurs, either during or following the conversations, Dexter also takes a sample of their blood and places it between two glass specimen slides. He takes the slide home and stores it in a trophy-like box filled with his other victims' blood samples. Like the conversation and the nudity, this particular behavioral pattern also stands out as clearly unnecessary to the act of murder. Moreover, it evolved over time. Dexter did not take a blood slide from Mary, his first kill, but he did with Mike, and we continue to see him taking them from a majority of his victims.

This element is ripe for analysis. The taking of a blood slide psychologically reaffirms the trait of domination or control, as well as order. There is a certain sense of power and forced intimacy Dexter supposes in the performance of such an unusual action without explanation or obvious reason provided to the victim. Viewers can assume that cut provides Dexter with an opportunity to act out his childhood experience as a witness to his mother's murder, this time in control as the aggressor. As we saw in "Born Free" (1-12), at some point during the crime young Dexter had endured a cut to his left cheek. Moreover, there is clearly some need to memorialize the murders and retain physical access to the memory in the future—like a prize. They help Dexter to relive the thrill of his kills. Finally, the slide aspect suggests a deviancy, a sort of abnormal gratification from blood or the orderly placement of blood. Dexter's career as a blood spatter analyst supports this conclusion.

There are times, however, when Dexter does not seem to experience these needs, which explains the instances when no blood slides are taken during the kill. This is most apparent in unplanned or personally meaningful or unmeaningful kills. In regard to unplanned kills, such as Esteban and Chico, the drug dealers who arrived at the cabin where Sergeant Doakes was held captive in "Left Turn Ahead" (2-11), Dexter killed out of practical necessity or impulse. The brooding fantasy or psychological need to kill was not present. As such, Dexter had no desire to memorialize the event. The same explanation can be applied to Dexter's meaningful kills. He did not take slides, for instance, from his brother the Ice Truck Killer, Lila his one-time girlfriend and Narcotics Anonymous sponsor, or Camilla Fig, family friend and retired police department employee. All of these individuals were personal to Dexter and he had no desire to recollect the kills. In the same vein, Dexter does not take slides for unmeaningful kills. For example, with Ken Olson in "Dex, Lies, and Videotape" (2-6), Dexter said, "No, I'm gonna kill you. I have to, I just don't need to . . . It's very empowering." This statement and Dexter's failure to take a blood slide suggest a lack of fantasy prior to the kill, and once again, no need to memorialize it.

The final piece of Dexter's signature is the excessive use of force postmortem. Dexter's current MO tends to involve a quick killing blow to the victim, usually a fatal stab wound to the chest, neck, or head. Any postmortem mutilation following the fatal blow is in excess of that necessary to accomplish the murder and by definition becomes part of Dexter's signature. Following the fatal blow, Dexter saws or cuts up the body into smaller pieces. This is referred to by forensic experts as "overkill." It produces a great deal of mess and blood that he easily cleans up using the plastic and garbage bags. Dexter's excessive use of force suggests psychological traits toward extreme violence, aggression, and anger. This behavior could also function as self-protection, maybe a clean and efficient way to follow Harry's Code and dispose of the body. But disposing of the body in one piece would arguably produce the same effect more quickly. Dexter does, after all, dispose of the body parts in the same location and leaves identifying marks, i.e., teeth and fingerprints, intact. This overkill suggests a need to not only kill his victims, who are murderers of innocent people, but literally slaughter them, defiling their bodies and rendering them unrecognizable. Like the blood slides, the process of this act may point toward a deviant gratification from blood.

Experts believe that an analysis of the signature elements, like those just described, can also reveal the criminal's fantasies. This is important because fantasies are thought to be the driving force behind the crimes committed by serial offenders. If the fantasy is that of humiliation, for example, the criminal may pose his victims in degrading ways before or after he tortures, kills, or rapes them. When he offends again, the fantasy will be repeated and the degrading poses will be his signature. The signature aspects may evolve or become more complex over time, but their underlying theme remains the same.

In regard to Dexter, we can piece together each of his signature aspects to deduce the fantasies that drive him to murder.

From them we might conclude that Dexter has fantasies of dominating, shaming, manipulating, and controlling murderers of innocent people. Furthermore, he probably fantasizes about replicating the fear within them that their own victims felt. Finally, Dexter has fantasies of being both an aggressor and avenger of the innocent. This is evident in "The Dark Defender" (2-5), where Dexter dreams about saving his mother from her killers while dressed as the superhero. These fantasies are consistent with those typical to survivors of childhood abuse who sometimes have fantasies of being in control in the role of the aggressor as adults. As a young boy, Dexter witnessed the brutal murder of his mother and sat in her blood with her sawed-up corpse for several days before being rescued by Harry. It is not unimaginable that he would have both a strong unconscious drive toward aggression as well as conscious fantasies, or daydreams, now as a young and capable man psychologically tormented and angry about his mother's murder.

Although Dexter plays out these fantasies in most of his murders, he does not, or sometimes is not able to, conduct all of the signature aspects in his crime. This is consistent with real-life serial killers as well. Crime scene investigators believe that serial criminals do not always leave signature aspects at all crime scenes. From time to time the criminal will not be able to complete the signature aspects of his crime. Factors such as time, victim behavior, or unforeseen events like intrusions can prevent him from completing the behaviors beyond those necessary to commit the crime. When this occurs, he is often less satisfied with the crime because he was unable to act on his fantasies.

In the case of Dexter, all of these factors are relevant. Time or unforeseen interruptions have occasionally precluded the completion of signature aspects, as in the murders of Valerie Castillo, Nathan Marten, and George King. With Valerie Castillo, wife and accomplice to Jorge Castillo in a coyote operation involving Cuban immigrants, Dexter ran out of time and was unable to perform his ritual overkill. With Nathan Marten, photographer and sex offender, the kill by strangulation was an impulsive reaction to catching Marten viewing photos of Rita's children. With this victim, the lack of pre-planning and time seemed to preclude the completion of signature aspects and Dexter did not seem as relieved by the kill. Lack of preparation, time, and anxiety all precluded Dexter's completion of signature aspects and satisfaction with the killing of George King, a.k.a, the Skinner. With this kill the tables were turned, at least initially. Dexter was caught by the Skinner and nearly became his victim, only to overpower the man at the last moment, breaking his neck and tossing him into the path of an oncoming police car just in time to escape from the scene unnoticed. In addition, some kills, like those of his brother, Brian Moser, a.k.a., the Ice Truck Killer, or Camilla Fig, do not seem to justify the signature aspects, since they are meaningful and personal. Dexter does not enjoy or get the same satisfaction from them and so would not get any gratification from his usual ritual.

Victimology

A third element of crime scene investigation is victimology, or simply the characteristics of the perpetrator's victim. Victimology may include the victims' age, gender, race, occupation, physical attractiveness, relationship status, or perceived vulnerability, to name a few. Sometimes there is an identifiable likeness in victims chosen by serial offenders because they prefer a certain type of victim, while other times there is not. For instance, some criminal behaviors are motivated by an emotion experienced by the perpetrator, such as rage or anger, and the victim may be chosen on the basis of availability. *Dexter* fans know that his victims do tend to have one personal trait in common: a history of killing innocent people. Only a few of the many do not share this history, including Camilla Fig and Nathan Marten, and in those cases Dexter's traditional MO and signature were noticeably absent.

If we were to examine only the cases of Mary and Mike, we might see more to the victimology than what is really there. Both of those victims were white and middle-aged. However, if we take a look at Dexter's other victims, we can immediately discount both characteristics. In regard to race, we need to look no further than the first season's Jorge Castillo and Alex Timmons, a sniper, who were, respectively, Hispanic and African American. Turning to age, we see that both of these victims were considerably younger than Mary and Mike, but if we still are not convinced we can look to Freebo, a drug dealer and murderer of two college girls in season three, who was likely in his twenties when Dexter killed him. It is easy to see how, without the benefit of insider knowledge, just studying the traits of a few similar victims could lead to inaccurate beliefs about victimology.

Still, victimology has its uses. In many cases, understanding a serial killer's victimology can lead to a greater understanding of his psychology. In season four, the Trinity Killer was so named because he was originally believed to kill in patterns of three—first a young woman, followed by a mother, and then a man. This basic victimology was first uncovered by Lundy and, paired with the MO, allowed the investigator to link many murders over a number of decades to Trinity. In Miami and too close to his man, Lundy was killed by Trinity's daughter Christine, but Dexter persisted where the investigator left off. He soon uncovered a fourth victim in Trinity's pattern—a young boy. We then learned that Trinity's victims' characteristics bore a shocking similarity to the psychological traumas he had experienced as a child. In fact, the young boy that began each of his killing cycles represented Trinity's childhood lost due to the tragic death of his family. The murders that followed represented each of their deaths in sequence. First, there was the accidental death of his sister, who bled out from a cut to her femoral artery after falling in the shower. Following her loss was that of his mother, who presumably jumped to her death from grief. Finally, his father died from a trauma to the head, possibly inflicted by Trinity.

Although Trinity's victimology was more apparent on the surface than Dexter's, we can also see a strong link in both serial killers between their psychology and their choice in victims. Of course, this is because we have the benefit, as viewers, of insider knowledge, which includes information about both killers' personal histories, MOs, and signatures. Combined, this information allows us to draw the most accurate conclusions regarding victimology. Most criminal investigators do not have the same benefit.

The Nail in the Coffin

We set out to discover the story told by Dexter's crimes. Using three popular aspects of crime scene investigation (modus operandi, signature, and victimology), we were able to analyze Dexter's criminal behaviors, psychological traits, needs, deviancy, and fantasies. If Dexter becomes sloppy, a similar analysis completed by his own police department could readily lead to his arrest. Due to frequent inconsistency in victimology and the evolution of MO over time, signature, according to some experts, can be the most useful tool for linking a series of crimes to one criminal and apprehending him.

This certainly seems to apply in Dexter's case. Clean crime scenes, dumped bodies, and dissimilar victim characteristics leave little or no lead with regard to MO or victimology for investigators. Dexter's signature, though, is more telling. Aspects of it, including his trophies and overkill, or excessive use of force, could be located, analyzed, and one day linked to our main character. In season two, at least one of Dexter's signature aspects, overkill, was revealed when his bagged, slaughtered bodies were recovered from the ocean. This discovery earned Dexter the title "the Bay Harbor Butcher" but was not enough to lead to his apprehension.

In addition to the possibility of one day revealing his identity, Dexter's signature tells his story—his traumatic life history and fantasies. As loyal viewers we sympathize with his pain and plight, and root for Dexter as he continues to foil the boys and girls in blue.

Marisa Mauro, PsyD, is a psychologist in private practice with a focus on forensics in Austin, Texas. She also works as a freelance writer and regularly contributes to her blog, "Take All Prisoners," on PsychologyToday.com. Previously, Dr. Mauro worked as a clinical psychologist at the California Department of Corrections and Rehabilitation. Much of her work there was focused on violent offenders, gang members, and inmates serving life sentences. She has also taught as an adjunct professor and conducted research on personality, academic success, career success, eating disorders, and suicide.

Dexter doesn't struggle with moral misgivings the way the rest of us do. He doesn't have the kinds of feelings and emotions that we do. Those limitations make him a little less human. But they also help to make him an exceptionally accomplished liar! His smarts help, too. Don't give Dexter all the credit, though. He's the star of the lie-telling show, but he has a whole cast of enablers. Rita, Deb, and many of the members of Miami Metro all contribute—however unwittingly— to Dexter's spectacularly successful deceits.

DECEPTION: IT'S WHAT

DEXTER DOES BEST

(WELL, SECOND BEST)

BELLA DePAULO

D exter Morgan, man of so little ordinary human sensibility, is an extraordinary liar. What he is covering up with his lies is staggering: Dexter kills people up close and personal. He does it over and over again. Yet hardly anyone ever suspects Dexter's dark heart and even darker deeds.

Dexter's job is in a homicide department; everyone around him is trained and experienced in the pursuit of murderers. Dexter's colleagues, including Dexter's own sister, Debra, interact with him every day, but they don't see a killer. Dexter's wife and kids, too, never suspected that Dexter chops people into their component body parts, ties them up in trash bags, and dumps them in the ocean.

How is this possible? How does this person, so baffled by human emotions and so bereft of natural interpersonal talents, walk mostly unchallenged among friends, family, colleagues, and homicide professionals? And what does this tell us about Dexter's real-life cousins in crime?

Lying in the Lives of Ordinary Humans

To get a sense of just how often real people lie, my colleagues and I asked 147 people (including college students and a diverse group of people from the community) to keep a record of all of the lies that they told, and all of their social interactions, every day for a week. Over the course of the week, the participants told about one or two lies a day, which amounted to about one lie in every four social interactions. Only seven people claimed never to have lied at all. (Maybe if our study lasted longer, even they would have 'fessed up to telling some lies.)

Most of the lies the participants recorded were little lies. For example, they lied about:

- *Their feelings and opinions* ("I told him I missed him and thought about him all the time when I really don't think about him at all"; "I told her that she looked good when she really looked like a blimp")
- *Their actions, plans, and whereabouts* ("Lied about where I had been; didn't tell them all of the places"; "Said I sent the check this morning")
- *Their achievements and failings* ("Led him to believe I had been a daring ski jumper"; "Tried to appear knowledge-able about operating room procedures when I only knew a little about them")
- *Their reasons and explanations* ("I told everyone at work I was late because I had car trouble"; "I told him I didn't take out our garbage because I didn't know where to take it")

There were some big lies scrawled in participants' lie diaries, but not enough to satisfy our perverse interest. So in the next set of studies, we asked people to tell us specifically about the most serious lie they ever told and the most serious lie anyone ever told to them. In response, we heard stories of far more consequential transgressions, though no one confessed to murder. We learned about many adulterers, people who lied about the severity of an illness (their own or someone else's), some who lied to almost everyone around them about their sexual identity, and much more.

The stereotype we have of liars is that they are crass, materialistic, exploitative, and uncaring. They want something—such as a better grade, a better job, money, or sex—and they will lie to get it. Although liars like that do exist, after studying thousands of lies, big and small, one thing became very clear to me: Lies told merely to fulfill immediate crass desires are the exceptions.

Instead, ordinary humans usually tell lies because they care. They care about what other people think of them. They want other people to think they are a daring ski jumper and not a couch potato. They don't want others to know that they were late for work because they are so disorganized that they couldn't get out the door on time. They don't want a potential employer to realize how little they actually know—not just because that would undermine their chance of getting the job, but also because they might appear to be the kind of person who would put a patient at risk just to get a paycheck. That hit to their reputation would hurt.

Ordinary people also lie because they care about other people's feelings and reputations. If that college student had told her boyfriend the truth about how she really felt about him—that she never even thinks about him—he would have been devastated. Even though she is not attracted to him, she doesn't want to wound him. People who lie to minimize the seriousness of their own illness or that of a beloved relative or friend are often trying to spare others from worry. It would be hard to argue that adulterers are not trying to satisfy their own needs and desires—and I'm not going to try. Sometimes, though, there is more at stake than the opportunity to continue their romps undeterred. Telling the truth about their transgressions would ruin their reputation and hurt the person who should have been the sole recipient of their intimacies. Some adulterers actually do care about both.

Dexter lies about some of the same kinds of things that the rest of us do. For example, he tells many lies about his actions, plans, and whereabouts; about what he knows and doesn't know; and about why he does some things and not others. His underlying motives, though, are simpler. Ultimately, all of his lies are told in the service of one goal—hiding who he really is and what he really does, so he can continue to do it. At times Dexter pretends to care about how other people feel and what they think of his skills and his character, but that's only because he *has* to fake all that to get away with his killing. Psychologically, that puts Dexter on a whole different planet from Deb, Rita, LaGuerta, Angel, Masuka, and you and me. As non-psychopathic humans, we almost can't help but care what others think of us.

The *Dexter Morgan Show:* The Writer/Director Tries to Make It Unremarkable

Dexter is the writer, producer, star cast member, and director of *The Dexter Morgan Show.* Like *The Truman Show,* it is a program that (almost) never goes off the air. Unlike every other person in show business, though, Dexter wants his performance to be utterly unremarkable. He wants viewers to turn away in boredom—nothing to see here. That's because the first step in getting away with a lie is to make sure that the question of whether or not you *might* be lying never even comes up.

The extraordinary Dexter Morgan works at trying to appear utterly ordinary. He doesn't say much and, as a guy, can get away with seeming like the stereotypical unemotional and unexpressive type. His clothes are uninteresting and so is his hair style (if you can call it that).

Appearing low-key and staying in the background is useful to Dexter because he has so little intuitive sense of what to say or how to act. There's a risk to doing too much of that, though—he could start seeming like a "loner" who "keeps to himself." That would be trouble! So Dexter does what he can to seem like one of the gang. He's the donut guy. That's easy enough—bring donuts and make people think you're a nice, thoughtful person. He goes out with the guys, knowing that he's not going to have a good time. He let his friends throw him a bachelor party and pretended to enjoy it, all the while wishing he could just go out and kill someone.

Perhaps the best props in Dexter's show have been Rita and the kids. How ordinary does that seem? The irony is that having a spouse or kids is actually *not* a great indicator of whether you might be a serial killer. In their book *Homicide: A Sourcebook of Social Research*, criminologists John Fox and Jack Levin note that many serial murderers "hold full-time jobs, are married or involved in some other stable relationship, and are members of various local community groups." What Dexter realizes, though, is that it is the conventional wisdom that counts. If other people generally believe that serial killers are loners and that men with families rarely do any harm, then the family man is the role to play.

What Makes Dexter Such an Extraordinarily Successful Liar?

To find out what makes Dexter such a great liar, we can start by looking inside him. To get away with a life of lies, Dexter benefits from what he does have—his smarts—and perhaps even more interestingly, from what he doesn't have—deep emotions and a conscience. Let's start with the have-nots.

NO EMOTIONS? NO PROBLEM

When ordinary people lie to someone face-to-face about where they were the night before or how their car got smashed, they risk being betrayed by their own feelings. If they are worried about getting caught in their lie, or if they feel guilty about what they did wrong or about the fact that they are telling a lie, they might come across differently than they would if they were telling the truth and not experiencing any of those emotions. Liars sometimes seem more tense than truth-tellers, and they can sound as if they don't really want to commit to what they are saying. Those kinds of differences in demeanor can tip off a listener that something is amiss.

Dexter, though, is emotionally stunted. He just doesn't understand human feelings. He doesn't often have them, and he usually doesn't know how to deal with other people's emotions.

When it comes to getting away with lies, emotional emptiness is not such a bad thing. That guilt that other people feel about their lies that can show in their behavior and give them away? Dexter doesn't have that. The apprehension about getting caught that can reveal itself in a nervous demeanor? Sure, Dexter is bound and determined to get away with his lies, but most of the time he doesn't experience much anxiety about the matter.

Dexter typically thinks of Harry's Code as a way to avoid getting caught. By season four, though, he has realized that the code also helps shield him from experiencing emotions.

Where Dexter runs into trouble as a plausible liar is when he has to fake emotions. The appropriate feelings don't come naturally to Dex, and sometimes he simply forgets that he's supposed to be feeling something and needs to pretend. That's one of the mistakes Dexter made that set off Sergeant Doakes's suspicions. After Angel was stabbed, his concerned friends and colleagues were at his side at the hospital. When word came that Angel would survive, everyone was visibly relieved. Well, everyone but Dexter. Doakes noticed.

Like an anthropologist trying to discern the ways of an unfamiliar tribe, Dexter studies his fellow humans for cues as to how to behave. After Dexter's first two stunningly unromantic marriage proposals to Rita were rebuffed, he knew he couldn't figure out this sentimentality thing on his own. Luckily, he heard someone else wax poetic about true love (never mind that the woman was a delusional murderer!). Then he came home to Rita and said the same thing in the same way. Proposal accepted.

NO CONSCIENCE? NO PROBLEM

When Robert Hare, one of the world's foremost authorities on psychopaths, wrote a book about them, he called it *Without Conscience*. That lack of conscience is probably the quality that most starkly separates psychopaths such as Dexter from everyone else. In fact, it may be Dexter's inability to experience the ordinary range and depth of emotions—especially feelings such as fear and anxiety—that accounts for his failure to develop a conscience.

Dexter, though, has a serviceable substitute—the Code of Harry. Dexter's foster father realized that Dexter's urges to kill would be uncontrollable, so he channeled and regulated them instead. Dexter is only allowed to kill people who deserve it. He can't get caught. Those are the two most important rules in the Code of Harry. The whole set of rules functions as a moral checklist. Dexter doesn't have to have an inner guiding light; he can just go down the list.

If it is your goal to kill people, lie about it, and get away with both the wicked deed and the lie, then not having a conscience, like not having emotions, is not such a bad thing. If you are an ordinary, morally grounded human who is tempted to transgress, your sense of right and wrong can give you pause. That feeling that you are about to do a bad thing is like a moral stomachache; it warns you that you had better stop indulging if you want to feel good again. Not so for Dexter. He has a stomach of steel. He will lie and manipulate and destroy evidence to stay in the clear, without even a twinge of guilt or shame. And if others, despite Dexter's best efforts, become suspicious anyway, well, let's say that Dexter may just take matters into his own hands.

DEXTER'S NO DUMMY

Watch Dexter as he sizes up a blood-drenched scene and in an instant deduces the entire choreography of the criminal and the crime. Listen to his repartee with his fellow serial killer who was a used-car salesman. The salesperson tossed out one lie after another, and Dexter batted each one away without missing a beat.[1] Notice how Dexter observes other people and commits their words and intonations to memory. Remember when Dexter was young and Harry told him how to come across as normal on a mental health assessment? Dexter nailed it.

All lines of evidence lead to the same conclusion: Dexter is no dummy. His smarts help him get away with his both his crimes and his lies. While other liars might stumble around as

---

[1] A note about those used car salespeople: they really are good liars! My brother Peter DePaulo and I learned this when we made videotapes of experienced salespeople pitching products they really did like and also pitching products they hated (but had to try to sell anyway). We showed those tapes to more than 100 people and asked them how deceptive they thought the salespeople were in each of their pitches. The salespersons were seamless. The observers noticed no difference at all in how deceptive the salespeople seemed when they were claiming that some car they hated was terrific than when they were honestly praising a car they loved.

they try to fabricate the perfect lie and struggle to remember what they already said and to whom—making it all the more obvious that they have something to hide—Dexter thinks quickly and sharply. The mental challenges of telling lies don't trip him up.

The significance of a good memory became especially apparent when Dexter suffered a concussion after his car accident in season four. Suddenly, he couldn't remember what he did with Benny Gomez's remains. How un-Dexter-like!

Dexter's cautiousness is smart, too. His trophy blood slides are so well hidden that only someone as determined as Doakes, who was willing to tear Dexter's place apart, would ever find them. His office is in good shape, too. When the feds descended upon the Miami Metro's homicide department to help with a particularly daunting case, Dexter gave them the password to his computer and walked away. He knew they weren't going to find anything.

A friend and colleague of mine, Weylin Sternglanz, had a great idea for his doctoral dissertation when he was a student in my lab. He thought that people trying to get away with their lies would be more successful if they admitted to a lesser offense than if they simply tried to deny that they had done anything wrong. It worked for Dexter—twice. Once, when Rita was becoming suspicious that something was amiss and asked whether Dexter was an addict, he said that he was. That answer satisfied her, especially after Dexter committed to going to the twelve-step meetings. Later, Doakes began tailing Dexter, certain that he would discover him doing something horrible. When instead his chase led him to the basement meeting of a Narcotics Anonymous group, Doakes thought all the pieces had fallen into place. Dexter wasn't avoiding him and acting suspicious because he was out committing crimes; he was just hiding his personal problem and the work he was doing to deal with it.

Rita, Deb, and All His Colleagues and Friends: Dexter's Unwitting Enablers

Having people around all the time can be quite an impediment, even to the determined liar. They see too much and know too much. Dexter has good reason to want his own space. Who wants some nice person around who, when the air conditioner breaks, might pull it out of the wall and try to fix it? Or who might wonder why you are getting home so late? Dexter lied to Rita about keeping his apartment because there, the Dark Defender could plot his evil deeds unmonitored and undeterred.

In other ways, though, the important people in Dexter's life enable his lies. They don't mean to, but they do. First, the mere presence of friends, a (now former) partner, kids, and a sibling he sees all the time shield Dexter from suspicion. They make him seem normal.

The second reason is perhaps not what you would think. Ask people if they can tell when someone close to them is lying, and often they will claim they have some special insight that strangers do not. They'll say something like, "Oh, yeah, I can always tell when he's lying." And why shouldn't they? They have much more experience observing, reading, and interacting with their close relationship partners than acquaintances or strangers do. And yet, when put to the test, romantic partners in particular are not very good at knowing when their loved ones are lying and when they are telling the truth. The problem is they *want* to believe that their partners would never lie—especially not to them. As a result they see their partners as telling the truth more often than they should, and more often than a stranger would.

Here's a clever example of a study that demonstrates romantic partners' obliviousness to one another's deceit. It was conducted by Eric Anderson, for his dissertation, when he was a graduate student in my lab.

Anderson's study modeled the dreaded question asked of one partner by the other, while pointing out a nearby stranger: "Do you think that person is attractive?" In the experiment, the person who was put on the spot—let's use the name Bernie since it could apply to a man or a woman—answered truthfully half the time and lied the other half. The romantic partners of all the different Bernies were just a shade better than chance at knowing when the answers were lies. (They were right 52 percent of the time, when they would have gotten 50 percent right simply by guessing.)

Each of the 100 couples was joined by a stranger who also tried to determine whether Bernie was lying. The strangers were not very good at detecting deception either, but at 58 percent, they were better than the partners.

Anderson, though, did not stop at asking the participants directly whether they thought that Bernie was lying or telling the truth. He also asked them some indirect questions, such as how confident they were about each answer, whether they had gotten enough information to make an accurate judgment, and whether they felt at all suspicious. When the romantically involved participants said that they were not very confident, that they needed more information, and that they felt a bit suspicious, their partner was more likely to be lying than to be telling the truth. So even though the sweethearts were hardly better than chance when they were asked directly whether their partners were lying, they did seem to know, at some level, that something was not quite right. Interestingly, the strangers did not show as much sensitivity to the more subtle signs that something was amiss.

As the people around Dexter observe his behavior, we would probably expect Rita (were she still alive) to be the first to notice when something seems not quite right. Part of the tension and drama in the developing relationship between the two came from Rita's growing sense of unease about what was really going on with Dexter. Yet, Rita might also be the last to con-clude that Dexter was lying. Give her something else to hang her suspicions on—oh, he's using!—and she'll grab it.

Deb is close to Dexter, too. Maybe she also has a deepen-ing sense of foreboding about the brother who is so important to her. But she is no more eager than Rita was to add up all the clues and label Dexter a monstrous liar.

Dexter's Cousins in Crime

In real life, there are people like Dexter who kill repeatedly over many years, yet live unsuspected among family and commu-nity. The BTK killer was one of them. BTK is the name that Dennis Rader gave himself because he bound, tortured, and killed his victims. He was married with two children and active in his church. He murdered ten people but was not caught until thirty-one years after his first kill. John Wayne Gacy was another. He was a married man who murdered thirty-three men and entombed many of them under the crawl space of his home. His wife remained clueless.

These and other psychopathic killers are Dexter's cousins in crime. So are some other big-time miscreants who pile lie upon lie in the service of other horrible deeds—for example, perpe-trators of massive Ponzi schemes that leave hundreds destitute and humiliated. What makes these people Dexter's blood rela-tives (so to speak) is not so much the nature of their deeds as the character of their feelings about their crimes. They don't feel bad about them.

Some even bask in the joy of their deceptive triumphs. An example is Clifford Irving, who landed a huge advance to write an "authorized" autobiography of Howard Hughes, a man he'd never met and knew he never would. Irving explained how he felt immediately after he confessed: "I almost wanted to cry out: 'Sure, I did it. And I'm glad I did it. You want me to grovel? I can't. You want me to feel guilty? I don't. *Because I enjoyed every goddamn minute of it.*'" No conscience, no remorse.

Ordinary people who do have a conscience can still become big-time liars, but for them the experience is much different. Every step they take into the muddy moral quagmire of cheating and deceiving threatens to sink them ever more deeply into guilt and shame. They end up feeling dirty—and physically ill. John Dean, White House counsel to President Richard Nixon from 1970 to 1973, was a key player in the infamous Watergate scandal, but not a very happy one. His fellow perpetrators were sometimes exasperated by his moral misgivings. Ultimately, Dean would star in an iconic moment in American history when he exposed the "cancer on the presidency" during the Watergate hearings.

Dean described how he felt when the cover-up was in its last throes, but just before he had decided to tell the truth. His account could hardly be more different from Clifford Irving's: "My thoughts, I realized, were no longer measured or rational. Every breath I drew in seemed cold, and the chill latched on to my thoughts and dragged them down into my stomach, then around up my spine. My cool, my detached calculation, was dissolving in fear."

Offenders without a conscience are the most dangerous criminals because only we can stop them. Culprits such as John Dean who do feel remorse will sometimes stop themselves.

So am I tossing Dexter into the bin with the worst of the worst? Maybe not. Dexter is not a hardcore unwavering psychopath. He has grown over the course of the series. He's started to feel something akin to real fondness and concern for other people. He's begun to worry that—should he ever get caught—his undoing would be devastating to other people, too, and not just to him. All those emotions make Dexter more human. But they also threaten to make him a less effective liar. Ironically, then, Dexter's growing humanity may be his undoing.

Alternatively, maybe Dexter's newfound feelings for other people will motivate him to stop killing. Perhaps he *will* stop himself. Then he won't need to lie so much. With Dexter (and his brilliant writers), you just never know what's going to happen next.

Bella DePaulo (PhD, Harvard) is the author of *Behind the Door of Deceit: Understanding the Biggest Liars in Our Lives* and *Singled Out: How Singles Are Stereotyped, Stigmatized, and Ignored, and Still Live Happily Ever After*. She has published more than 100 scholarly articles. DePaulo's work on deception has been described in the *New York Times*, the *Washington Post*, the *Wall Street Journal*, *Time* magazine, the *New Yorker*, and many other publications. Dr. DePaulo has appeared as an expert on deception on ABC, NBC, CBS, CNN, PBS, the BBC, and other television outlets. She has also lectured nationally and internationally. Dr. DePaulo used to believe that she loved only true crime stories until she discovered Dexter.

How is it that we manage to balance our paid employment with all of the other parts of our lives, such as friends, family, and other interests? That's a topic that many of us obsess about. Scholars have filled books and academic journals with their research and writing on the matter. But this chapter may well be the first one devoted to a critical discussion of how juggling is accomplished by a serial killer!

THE SCIENTIST AND THE SERIAL KILLER

A Study in Work-Life Balance

MORRIE MULLINS

> "Dexter Morgan: Blood tech, husband, father, serial killer . . . Which one are you?"
>
> —Harry Morgan, "Hello, Dexter Morgan" (4-11)

L ife is complicated. Every day, we juggle demands from bosses, coworkers, friends, family, and neighbors. Everyone wants something, and they want it now—or sooner, if possible. Our task is to figure out how to balance all of these demands. How do we keep our work and non-work lives separate? Is it even possible?

Work-life issues have been an increasing area of interest for psychologists over the past few decades. In 2004, a theme of the American Psychological Association's annual conference was the interface of work and family. Issues of how people manage their increasingly busy and over-scheduled lives have only become more central to the field, and with the huge numbers of families in which parents are trying to manage dual careers, raising children, and being members of their community, that shows no sign of changing.

Enter Dexter Morgan. At work, Dexter is a quiet lab tech with the Miami Metropolitan Police Department, a pleasant-if-eccentric analyst of blood spatter. He gets along with his coworkers (for the most part), doesn't make a lot of noise, and is good at his job. At home, Dexter has a different role. He hunts and kills criminals that the system is unable to bring to justice, dismembering them, dumping them in the ocean, and retaining only a collection of blood slides as mementoes. These two lives—the scientist and the serial killer—have to coexist. Like all of us, Dexter has to find a way to make the things he does to pay the rent fit into the same brain that carries all of his non-work needs and desires.

Dexter is an extreme example of work-life balance,[1] since most of us don't have a Dark Passenger to exacerbate the conflict. When we met him, he was already established in his career, having developed a routine that allowed him to manage both his work and non-work activities. The complications involved in this routine became a source of both internal and external conflict over the course of the first four seasons. As a result, Dexter offers an excellent vision into how people try to manage the demands that arise from different areas of their lives.

---

[1] In the research literature, the terms "work-family balance" and "work-nonwork balance" are more common. I've chosen the less precise but more generally descriptive term "work-life balance" because for much of the early run of the series, what Dexter does outside of work is rarely either "family" or "non-work" as we might understand the terms. My choice of wording isn't meant to imply that work is not a part of life, since obviously it is—Dexter is just a very special case, for a variety of reasons!

A number of theories have been presented to try to describe the why and the how of work-life balance. I will discuss three of these theories—the compensation model, the segmentation model, and the spillover model—drawing on examples from Dexter's life and the lives of those around him to illustrate how we can try to understand the interplay of work and non-work in our lives, as well as in Dexter's.

A final note, then, before I begin: Although work-life issues occur throughout the first three seasons of *Dexter*, they really come to a head in season four. Married, with kids, everything Dexter had to deal with previously is suddenly taken up several notches. Because of this, I'm going to primarily rely on the first three seasons to describe the models, then treat the fourth season on its own. This approach has the added benefit of allowing anyone who hasn't seen the fourth season to know when to stop, to avoid spoilers!

The Compensation Model: Does Dexter Compensate?

Compensation theory says that we seek to "round out" our lives by obtaining experiences we can't get in one part of it through another. We work because our home lives don't give us enough of a sense of accomplishment, for example, but because the workplace isn't notably good at meeting emotional needs, we rely on our families to fulfill those. Each compensates for the other.

Dexter, at the beginning of season one, embodied a compensation perspective. He worked in part because the culture demanded that he do so. If he wanted to have a place to sleep and food to eat, he needed a job. There may never be a shortage of work for people who want to kill murderers, rapists, and other forms of human sludge, but it's never been the kind of employment that pays well.

A natural interest in blood and the ability to examine horrific scenes in a detached fashion, plus a quick scientist's brain, made work as a blood spatter analyst a good fit. Add in that Dexter had a strong role model for police work in his adopted father, Harry, and Dexter has found a job that allows him to meet a number of basic needs and to fake several others.

One of the things that motivates "normal" people is human contact. Most of us have social needs; human beings tend to be gregarious, or herd-like. The ones who aren't, who float toward the fringes of society, attract attention. A classic sound-bite from neighbors of captured serial killers is, "He was quiet, kind of a loner." Which, of course, implies that there is something wrong with such a person, that someone who doesn't interact socially is somehow broken.

It's a description that certainly applies to Dexter, who neither wants nor needs human contact (at least at the beginning of the series), and who feels a compulsion to kill. Because social interaction is assumed to be a basic human need, and because its lack can draw attention, Dexter needed to put himself in situations where he could be part of "the group" and thereby hide himself out in the open. This helped him satisfy another basic need: safety. Harry taught Dexter many things, but the most important was to follow the code. One aspect of the code involved blending in, appearing normal to a world unlikely to appreciate Dexter's perspective and distinct set of values.

So, from a compensation theory perspective, work satisfies Dexter's basic physiological needs (food and water) by providing an income, and it satisfies some of his safety needs by appearing to meet the social needs that he doesn't possess, whose absence could give him away.

What work does not do is fulfill him. Some would suggest that we work in order to gain esteem, or to improve how we view ourselves as providers and contributors to the community. Self-esteem, as a value judgment of personal worth, is not relevant to what Dexter does at Miami Metro; he has a job to do, and he does it while maintaining something close to an emotional flat-line. Dexter does his job well not because he needs to feel good about himself, and not because he wants people to speak well of his work, but because being good at it allows him to blend in more effectively. People remember negative information much more strongly than positive information. Being mediocre or bad at his job would cause Dexter to stick out.

As such, Dexter doesn't meet any classic psychological needs with his work. There is his psychological tie to blood, but in terms of the things we traditionally think of as moti-vators and contributors to self-evaluation, working at Miami Metro simply doesn't serve a "normal" purpose for Dexter. Outside of work, though, how he feels about what he does and how Harry would feel about him do seem to matter. The code guides how he views himself and his place in the world. He spends his non-work time trying to understand and live with the pathological need to kill, and it is only with the kill that he feels like he is truly himself, at peace, doing his proper thing in the world. He's not doing it for the world, of course—killing is deeply personal for him—but if it's good for someone else, he doesn't mind.

One of the interesting elements of Dexter's development is his growing ability and willingness to connect with other peo-ple. He moved from having no relationships of note in season one (other than the ongoing and, at the beginning, fairly super-ficial relationship with Debra), to a developing relationship with Rita that spanned four seasons. He found and attempted to connect with individuals like Lila Tournay and Miguel Prado. The way these people viewed him did, at times, seem to matter. Their regard wasn't something he sought through his actions at work, though. Certainly in the case of Lila and Miguel, it had more to do with their ability to understand and appreciate what he did when he left the office behind.

Compensation theory is interesting, but even in Dexter's case it falls short of explaining the complexity of what drives us. It deals in needs, which may or may not be necessary to consider for two reasons. First, Dexter's needs do not easily align with those that drive most of us; the code and Dexter's Dark Passenger warp the concept of "needs" in a number of ways. Second, the needs themselves devolve quickly to a level so basic as to be potentially meaningless. Needing food, air, water, and contact are not all that interesting.

At the theoretical level, the focus becomes even more questionable. Many need-based theories have been criticized for a lack of testability, and haven't always held up well in practice. Even here, the "needs" met by having a job are ones that could potentially be met in other ways. Having a workplace is not a requirement to keep from appearing to be a shut-in, and it's quite the logical stretch to suggest that the only way Dexter could have put food on the table, paid rent, and looked like a "normal" member of society would have been to obtain an advanced degree in forensic science. Although it's true that his job also provides him with resources (such as criminal databases) that make it easier for Dexter to identify code-appropriate targets to kill, the give-and-take implied by compensation theory has always felt a little like trying to fit a square peg into a Honda-shaped hole. The mere ability to create an explanation—which compensation provides—does not in any way guarantee that explanation's completeness.

The Segmentation Model: Leaving Work at Work

If you've ever had a friend say, "At five o'clock, work is over. I leave it there. Once I get home, I'm all about my family," then you've heard the basic logic of the segmentation theory. Segmentation theory says that people cope with competing work-life demands by keeping the two areas as separate as possible.

They don't answer work emails at home, they don't take work calls on vacation, and they can be pretty fiercely protective of their personal time. The opposite also tends to be true; when they are at work, they are very present. They don't talk about family, don't allow themselves to schedule family-related obligations during work hours, and maintain high levels of professionalism at all times.

It's an ideal world, isn't it? One in which we can keep the two domains completely separate? I'm sure I'd like to live in that world, but I'm as guilty as anyone of answering work emails at ten, eleven, twelve o'clock at night. My boss makes fun of me because a couple of times, I've sent her emails with 2 A.M. time stamps! A lot of us talk about segmentation, a lot of us try it, but not a lot of us succeed.

Dexter tried it. He even made it work, for a while. If you go back to the early seasons, it's pretty clear that the life he set up for himself was one where his work activities—visiting and modeling crime scenes, writing reports, meeting with his coworkers— remained, by design and necessity, separate from his non-work activities. Even when apparent bleed-over exists, as when he went out for drinks with Batista or Vince, or when he took part in the bowling team, for Dexter this wasn't bleed-over. None of that was "personal" to him. It was *all work*, because *everything he did to protect his ability to hunt and kill to satisfy his Dark Passenger was work*.

As such, Dex has a huge advantage on the rest of us. He can draw a very solid line in his life. The things on one side of it are the things that he does to enable him to feed his need to kill. The things on the other side are all part of the killing.

I would doubt, however, that most of us are all that interested in an "advantage" that stems from sitting in a pool of mom's blood in a cargo crate, then growing up into a person who is (nearly) incapable of feeling emotions.

Making segmentation work almost requires a mental switch that we can turn on and off at will. When it's on, we're one person. When it's off, we're someone else. Without emotions, and with the code to guide him, Dexter can manage this kind of segmentation. For those of us who lack the emotional detachment that allows Dexter to be both a serial killer and a functioning member of normal-appearing society, it's much more difficult.

There are situations in which this is possible without the type of pathology we see in Dexter. Jobs that are not cognitively or emotionally demanding, in which we have no responsibilities for or to other people except those we have in the moment, are ones that can be left behind at the end of the day. Such jobs are vanishingly rare, though, and soon may be limited to entry-level service and retail jobs and those that primarily involve manual labor.

Technology alone makes it difficult to keep our work and non-work lives separate. The various brands of "electronic leashes" we carry on our belts or in our pockets make us reachable anywhere and everywhere. The number of places we can go to shelter ourselves from the demands of coworkers and bosses shrinks a little more every day—we can't even take shelter on airplanes any more, since they became Wi-Fi enabled! Society itself works against segmentation, and despite our best attempts, we will find ourselves bringing work home with us. Trying to keep our family problems out of the workplace is similarly problematic. Sick kids, text messages and emails from friends or family members during work hours, and community volunteering—all of these are enabled by technology, just like intrusions of the office at the dinner table.

Even Dexter isn't immune. His ability to segment his work and non-work lives was challenged for the first time by his brother, the Ice Truck Killer, and how Dexter's relationship with Debra put her life in jeopardy. Dexter's work with Frank Lundy (and Debra's relationship with Lundy) further strained his ability to keep work and non-work separate, and his friendship-cum-mentorship of Miguel Prado threatened to obliterate the boundary Dex established between his work and his killings.

In the end, what do we know about the segmentation model? We know that it's an interesting idea, and something that we can strive for. Unfortunately, a hard separation between work and non-work requires (a) little or no emotional involvement in work, (b) a job low enough in complexity to make leaving it behind feasible and, at the very least, not undesirable, and/or (c) significant psychopathology. In a world where BlackBerrys and iPhones and email make us accessible twenty-four hours a day, seven days a week, true segmentation of work and non-work activities is harder and harder to obtain.

If you've managed to succeed in creating this kind of balance with a job you love, trust me when I say that I envy you, and suspect you're in a very happy minority. Dexter would probably envy you as well—if he felt emotion, that is.

The Spillover Model: Blood Isn't the Messiest Thing, After All . . .

Compensation, with its focus on needs, ends up being too simplistic. Segmentation, which suggests that we can create a hard separation between our work lives and our non-work lives, ends up feeling utopian, if a step in the right direction. The reason that segmentation fails is that the roles we adopt in one environment do not cease to be part of who we are when we leave that environment. A manager does not stop being a manager when she leaves the office; the doctor who is not on-call will not turn a blind eye when the man at the next table chokes on a chicken bone while she's out to dinner with her family. The reality is, who we are is defined by a multitude of roles, and our task is figuring out how to manage those competing and potentially conflicting roles on a daily basis.

Spillover theory would suggest that because our roles are part of our self-definition, attempting to isolate them by linking them solely to specific activities is almost always going to fail. What we need to do instead is accept that spillover is going to happen. Work will influence non-work, and vice versa. Barring fringe cases, we are generally not able to keep the domains separate—and it may be the case that we shouldn't try.

One of the important things to recognize about spillover is that it isn't necessarily negative. When we think about work affecting non-work life, the easiest examples are the most painful. Debra was targeted by the Ice Truck Killer because of her connection to Dexter. Dexter's vigilante activities led to conflict at work with Doakes, and the inevitable showdown at the cabin in the swamp. In fact, Dexter is something of a poster child for negative spillover. His interactions with Doakes, Lila, and Miguel all blurred the lines he carefully tried to draw between work and non-work life. All of them ended up dead.

You don't get much more "negative" when it comes to spillover than dead bodies of good people. Lila notably doesn't fit into that category, but her knowledge of Dexter's nature put Astor and Cody at risk, much as Brian's did Debra at the end of season one. Ellen Wolf died because Dexter allowed Miguel too much insight into his non-work life.

However, we also see examples of positive spillover in Dexter's life. It could even be argued that positive spillover, rather than segmentation, is what Dexter was striving to achieve when we first met him.

Take, for example, his interactions with Batista, Vince, LaGuerta, even Debra. The lengths to which Dexter went to make himself appear normal—going out for drinks, joining the bowling team—can be read as an attempt to keep his work and non-work lives fully separate, but they can also be read as a way for him to create a unified picture of the roles expected of a functioning member of society. Dexter wasn't compartmentalizing his work role from his non-work role, viewed this way; he was creating one integrated set of roles that matched the expectations people had of him. He designed spillover into what he did, because that was how he believed (based on Harry's training and his own scientific observations of the world around him) that he ought to function.

Positive spillover from work to non-work occurs for Dexter because of the resources work offers him, too. Earlier, I mentioned access to criminal databases as a perk of his job. These databases undoubtedly make his unpaid vocation easier to accomplish. Access to DNA testing equipment, satellite imagery, detailed crime scene photos, and criminal histories makes it possible for Dexter to meet one of the key requirements of the code: being certain.

Work can therefore positively affect his non-work activities, but is the opposite true? Does killing people have any positive effect on how Dexter does his job?

The man himself would deem the question irrelevant, since the job is a part of the mask he wears to keep himself hidden in broader society. It's clear at several points, though, that positive spillover from murder to forensic analysis does exist. The pathological need to kill would, if left unfulfilled, drive him to distraction. When he is unable to kill, his focus drifts. If he weren't able to isolate targets, learn their patterns, hunt them down, and make an end of them, would he be able to function at all?

The strong suggestion, based on what Dexter himself says and what Harry told him, is that he wouldn't. He would end up in jail, or dead. The act of killing creates positive spillover to his work, because it allows him to do his job, help solve crimes, and save lives. Dexter may or may not care about the outcomes associated with his success at his job, but that doesn't change the reality of those outcomes. His ability to continue to do the right thing for such very wrong reasons is one of the things that makes him a compelling character.

In rewatching episodes before writing this essay, it often seemed to me that the way the lives of all the characters in the show—not just Dexter—developed was based on the idea that the isolation of one life domain from another is simply impossible. Things will always spill over. That idea created much of the dramatic tension around Dexter himself, but also provided us with memorable incidents in the lives of other characters. Batista's divorce led to a number of work-related problems, including his job-threatening fling with Lila and near arrest by undercover vice officer Barbara Gianna. Debra's romantic history is rife with work spilling into her personal life, as she has moved from the Ice Truck Killer, to an FBI Special Agent, to a confidential informant—to say nothing of poor Gabriel, the children's book writer whom she almost chased out of her life because she looked at their relationship with a homicide detective's eyes. Even patriarch Harry Morgan seems to have had trouble keeping work and non-work separate—and good for Harry. If he hadn't carried that frightened, bloody child out of the cargo crate and adopted him, we wouldn't have ever met Dexter.

Season Four

For all Dexter's trouble with maintaining normality and keeping his work and non-work activities separate, things didn't become really complicated until he married Rita at the end of season three. With the arrival of Harrison, everything in Dexter's life changed. Late-night excursions to hunt and kill bad guys became endurance tests. He fell asleep while staking out a target, then again at the wheel of his SUV. He was so sleep-deprived from getting up with Harrison that he took the wrong files to a trial and allowed a killer to go free, and when he brought his own personal justice to the killer, he forgot what he did with the body!

Prior to season four, Dexter mainly had to deal with work versus non-work. In season four it became a matter of work-nonwork-*family* balance, and things grew exponentially more complicated. Issues from his past continued to re-surface, his need to protect children revealed a chink in his psychological armor, and this man who denied being able to feel emotions seemed to feel something very close to love.

The examples of conflict between work and non-work in season four alone would have been enough to fill a chapter. Take Quinn, whose involvement with reporter Christine compromised his judgment and allowed her to protect her serial-killer father by killing Lundy and shooting Debra. The stories Christine ran relating to the investigation, based in part on information she gleaned through her relationship with Quinn, let her father know exactly how far ahead of Miami Metro he was.

Debra's trouble with men continued. With Lundy's re-appearance in Miami to search for the Trinity killer, she found herself torn between him and Anton. She slept with Lundy, only to have him gunned down in front of her, then told Anton the truth and found herself alone yet again. Her inability to separate work from non-work did not go unnoticed, either; when she claimed a phone call was personal, rather than work, she got this response from Batista: "For you? Same difference" ("If I Had a Hammer," 4-6).

Batista and LaGuerta's intimate relationship spilled over into conflict with Matthews. LaGuerta followed departmental policy and submitted notice of their relationship, only to learn that one or the other of them would be re-assigned to prevent the relationship from affecting their work. A failed attempt at re-assignment (and two signed affidavits) later, they found their careers in jeopardy and quietly married in LaGuerta's office to prevent administrative consequences for perjuring themselves. While the philosophy of, "If it's going to spill over, let it spill over all the way!" may be interesting dramatically, I have little doubt that this series of decisions, culminating in their marriage, is only going to create more work-family conflict for these two in the future.

Central to the season, though, was the Trinity killer—Arthur Mitchell—and what Dexter hoped to learn from him.

Trinity was the most successful serial killer in history, having murdered people using the same pattern in different cities across the country for at least thirty years. Because two of the methods he used looked very much like suicide, a third looked like something that could happen at any bar, and the last was not even noticed because of how he disposed of the bodies, no one but Frank Lundy had picked up on what Trinity was doing.

Trinity was much more interesting than a simple murderer, though. At least, he was to Dexter. Struggling with his new life as a family man, a blood tech, and a serial killer, and trying to balance these roles, Dexter became particularly interested in Trinity when he tracked the man behind the thirty-year spree back to where he lived. Rather than the loner he and Lundy expected, Dexter found a man with a wife and two children, a house in the suburbs, a vibrant work life, and a deep involvement in the community. At a glance, it appeared that Arthur Mitchell had achieved what Dexter was striving for: he juggled not only work and family, but also being a successful serial killer. Clearly, there was much to be learned from Arthur Mitchell.

The assumption at this point was that Arthur had accomplished segmentation; he was able to kill on a regular basis, with no ill effects on his family life. His family certainly looked happy enough, on the surface. Digging a little deeper, though, revealed a truth that Dexter didn't want to hear.

Arthur's family feared him. With them, he was not the kindly man he appeared to be when serving as the deacon at his church or helping to build houses with the "Four Walls" charity. While he fooled the people who only knew him in those contexts, much like Dexter fools almost everyone at Miami Metro, the people around Arthur the most saw through his façade. He hit them. He locked his daughter in her room. When his son displeased him, Arthur broke the boy's little finger. There was no segmentation of serial killer from family man; at home, in the house he provided for them, the truth of Arthur's pathology, his evil, came through. This was what Harry had warned Dexter about, and what Dexter had feared to be true all along.

In its totality, season four seemed to reaffirm the message that spillover is always going to happen. The various roles we play will affect one another—sometimes for the better, often for the worse. Attempts to keep disparate parts of our lives from touching one another are doomed to failure; for the Morgan family, those failures tend toward the bloody.

Dexter struggles with the same things all of us do. We have conflicting roles and demands. We try to balance them. We may find ways that work compensates for things that are lacking in other areas of our lives, or that family and friends provide us with satisfaction our work cannot. We may try to keep different aspects of our lives separate, with varying degrees of success. In the end, though, we find ourselves facing the same kind of question I began this essay with: "Blood tech, husband, father, serial killer . . . Which one are you?" The answer Dexter gave is full of complicated truth, and is one that every one of us has to face.

"All of them."

Morrie Mullins, PhD, is an associate professor of industrial-organizational psychology at Xavier University in Cincinnati. When he's not doing academic research on personnel selection and mentoring students, he's probably writing fiction, immersing himself in pop culture, or spending time with his wife and dogs. His definition of "work-nonwork balance" involves having enough time and energy to work on his stories and watch TV after he gets home. Contrary to what his students may believe, he is emphatically *not* the biggest Star Wars geek in twelve systems.

Who is Dexter, really? What is his true self? The easy answer is that Dexter is a killer—that's who he really is, and all the other roles he plays (brother, boyfriend/husband, friend, worker, coworker, parent) are just performances. But was that killer instinct irredeemably part of him from birth, or could Dexter have been shaped in some other dramatically different way? If the roles he played were performances initially, did Dexter grow into some of the characters he only pretended to be? Do we?

ON BECOMING
A REAL BOY

Emergence and Evolution of Self in Dexter

STEPHEN D. LIVINGSTON

"GHOST" HARRY: You're juggling too many people, Dexter.

DEXTER: I know. Arthur, Beaudry, Rita, now Batista . . .

"GHOST" HARRY: I'm not talking about them. I mean Dexter Morgan. Blood tech. Husband. Father. Serial killer. And now Kyle Butler, extortionist? Which one are you?

DEXTER (looking into multiple mirrors): All of them.

— "Hello, Dexter Morgan," 4-11

I ssues of self and identity have historically ranked among the most beguiling and bemusing of the topics studied by psychologists and philosophers. *Self* is such a tricky concept in part because it is so broadly used. Even a cursory peek at the psychological research literature reveals dozens of theories and concepts that employ the term: *self-esteem*, *self-concept*, *self-discrepancy*, *self-regulation*, *self-awareness*, etc. There are also everyday uses of the term: we often speak of "feeling self-conscious" or "acting selfishly." In modern psychology, self is often defined as the mental apparatus that permits individuals to experience abstract, inwardly directed thoughts and feelings. Research in comparative psychology reveals that some non-human animals, including chimpanzees, gorillas, elephants, dolphins, parrots, and cephalopods (octopi and squid), have a demonstrable ability to recognize themselves. The fact that selfhood, like the lens-bearing eye, has independently emerged in numerous distinct evolutionary lineages suggests that it is very useful feature. It is also notable that the species with self-recognition abilities tend to be, like humans, highly social. However, it has typically been argued that such non-human selfhood is fairly rudimentary: the complex reflective self is thought to be unique to human beings, and core to our historical success as a species. Selfhood appears to be a key contributing factor in our abilities to form preferences, to evaluate ourselves against internal and external standards, to plan for the future, and to relate to others.

As is the case for all of us, young Dexter Morgan's personality is shaped by juvenile life events and early instruction. As an adult, Dexter tries to plot a life course that navigates somewhere between his own desires and the demands of other people. He experiments with different identities, and strategically presents different facets of himself (real or feigned) to different people. He changes as a result of forming and maintaining close interpersonal relationships. His life is, of course, more complicated than most in that Dexter must routinely disguise core aspects of his personality and behavior in order to maintain his homicidal lifestyle. But these life challenges parallel those that we all face, including the difficult problem of distinguishing the "real me" from those aspects that we display to others and those aspects that are imposed upon us by other people.

Born in Blood or Self-Fulfilling Prophecy?

A key factor in the development of self is parental influence. In Dexter's case, we see an early emotional shutdown caused by the traumatic loss of his original family. When Dexter discovered a newspaper article detailing the massacre that separated him from his mother and brother, his juvenile feelings of fright and loss overwhelmed him: "No wonder I felt so disconnected my entire life. If I did have emotions, I'd have to feel *this*" ("Truth Be Told," 1-10). His adoption by the Morgans provided him with a surrogate family, and Harry helped shape Dexter's personality. However, it can also be argued that Harry shaped Dexter's homicidal tendencies. Harry's experiences as a police officer, dealing with violent criminals who emerged from violent backgrounds, likely shaped his expectations about Dexter's developmental course. When the teenaged Dexter showed violence toward animals, Harry was not surprised: "What happened to you changed something inside you. It got into you too early. I'm afraid your urge to kill is only going to get stronger" ("Dexter," 1-1). As an adult, Dexter continues to accept Harry's prediction as a binding truth:

> DEXTER: I am who I am, and nobody's going to change that.
>
> LILA: Jesus, Dexter, what are you so fucking scared of? You make yourself into a monster so you no longer bear responsibility for what you do. 'I can't help it: I'm a monster.' 'Oh, of course I was going to do that: I'm a monster.' ("See-Through," 2-4)

For all of her faults, Lila raised an important point. The definition of self that we choose (or that is chosen for us) sets clear limits on our acceptable range of behaviors. The concept that expectation shapes action is a classic idea in sociology and psychology, and one that has gained popularity outside of academic discourse. You may have heard of the concept of a *self-fulfilling prophecy* (hereafter SFP), as coined by sociologist Robert Merton.[1] In an SFP, a perceiver (Harry) has an expectation (future interpersonal violence because of early trauma) about a target (Dexter), which leads the perceiver to act toward the target in a manner that befits the expectancy (encouraging Dexter to embrace his violent impulses toward people). The target tends to react accordingly (Dexter feels empowered to kill, and does so), thus behaving in a way that confirms the original expectation. The perceiver's belief is now justified by external evidence (Dexter killed because he is a violent person), and the SFP cycle begins anew.[2] Is what we see in the Harry/Dexter dynamic all that different than the parent who enrolls a child in piano lessons because they believe their child has (or should have) musical talent? At a basic conceptual level, I would argue that it is not. An originally subjective (and/or false) belief creates real behavior with real social consequences.

The dynamics of SFPs may make an existing problem even worse. In the episode "See-Through," we saw in flashback that Harry actively tried to thwart an attempt to get professional treatment for Dexter. Harry's wife, concerned that "something is off about him," arranged for Dexter to be assessed by a psychologist. Harry coached Dexter to lie about his problems: "Whatever you think is right, is wrong. When he asks you a question I want you to think of your answer first, and then tell him the exact opposite." Dexter was congratulated by Harry on his successful deception, and told to keep up the same ruse when dealing with others. One wonders how dramatically different

---

[1] Merton, R. K., "The self-fulfilling prophecy," *The Antioch Review*, Vol. 8, 1948; Merton, R. K., *Social theory and social structure*, 1957.

[2] Darley, J. M. and R. H. Fazio, "Expectancy confirmation processes arising in the social-interaction sequence," *American Psychologist*, Vol. 35, 1980; Snyder, M., and A. A. Stukas, Jr., "Self-fulfilling prophecy," *Encyclopedia of Psychology*, Vol. 7, 2000.

Dexter's life course would have been had he entered into treatment for his problems years prior to first taking a human life.

There is an implication in the TV series (and an outright declaration in the novels) that Rita's children, Cody and Astor, have their own violent tendencies as a result of the early environment created by their abusive father. Instead of horror at this realization, the Dexter of the novels experiences delight: "I found myself wanting it to be true. I wanted [Cody] to grow up to be like me—mostly, I realized, because I wanted to shape him and place his tiny feet onto the Harry Path . . . I knew it was wrong—but what fun it would be!" (*Dearly Devoted Dexter*). The Dexter of the books experiences a reproductive urge, but the urge is aimed at psychological rather than biological offspring: he wishes to pass on the Code of Harry. (In *Dexter By Design*, he has an internal struggle about this choice, which apparently quickly passes.) The Dexter of the TV series has a more complex relationship with the Code, in part because he recognizes how much it has kept him isolated from other people and from a "real" life. However, it is hard to imagine that Dexter will escape the fatalistic conclusion that young Harrison will grow up to be like him: not only was Harrison born of Dexter's DNA, but his presence at Rita's murder site carries the expectation that his personality will be similarly "born in blood."

Dramatically Deceptive Dexter

The idea that we derive knowledge about the self by observing the reactions of important social others holds a central place in many influential classic theories, including the symbolic interactionism of sociologists like Charles Cooley and George Herbert Mead, the pragmatic philosophy and psychology of William James, and the psychoanalytics of Melanie Klein and Jacques Lacan. One logical consequence of self as a social construction is that an individual is typically highly sensitive to the perceptions of other people. James (one of my favorite psychological thinkers) distinguished between "self as subject" and "self as object." *Self as subject* refers to the singular, continuous, embodied self perceived during reflective consciousness: you are in some sense the same person today as you were yesterday; you are distinguishable from other people. *Self as object* refers to the multiplicity of constructions existing in the minds of relevant social others: you are different things to different people. For example, I am a son, a younger brother, a husband, a friend, a colleague, a teacher, or merely the faceless author of the text you're reading. Dexter Morgan is a son, a brother, a husband, a father, a forensic technician, and a murderer. In James's words: "a man has as many social selves as there are individuals who recognize him."[3] In Dexter's: "Brother, friend, boyfriend . . . All part of my costume collection" ("Let's Give the Boy a Hand," 1-4).

Echoes of these older ideas are found in modern social psychological theories. For example, self-discrepancy theory (SDT)[4] predicts specific emotional and motivational consequences from contrasting our current self (our "actual self," in the language of SDT, keeping in mind that our self-view may not always be objectively accurate) with our positive aspirations (our "ideal self"), what societal pressures compel us to be (our "ought selves," of which there may be many, analogous to the Jamesian "social selves"), and perhaps even what we dread becoming (the "feared self").[5] Dexter has tried on various personas, to varying degrees of comfort and success. Like all of us, he has internalized values from significant others. Much of the

---

[3] James, W., *Psychology: The Briefer Course*, 1892/1985.

[4] Higgins, E. T., "Self-discrepancy: A theory relating self and affect," *Psychological Review*, Vol. 94, 1987.

[5] Carver, C. S., J. W. Lawrence, and M. F. Scheier, "Self-discrepancies and affect: Introducing the role of feared selves," *Personality and Social Psychology Bulletin*, Vol. 25, 1999.

change we see in him during the series has resulted from his looking to these other people, who represent externalized versions of Dexter's different selves, for inspiration on how to live. Harry, who comes to personify Dexter's conscience, represents an ought self. Arthur Mitchell changed in Dexter's eyes from an ideal self (the prolific serial killer who has everything under tight control) to a feared self (the monster who terrorizes his own family to maintain that control).

There is also a long tradition of using the metaphor of theatrical presentation when discussing social behavior. Erving Goffman, a pioneering intellect in micro-sociology—the study of individual and small-group interactions—was a strong proponent of this dramaturgical perspective. In his influential first book *The Presentation of Self in Everyday Life* (1959), Goffman argued that much of human interaction can be likened to theatrical performance, in which we variously play the roles of involved actors or passive audience members. For all the reverence in Western society given to being "true to oneself," intentional artifice pervades much of our lives. We dress, talk, act, and react in ways designed to evoke desired responses in others. In Goffman's words: "control [over the behavior of other people] is achieved largely by influencing the definition of the situation which the others come to formulate, and [the individual] can influence this definition by expressing himself in such a way as to give them the kind of impression that will lead them to act voluntarily in accordance with his own plan."

Goffman himself admitted that he was by no means the originator of this idea: "[t]he general notion that we make a presentation of ourselves to others is hardly novel." Nearly 350 years before, in *As You Like It*, William Shakespeare famously wrote that "All the world's a stage/And one man in his time plays many parts." That classic collection of military wisdom known as *The Art of War* is laden with encouragements to deceive one's enemies (and even one's allies!) by making false shows of strength and weakness (e.g., "all warfare is based on deception"; "practice dissimulation, and you will succeed"). The English word *person* originates from the Latin word *persona*, which meant both "dramatic character" and "mask" prior to its use as a general term for "human being." We still commonly use *persona* as a general term for a public social role enacted by an individual. Clearly, the recognition that human life is anchored in strategic presentation is no recent insight.

Indeed, if you examine your own life, you might find some similarity to Dexter (hopefully not *too much* similarity). Dexter feels pressure to keep his secrets secret, but he also longs to reveal those secrets to the world. He alters his actions to fit his audience, much like you may present yourself differently when at work (industrious), on the athletic field (competitive), with your parents (respectful), and at the local tavern (fun-loving). Beginning in adolescence, all people experience a growing realization that there is a multiplicity of selves from which to choose, and that peers, parents, and important social others put constraints on which self we display at any given time. This often causes distress, as the young person is unsure which set of behaviors makes up the "real" self. Older adolescents typically arrive at the conclusion that frequent and strategic shifting of behaviors across situational and relational contexts is both necessary and desirable, and that it need not indicate that one is somehow fake or dishonest. (As the poet Walt Whitman famously wrote, we contain multitudes.)

Psychoanalyst Erik Erikson argued that this problem of *identity achievement* vs. *identity diffusion* (or *role confusion*) is the core developmental conflict of adolescence. Extending Erikson's ideas, developmental psychologist James Marcia proposed further subdivisions of identity maturation, including *identity foreclosure*, which occurs when a person adopts some value system, occupational aspiration, etc.—typically imposed by parents—without ensuring that it truly fits the self. Here, Marcia describes the adolescent in the grips of identity foreclosure:

> It is difficult to tell where his parents' goals for him leave off and where his begin. He is becoming what others have pre-pared or intended him to become as a child . . . one feels that if he were faced with a situation in which parental values were nonfunctional, he would feel extremely threatened.[6]

Compare Marcia's description with this candid self-assessment of Dexter's in an early episode: I'm not sure where Harry's vision of me ends and the real me starts ("Let's Give the Boy a Hand"). And as described in Marcia's theory, we usually find Dexter gets into considerable trouble when he encounters problems to which the Code of Harry is inapplicable.

Foreclosure need not occur only once, or only during ado-lescence, and indeed identity foreclosure is not experienced by all people during normal development. It is a typically a brief period in a person's life, and is usually followed by experimen-tation with possible alternatives (a period Marcia termed *iden-tity moratorium*) and then strong commitment to some specific identity. But Dexter has not clearly reached a point of identity achievement: he's still not entirely sure what he wants to be when he "grows up."

Yet perhaps because he does not have a strongly defined sense of personal identity, Dexter is especially successful at acts of social disguise:

DEXTER: The only real question I have is why, in a build-ing full of cops, all supposedly with a keen insight into the

---

[6] Marcia, J. E., "Development and validation of ego-identity status," *Journal of Personality and Social Psychology*, Vol. 3, 1965.

human soul, is Doakes the only one gets the creeps from me? ("Dexter")

This is an excellent question, and reflects the success of Dexter's attempts at disguise. In Goffman's formulation: "an individual who implicitly or explicitly signifies that he has certain social characteristics ought in fact to be what he claims he is . . . others find, then, that the individual has informed them as to what is and as to what they *ought* to see as the 'is'" (emphasis original). Dexter acts friendly—witness his daily donut ritual—dresses well, and performs his job quite successfully. The positive stereotype that police are "good guys" concerned with upholding the law is believed by most people, including the police themselves. Dexter thus benefits from a sort of "innocence by association."[7] Dexter is not merely friendly with law enforcement but a functional member of the group, a sort of wolf in blue wool.[8]

Dexter most often has difficulty in presenting a convincing front when it comes to sexual matters. He often spouts sexual innuendo without even realizing it, to the amusement of his sister and coworkers. He originally chose to date Rita because, after being repeatedly abused by her former romantic partner, she was largely disinterested in sex. Once Rita showed signs of sexual receptivity, Dexter fretted about the consequences: "I can't have sex with Rita. Every time I sleep with a woman, she sees me for what I really am—empty. Then she's gone" ("Shrink

---

[7] Winslow, M. P., "Reactions to the imputation of prejudice," *Basic and Applied Social Psychology,* Vol. 26, 2004.

[8] This sort of disguise is not unheard of in the real world of serial killing, as evidenced by two current cases: in Brazil, a retired police sergeant is the prime suspect in the killings of thirteen gay men; in Canada, the former commanding officer of a major air force base is charged with the murders and sexual assaults of four women, as well as scores of robberies. Nor is it unusual to find serial killers employed as health care professionals.

Wrap," 1-8). For all of the braggadocio and boasting we find in everyday conversations about sex, it is an act that makes us highly vulnerable both physically and psychologically. While Dexter does not have a normal degree of interest in sex, he does have a very normal fear about it: that our new sexual partners will discover something strange about us—say, a physical abnormality or some unusual kink—and that this discovery will lead to the dissolution of the romantic relationships that we wish to maintain.

The Mask Is Slipping

Many psychologists and philosophers, working from the assumption that the self is a partial product of socialization, have suggested that the self need not be contained within the boundaries of the physical individual. Some theorists have suggested that the closeness of relationships can be usefully quantified in terms of how much the other person is included within a self-representation. Think back to high school math class and Venn diagrams, which use overlapping circles to illustrate associations between objects or categories. In psychological terms, the more overlap of the circle representing "ME" and the circle representing "YOU," the closer our relationship is likely to be.[9] Anecdotally, many of us will have witnessed how new romantic partners happily refer to themselves as "we" or as "a couple" after they reach some basic level of commitment. In the general phenomenon of *deindividuation*, people temporarily lose their sense of being a distinct person and instead come to think of themselves as part of a social unit. Psychologists have found interesting cognitive consequences of such perceived "we-ness." For example, a classic study by Festinger, Pepitone, and Newcomb

---

[9] Aron, A., E. N. Aron, M. Tudor, and G. Nelson, "Close relationships as including other in the self," *Journal of Personality and Social Psychology*, Vol. 60, 1991.

showed that the more individuals identified with the tasked goal of a discussion group, the more difficult it was for them to accurately recall which members of the group said some specific statement.[10] Similarly, Brenner found that the accuracy of recall for a romantic partner's scripted speech (i.e., vocabulary words read from index cards) was intermediate between memory of one's own speech and memory of a stranger's speech.[11]

Self-disclosure is an important ingredient in psychologically intimate relationships. Dexter clearly desires to unburden himself of his secrets. Witness the joy in his confession to psychiatrist Emmet Meridian: "I'm a serial killer. Oh God . . . That feels so *amazing* to say out loud!" ("Shrink Wrap"). Yet in his relationship with Rita, Dexter was on the horns of a dilemma. Total self-disclosure would surely have meant an abrupt end to the romantic relationship (and to his life outside of a prison cell), and yet total non-disclosure would also have ultimately killed that relationship. Throughout the series, Dexter dropped occasional hints to Rita about a darker side that he keeps hidden, perhaps hoping that she would show signs of receptiveness, but Rita typically ignored these hints or dismissed them outright:

DEXTER: I have a dark side, too. [RITA laughs.] What? I do!

RITA: Somehow, I doubt that. You have a good heart, Dexter. You're not like Paul. You don't hurt people.

DEXTER: Innocent people. I don't hurt *innocent* people. ("Circle of Friends," 1-7)

---

[10] Festinger, L., A. Pepitone, and T. Newcomb, "Some consequences of deindividuation in a group," *Journal of Abnormal and Social Psychology*, Vol. 47, 1952.

[11] Brenner, M. "Caring, love, and selective memory." *Proceedings of the 79th Annual Convention of the American Psychological Association*, Vol. 6 (Part 1), 1971. See also Aron, et al., 1991, Experiment 2.

In season two, a great deal of Dexter's initial attraction to Lila stemmed from his belief that he could reveal more of his true self to her than he ever could to Rita. Consider the scene where Dexter showed Lila remains of the "Bay Harbor Butcher" (his) victims, and she expressed fascination rather than revulsion:

DEXTER: You're not disgusted? Appalled? Horrified?

LILA: It's incredible.

DEXTER: But the person who did this . . .

LILA: Is a person just like me . . . like you. We're *all* good, Dexter, and we're *all* evil.

DEXTER [V/O]: I thought I closed the door to anyone ever seeing me for who I am, but this woman sees me. She doesn't know it, but she's looking behind the mask—and she's not turning away. ("See-Through")

A recurring theme in the TV series (and in Jeff Lindsay's books) is that Dexter can quickly see through the veneers of other killers, and they can similarly penetrate his disguise. Lila, Brian Moser, Arthur Mitchell, and even Sergeant Doakes all carry their own "Dark Passengers." This shared strangeness leads Dexter to feel an affinity for each of them despite their strong antagonism toward him.

Doakes was sharing space with something, just like I was. Not the same thing, but something very similar, a panther to my tiger . . . A reasonable being might think that he and I could find some common ground; have a cup of coffee and compare our Passengers, exchange trade talk and chitchat about dismemberment techniques. (*Dearly Devoted Dexter*)

Early on, we saw that Dexter has purely instrumental goals in his human relationships. He expresses a strong fondness for children, perhaps because of their general innocence and lack of guile. But adults are another matter entirely. As Dexter narrates in the book series:

> I genuinely wouldn't care if every human in the universe were suddenly to expire, with the possible exception of myself and maybe Deborah. Other people are less important to me than lawn furniture. I do not, as the shrinks put it so eloquently, have any sense of the reality of others. And I am not burdened with this realization. (*Darkly Dreaming Dexter*)

Although the Dexter of the TV series is not quite so callous, aside from his sister Debra almost all people of any consequence in Dexter's life when we first encounter him can be categorized as obstacles to be overcome (e.g., Doakes), props to be used (e.g., his police coworkers), or victims that can satisfy his lust for killing. Dexter feels little empathy for others, and this indifference might stem from a failure to incorporate other people into his self-representation.[12] His relationship with Rita started solely because he sought camouflage: most people want partners, and so to appear normal he must take on a partner as well. We saw this lesson imparted by Harry in a flashback to Dexter's adolescence:

DEXTER: I just like being alone.

HARRY: But most normal people don't, and it's important that you seem normal.

---

[12] Cialdini, R. B., S. L. Brown, B. P. Lewis, C. Luce, and S. L. Neuberg, "Reinterpreting the empathy-altruism relationship: When one into one equals oneness," *Journal of Personality and Social Psychology*, Vol. 73, 1997.

DEXTER: Even though I'm not.

HARRY: *Because* you're not. ("Love, American Style," 1-5)

As the series has continued, we have seen a progressive evolution of Dexter's character and his attitudes toward engaging with other people. This evolution evokes the distinction made by German philosopher Martin Buber between *Ich-Es* ("I-It") and *Ich-Du* ("I-Thou") relationships.[13] Buber suggested that we attain a form of spiritual, even religious, transcendence when we move from treating another person as an exploitable thing (an "It") to engaging with that person as a being of intrinsic worth (a "Thou"). Dexter yearns for such transcendence, to emerge from his self-imposed cocoon, even though it presents clear risks:

> The relationships I cultivate . . . They're not just disguises anymore. I need them, even if they make me vulnerable. ("The British Invasion," 2-12)

> The Dark Passenger's been fighting against it, trying to keep me all to himself. But it's my turn now, to get what I want. To embrace my family. And maybe one day, not so long from now, I'll be rid of the Dark Passenger. It all begins with a getaway. Time away from the old me. ("The Getaway," 4-12)

However, we have seen that Dexter's attempts at forming relationships—such as with Lila (season two) and Miguel Prado (season three)—have typically led to tragic results. This pattern culminated with the death of Rita at the hands of Arthur Mitchell, the Trinity Killer, which clearly could have been avoided had Dexter not engaged with Mitchell in the first place. We witness Dexter's optimism about starting a new life, *sans* the Dark Passenger, quickly dissipate after discovering Rita's body:

---

[13] Buber, M. *Ich und Du* [*I and Thou*]. 1923/2004.

> Harry was right. I thought I could change what I am; keep my
> family safe. But it doesn't matter what I do, what I choose . . .
> *I'm* what's wrong. This is fate. ("The Getaway," 4-12)

The loss of Rita in some ways reset Dexter to his beginnings. Rita can no longer act to constrain his violent impulses or reinforce his positive behaviors. Robbed of his long-term partner, he must work hard if he is to develop another, similar relationship. Dexter's return to a fatalistic outlook in "The Getaway" ("*I'm* what's wrong") may create strong reluctance to engage in this process and reveal himself to a new woman, for fear of hurting a new partner (or himself) by being honest. But whether he withdraws inwardly, embracing the Dark Passenger, or expands outwardly, finding solace in those who love him, Dexter's self will continue to grow and change. For all of us, creating and maintaining a cohesive sense of self is a work in progress.

AUTHOR'S NOTE: Sincere thanks are due to Clarissa Thompson and Sabrina Bellhouse, both excellent psychologists and dedicated Dexter fans, for their constructive comments on an earlier version of this manuscript.

Stephen D. Livingston, BSc, MA, is a social psychologist and science writer with expertise in the domains of prejudice and persuasion. He studied biology and psychology at the University of Winnipeg, and social psychology and political science at the Ohio State University. He was most recently an assistant professor of psychology at the University of Toronto Scarborough. You can read more of his writing in *Tinted Lenses*—a blog that discusses bias in everyday life—at www.Psychology Today.com.

Is there hope for someone as damaged as Dexter? Jeremy Clyman argues that there is. Dexter has three angels in his life—Camilla, Debra, and Rita. They all truly care for him. Collectively, they have the potential to persuade Dexter that the world is actually not so terrible, and neither is he.

THE ANGELS

ON HIS SHOULDER

JEREMY CLYMAN

Dexter is a likable serial killer of killers. This is a statement of the obvious. But let's not let this single characteristic—the tendency to kill—dictate our view of his entire identity. Just for a moment, suspend this rather startling, perhaps horrific point, as it distorts our view of who he truly is and what he truly wants. Suspending judgment helps us to realize that the true function of Dexter's midnight murders is to assert an excessive need for control of his surroundings. He kills because he doesn't want the family of a killer's next victim to endure the trauma and loss he suffered as a child. And this relentless cycle of death is driven by an equally relentless search for identity. Questions of identity are often lurking behind the expression of excessive needs. In other words, Dexter feels such a strong desire to control his outer world (bringing justice to murderers) because it helps to appease the sense of inner chaos he feels over not knowing who he is.

Dexter is in his early thirties and yet he is a blank slate when it comes to answering the question "Who am I?" More than enough psychological studies indicate that the answer to this question involves other people, namely significant attachment figures (a.k.a. friends and family). Identity is more a reflection than anything else. Who we think we are is significantly informed by the feedback we receive from others.

Thus, to a degree, the evolution of Dexter's identity is in the hands of those around him. And a glance into his internal world reveals a battle between the "angelic" and "devilish" members of his external world.

Much research exists on the human need to organize beliefs about the self, other people, and the world into a coherent narrative. Healthy identity flows from an integrated view of all three, and leads to deeper insight into oneself, an attitude of flexible optimism toward others, and a hopeful belief in the world. Devil figures, either implicitly or explicitly, engender an unhealthy narrative in which the opposite happens. The self is viewed with ignorance, others are cast in a suspicious light, and the world is perceived as a hopeless place. The result of such a narrative is dissatisfaction with oneself and disconnection from the world.

Dexter's identity is primarily ruled by devils. First there are his different selves—the traumatized child that feels helpless and frightened, the alienated adolescent fearful of his own rage, and, of course, the adult calmed by murder—which create a lot of inner turmoil and negative emotion. Watching his mother die, experiencing alienation from his peers, and harboring secrets about his identity are all experiences that he needs to explain to himself in order to reduce their emotional intensity. The explanation offered by his (sometimes) misguided father Harry—another devil, though a complicated one—was that Dexter had within him a dark force that could be channeled but never fully controlled—that this was who he was, and he could not change that. His psychotic brother Brian's appearance reinforced the validity of this explanation, since he and Dexter shared the same genes as well as the desire to kill. Even more devils followed. His nightmarish Narcotics Anonymous sponsor, Lila, taught him to regret intimacy when she inexplicably transformed from an understanding lover into a violently mistrustful, sometimes paranoid stalker of *Fatal Attraction* proportions. Miguel, the monster-in-hiding, furthered this pessimistic view of humanity by teaching Dexter that friendship can be a seductive form of betrayal. Whether through misguided advice or idiosyncratic misdeeds, these figures relayed the same message: "Like us, you, Dexter, are a tragic figure doomed to live within a broken mind, amongst enemies disguised as friends, within an unforgiving world that would reject you if it knew the truth."

These voices have coalesced in the back of his mind, creating an overwhelming self-loathing that dominates his identity, particularly his interpretation of his need to kill. It may appear on the surface that Dexter pursues death and blood in the same way that a heroin addict pursues his next fix. Not true. Recall those moments in which Dexter has reflected upon his murderous nature. He does not experience the pleasure and relief of an addiction satiated. Instead, he wrestles with himself in the ways that tormented souls with forgiveness issues wrestle with themselves. He seeks Harry's approval, he evaluates his behavior through a strict moral lens, he saturates his psyche with negative self-talk about being a "monster," and he fearfully ponders the potential consequences of his actions on those he loves. What he's really doing when he's killing is attempting to organize his "devil" voices into a coherent narrative. He wraps these destructive voices into a neatly compartmentalized package—his Dark Passenger—and engages in a life that takes him further away from what he really wants: to see himself as normal, connected, and loved.

To do this, he needs to allow his self-concept to be influenced by those who already see him this way and can help him develop healthy views of himself, others, and the world. By listening to his angels—Camilla, Debra, and Rita—Dexter moves ever closer to this destination that he so desperately desires, and for which we as an audience so cheerfully root.

Camilla: The Invisible Mother

Camilla was a sweet, homely, donut-loving file clerk who only seemed insignificant. Behind her kind blue eyes rested the concern and protective instincts of a mother—in this case, an invisible one. When lung cancer got the better of her in season three and she slowly but surely began to die, Dexter discovered that she knew of his traumatic beginnings (witnessing the brutal slaughtering of his mother), his connection to the Ice Truck Killer, and perhaps even his secret life as a killer. This startling epiphany changes the meaning of their previous water-cooler chats and mindless transactions significantly. It indicates that their encounters contained subtle but clear injections of the mother-child bond: namely, intense love, acceptance, and support that never wavered no matter what Dexter did.

Dexter couldn't receive this from his real mother after her death, but he received it from Camilla. We saw evidence of her perpetual but invisible mothering from their first encounter in season one. Camilla said, "Been keeping your fingernails clean . . . good boy" ("Dexter," 1-1). Later in season one she requested that he "find a nice girl . . . settle down" ("Truth Be Told," 1-11). At the time these mundane comments seemed to be nothing more than mildly humorous reminders that Dexter believed these things to be well beyond his reach. But in light of the revelations in season three, we realize these comments were, in fact, the stereotypical fretting of a mother-in-disguise. What's more, evidence suggests these implicit signals penetrated Dexter's psyche. While he rushed past his workmates without so much as a "hello" during his daily morning donut rounds, he never failed to stop, sit, and chat with Camilla. Still better evidence surfaced in season three when Camilla was on her deathbed. Dexter sat by her side like a loving son and raced around town hoping to satisfy her request for the best key lime pie.

When Dexter reluctantly met her final request, a peaceful death by his hand, Camilla taught him something that all mothers teach their children: that his behaviors, no matter how extreme, do not define him. Though he may travel with a Dark Passenger, that does not make him unlovable. Camilla normalized his fears and secrets. He may think of himself as an evil "monster," but Camilla helped him see that the act of killing is not so black and white. Spoon-feeding Camilla poisoned key lime pie was not committing a horrific act. Quite the contrary, he was saving a generous and prudent woman from further torture. Her undying gratitude (pardon the pun) confirmed that this act was more humane than a nurse's morphine or a friend's prayer could ever be.

On some level, Dexter's surrogate, symbolic mother taught him another lesson contrary to his common perceptions of self. All those years that Camilla sat at her desk with little donut crumbs bordering her mouth, Dexter resided at the heart of her internal world—she thought about him when he wasn't around and she protected him in ways he didn't realize (i.e., by destroying the police file of his mother's murder). Dexter knew that Camilla's opinion of things mattered—that she was a good person. Once he knew of his high standing in her mind, he had no choice but to logically conclude that he was also a good person, since she deemed him deserving of her focus and affection. As much as his self-loathing may resist such an idea, his sophisticated deductive reasoning abilities must conclude that he is worthwhile and lovable.

These elements of attachment may seem silly and simplistic, but research on the subject of attachment and personality development, including Daniel Siegel's in *The Mindful Brain*, suggests that a strong, secure attachment experience can completely change an individual for the better. It can be the difference between a productive, fulfilling, and moral life, and one of wasted talent, ineptitude, and misery. According to this literature, however, in order for the attachment process to significantly affect personality development, a minimal mother-child bond must exist during a specific "critical" developmental period in early childhood. In Dexter's case, the interesting question of "too little, too late" arises. He received from Camilla exactly what a child receives in a healthy attachment process, but he did so as a fully formed adult in the short but intense period of her hospitalization and death. Although Dexter's learning environment was far from ideal, he seemed to fully commit to Camilla, appearing at her bedside with consistency and forcing himself to feel the vulnerable feelings of despair as her condition worsened.

Debra: The Better Half

As his second brightest angel, Debra props Dexter up, literally and figuratively. Dexter's self-esteem is in the basement. He is surprised by every compliment Debra gives him—his eyebrows raise with incredulity every time she expresses her appreciation that he is such an awesome big brother—and he operates from the assumption that he is an outcast and that his friendships are not legitimate. The "devil" voices have worked him over pretty good. He needs someone to restore his belief in himself, and Debra's defining feature—her evolution from self-flagellating street cop into resilient detective—serves this purpose admirably.

When we met Debra in season one she was working undercover as a prostitute. This "disguise" was also symbolic. Like the stereotypical prostitute archetype, Debra was vivacious and over-the-top profane. She was filled with insecurity, dated a revolving door of tattooed losers, and failed to play the political games at work to the point of self-sabotage. Over the course of the four seasons that followed, she evolved tremendously. Her judgment in bed vastly improved (at least after the manipulative "Rudy"). She dated Lundy, a famed serial killer hunter, who helped her access peace and tranquility, and then a laid-back musician, who loved her for exactly who she is. Her professional gains have been even more significant. By season three Debra had transformed into the kind of serial killer hunter that Lundy could be proud of, and that Dexter feared would beat him to the bad guys. Everything about her persona screams "detective," from her dry-cleaned button-down shirts to her tenacity in the interrogation room to her tendency to drown herself in boxes of evidence. She's like a gladiator preparing for battle.

Now, how does this very Debra-specific evolution positively impact Dexter? First, Debra changes the meaning of what it means to be a "Morgan." They are both Morgans—the beneficiaries of a dysfunctional psychological will bequeathed by Harry. They both struggle to identify and express their emotions, to trust others, and, most importantly, to view themselves without distortion. Early on, Debra viewed herself as worthless, undeserving of her father's love. For instance, early in season one Debra developed some decent leads related to the Ice Truck Killer case but Lieutenant LaGuerta shut her down simply because she liked asserting her political power and did not like Debra. Instead of confronting her boss's impulsive stone-walling with the confidence her strong ideas warranted, she withdrew and complained to Dexter. Her self-perception was laced with insecurity and a sense of helplessness. For a while she became entrenched in a doomed cycle—she relentlessly pursued bad guys, but she was so plagued with self-doubt and chronic dissatisfaction that each successful collar failed to address how her father never fully appreciated her. As discussed, Harry infected

Dexter with a different but equally destructive self-perception. Dexter sees himself as dangerous and incapable of fitting in. Similar to Debra, he became entrenched in his own doomed cycle, in which a code of killing kept basic human connection at arm's length. As Debra continues to overcome her insecurity and helplessness and gain composure and assertiveness, she is exorcising Harry's toxic heirloom. She is helping Dexter to realize that he, like his fellow Harry-survivor, can evolve into a conqueror of their "dark passengers" instead of their prisoner.

The other way Debra helps is by fully embracing an aspect of herself that Dexter struggles to embrace within himself. Dexter battles most viciously with the part of him that wants to live within the bounds of law and order, and he rejects what most citizens take for granted about the justice system. He pursues criminals because he views the system as a dilapidated dam, leaking injustice from all sides. On the other hand, Debra's belief in law and order is rock solid. Almost everything about her is squeaky clean and by the book, a tribute to her conviction in the justice system. She relentlessly pursues bad guys, strictly abides by the "cop" code, and never does drugs or anything remotely corrupt (with the exception of an occasional drink). In season two when she fell into a psychic funk and thought of herself as the idiot cop who failed to realize her boyfriend was actually a serial killer, she emerged from her identity crisis because of— among other things—around-the-clock exercise. While Dexter chooses to kill as a means of managing his mounting distress with life, Debra chooses one of society's most popular and palatable outlets.

To live more effectively within society and be mentally well-rounded, Dexter needs some of Debra's societal faith and optimism. Fortunately for him, a slow but steady internalization of Debra's gung-ho societal attitudes has unfolded. This was most vividly articulated in the climactic scenes of season one. When Rudy, Dexter's long-lost, sociopathic brother, surfaced with plans to form a brotherly version of Bonnie and Clyde, he seduced and abducted Debra in the hope that Dexter would play the villain by killing her and, by extension, commit to a life of code-less murder. Dexter chose the hero option and, in between tears, killed his brother and watched the blood drain from his body.

Let's recount this sequence with an eye toward symbolism and in the context of Dexter's battle with self. Rudy clearly represents the worst of Dexter—the anti-social part that wants to reject a law and order that abandoned him as a child when he needed it most (during his mother's brutal slaying). Debra, we now know, represents the pro-social part of Dexter that fully accepts a law and order that is mostly just and deserving of a second chance. When Dexter chose Debra, he was not just choosing his little sister over his big brother. He was embracing an aspect of himself and a way of life.

Debra props Dexter up in more literal ways as well. She builds his self-esteem like a psychological cheerleader on steroids, through myriad channels, both unintentional and intentional. She does this unintentionally through the rather large chip on her shoulder that stems from suffering second-place syndrome as a child. Indeed, flashbacks expose a family dynamic in which Harry clearly prioritized Dexter. When at crime scenes, Harry yelled at Debra to get back in the car while he eagerly showed Dexter various investigative details. On his death bed, Harry talked right through Debra to Dexter about adhering to "the Code." The silver lining to Debra being treated as invisible is that Dexter stood out as special. She is a walking reminder of how much Harry cared for and favored him.

Debra also cheerleads intentionally through their steady banter. She relays a positive image of Dexter, to him and to everyone around them, with the passion and persistence of a gifted politician. In her eyes, he is a hero who saved her life (from Brian) and then prevented her from "spinning out of control" in the aftermath. He is a brilliant forensics analyst who can do no wrong in catching bad guys, and to whom she turns when seeking expert guidance on her criminal theories. Her cheerleading reached fever pitch in the season four finale when she gave Dexter the "you are, have always been, and will forever be the best thing in my life" speech. All of this affords Dexter a mini-vacation from his negative self-perception in which he can see himself as a protective big brother, blood genius, and fellow survivor of an emotionally tumultuous upbringing.

Remember toward the end of season two when Dexter's self-loathing was on the verge of overtaking his will to live? There was upheaval in his inner world as his sense of safety and stability was shaken by a profound sense of failure. The media's coverage of his well-intentioned killings led to less purposeful copycat killings. He was on the verge of being dishonorably captured by the FBI, he could not protect his loved ones from Lila's erratic behavior, and his moral code was in shambles as Sergeant Doakes, his relatively honorable colleague, sat in a locked cage. He was on the verge of confessing his sins to the authorities—for him, a form of psychic suicide. And then Debra came over for dinner. She relished the way he cooked her steak, but more importantly, she reminded him that he is loved—that he is the kind of noble warrior that provides for those who depend upon him. This affirming view of Dexter, in recalling his purpose and his virtues, saved him from self-destruction.

Rita: The Infiltrator

Rita was the brightest of Dexter's angels. She was the only person in Dexter's life who offered romantic intimacy and a gateway into the family man lifestyle he never thought possible. In short, she infiltrated his psychological defenses and effectively pushed him to grow into a better man through a Rita-specific formula of vulnerability, emotional space, and trust. She chipped away at Dexter's existential loneliness, proving herself to be a perfect fit—even soul-mate material—for the idiosyncratic Dexter.

As a single mother and victim of past domestic abuse, Rita began season one just as averse to intimacy as Dexter. Her regrettable marriage to ex-convict Paul induced a virtual phobia of conflict and plummeting self-esteem. And that damage doesn't even take into account the physical bumps and bruises. Moreover, she was bleeding to death from a thousand emotional cuts. In an early episode, Rita politely asked her inconsiderate neighbor to silence her perpetually barking dog. Rita's request was met with laughter and a door in the face. Then, her ex-husband's drug dealer slithered into view to hijack her car. In both cases Rita passively withdrew, because there wasn't a combative bone in her body. A single working mother who tormented herself over how to protect her children from a nasty, erratic world, who had to commute to work sleep-deprived, and on a crowded bus—was this not the perfect rescue scenario for Dexter's compulsive protective tendencies?

Halfway through season one Rita broke out of her shell to enact a patient yet spirited campaign to consummate their relationship. Dexter fought her off. He's a tough nut to crack and numerous times she was left naked, confused, and alone in the dust of his mad dashes toward the door, driven by fears of rejection. This "reluctant beginnings" phase of the relationship carried two sweeping, internal changes: Dexter amended the Harry Code with a sub-code—let's call it the Rita Act—in which he attempted to control and protect through non-murderous means. His responses to Rita-related conflicts were always compromises. He kidnapped the obnoxious dog (instead of killing it) and he provided Rita with a new car (instead of killing the drug dealing car thief). And when Paul threatened for custody, Dexter ended his reign of terror with a clever frame job involving a frying pan to the face and planted heroin. And

Dexter made these recalibrations because he was "hooked" by Rita's wounded child-like vulnerability.

. If Rita's damsel-in-distress persona was the hook, then her gentle, non-judgmental perspective was what reeled him in; it was like nothing his self-loathing had ever encountered. She assumed his goodness until proven otherwise and didn't violate his personal boundaries or "alone time." In fact, her acceptance of his workaholic, tightly compartmentalized lifestyle never wavered. In season four she trashed the traditional expectations and natural needs of a wife, accepting him for who he was, even if that meant having a husband who couldn't express his love in direct, traditional ways (he showed care for the relationship by punching a neighbor who kissed her) or fulfill basic familial obligations like sticking around for major holidays (apparently sociopaths like Arthur need to die tonight instead of tomorrow).

The vast expanse of emotional space that Rita provided along with the relationship he always wanted but never thought he could have allowed him to operate with greater comfort and confidence. He fell for her in a genuine and profound way that was first overtly expressed in the office of Dr. Emmett Meridian toward the end of season one. Yes, Dexter was there to kill the "evil" psychiatrist for preying on his clinically depressed patients, but before Dexter satisfied his internal needs he opened up to the therapeutic process. He experienced a breakthrough in which his loving feelings toward Rita and true capacity for intimacy were realized. Afterward, he ran over to Rita's house in the dead of night like Romeo to Juliet, and his leap of faith was immediately rewarded. Rita became his guide to the unchartered emotional territory of intimacy, showing him that sex and intimacy could be as appealing as blood and death.

During season two, the blissful boat of domesticity began to rock. Dexter's frame job of ex-husband Paul was a stray shoe short of flawless, and when Rita discovered the shoe that

Paul claimed fell off his foot after Dexter knocked him unconscious and dragged him out of the house, his seemingly paranoid accusations were validated. It seemed inevitable that Rita would turn Dexter in and end their relationship. But this is gentle, non-judgmental Rita we're talking about. Despite the moral qualms inherent in keeping Paul in prison (a move that proved complicit in his death) and despite the fact that finding the shoe recast Dexter's frequent midnight disappearances in a more ominous light, Rita chose to trust Dexter. Her we-need-to-stick-together mantra cushioned Dexter's serious trust and intimacy issues. Quite predictably, her reaction to the "shoe debacle" only solidified her loyalty to Dexter. One can imagine many moments in which Rita might have caved. She could have betrayed Dexter for the familiar comfort of Paul (i.e., "he says he's changed, maybe I should believe him"), or the psychological comfort of moral righteousness (i.e., "Dexter committed a crime so he's got to go"). Even when she learned that Paul died in a prison fight, she remained in Dexter's corner. Specifically, by exerting tremendous psychological effort, she effectively managed two overwhelming emotions: a sense of anger toward Dexter for putting Paul in prison, and a sense of guilt that she sat on the sidelines and allowed Paul to remain there.

For Dexter there were two key advantages to Rita's discovery: First, Dexter saw the moral sacrifices that Rita made on his behalf and concluded that their relationship and his role as boyfriend must have been worth the burden for her. Second, Dexter was forced to fabricate a much more palatable addiction than killing—heroin. The advantage to this lie is that it freed Dexter up to share himself with Rita through abstract discussions of his Dark Passenger. Even though Dexter was talking about killing and he knew that Rita thought he was talking about heroin, it still allowed him to be honest with her, and build emotional intimacy with her, in a way he otherwise couldn't have.

Next and most important came the "family man" phase of their relationship, in which Dexter was pushed toward further positive change. Yes, Dexter's "killer" identity could hide even more safely behind his new image as husband and father. But this cynically pragmatic view of his choice to marry Rita was soon swept away by lucrative emotional returns on his investment as a family man and the discovery that he's actually a pretty good dad.

His new family man persona has an effect far greater than his killings. Despite a childhood filled with abandonment and adversity, Cody remained a sweet and innocent boy. Dexter must have realized that his hugs, compliments, and presence at school events contributed to Cody's unexpected normalcy. And when Dexter's social ineptitude put him in conflict with newly adolescent Astor in season four and she said, "It's okay. You can be dumb," he knew that she really meant "I love you" ("Blinded by the Light," 4-3). Dexter may lack emotional intelligence, but his cognitive skills let him easily interpret the meaning behind her words.

Most important, Dexter's connection to and competence in taking care of Rita and the kids allowed him to see himself as "good." This ability increased along with his sense of connectedness—a sort of silver lining of competence within a cloud of happiness. This is largely because the calmness under pressure and hyper-vigilance about human nature that serves him so well as a serial killer also proved beneficial for fatherhood. He routinely saved hectic mornings with donuts and car rides to school. He managed Rita's insecurities with levity, teaching the children that disagreements don't have to escalate into fights. And when Cody ran away during season two, Dexter knew right where to find him. Dexter even channeled his traumatic experiences into the most insightful parenting moment of the series: at the end of season two he alerted Rita to the fact that neglecting to discuss her ex-husband and the entirety of his misdeeds didn't protect Cody and Astor, it actually protected Paul, at the kids' expense.

Now, it should be noted that any discussion involving the impact of other characters on Dexter's personality runs into an inherent obstacle. Dexter spends so much time in his own head and is so impaired at taking the emotional temperature of those around him that he is neither a reliable nor particularly observant judge of interpersonal interactions. Plus, the show's writers seem invested in minimizing Dexter's growth. Since setbacks, conflict, and vacillation about self are fodder for high melodrama, the writers seem to enjoy delivering sucker punches to Dexter's psychological advancement. Camilla died in season three, Rita was killed off in season four, and the moments of intimacy between Debra and Dexter always seem to end mid-sentence. As a result of all this, Dexter rarely notices the effects of the angels around him. Nevertheless, Rita, Debra, and Camilla have still penetrated Dexter's psyche in meaningful, sustaining ways. Camilla nurtured him and Debra kept him propped up while Rita shoved him into battle against his devils. As a result, Dexter has begun to rewrite a more mentally healthy narrative of his life that is based upon greater insight into himself, greater faith in other people, and greater hope in the world.

Dexter's angels all feed the part of him that keeps him separate from the true devils: those on his kill table. He does not kill "without reason or regret" like Rudy. He does not manipulate good people and kill out of self-interest like Miguel. He definitely does not terrorize his family like Arthur. Despite Harry's fearful, unfounded prediction that Dexter would become like these monsters, a world of difference exists between him and them. Dexter feels tremendous guilt on the rare occasions that he mistakenly harms the innocent and he cares more about saving victims than he does killing criminals. This is the real Dexter. Rita, Debra, and Camilla see this "truth," and this positive, hopeful vision of Dexter is reflected back to him, saving him . . . from himself.

Jeremy Clyman is currently pursuing his doctorate in clinical psychology at Yeshiva University in New York. In 2007, he earned a master's degree in print journalism from Northeastern University. He has written about psychology and cinema for numerous publications including *PsycCRITIQUES*, a research journal sponsored by the American Psychological Association. He also maintains a bi-weekly blog for Psychology-Today.com called Reel Therapy. He is grateful for the opportunity to join BenBella's team of gifted writers.

If you want to believe that you have nothing in common with Dexter, do not read this chapter. The authors argue that we all have our own "Dark Passengers"—okay, maybe not murderous ones, but dark all the same. So what do we do with our shadows so we are not so scared of them? Do we bring them out into the open, then try to banish them, as Freud might recommend? Or do we recognize that darkness is part of human nature, and we need to coexist with it or even put it to good use, as Carl Jung might advise? The battle between good and evil has enthralled generations of psychologists, and inspired tales that stretch from the myth of Zeus and the legend of King Arthur through Pinocchio *and the* Lord of the Rings *to* Star Wars *and* Harry Potter. *Dexter is a descendant of these classics—with his own unique and breathtaking twist.*

THE DARK

PASSENGER IN

ALL OF US

MELISSA BURKLEY AND EDWARD BURKLEY

> "I just know there's something dark in me and I hide it. I certainly don't talk about it, but it's there always, this Dark Passenger. And when he's driving, I feel alive, half sick with the thrill of complete wrongness. I don't fight him, I don't want to. He's all I've got. Nothing else could love me . . . Or is that just a lie the Dark Passenger tells me?"
>
> —Dexter Morgan ("An Inconvenient Lie," 2-3)

I n the Dexter series, one major character is never given any dialogue or physical screen time, and yet still manages to play one of the most important roles in the show. What character, you may ask, could play such an integral role and yet stay so suspiciously hidden? This entity is known to the audience as Dexter's Dark Passenger.

Although the audience never gets to meet the Dark Passenger, we are given brief glimpses of him through Dexter's eyes. As expressed in the ominous quote above, Dexter often describes a kind of "tug-of-war" that wages within his mind between what he is told is the "right" thing to do and what his Dark Passenger tells him to do.

Dexter's internal struggle between these opposing forces forms the foundation for much of the series and is a key reason for the show's appeal. Dexter is such a captivating character, in part, because he often experiences the same struggle found in us all.

The balance of good and evil within humankind is an age-old tale, bound by neither time nor culture. Tales of such a struggle can be found in both ancient myth and modern storytelling. The idea that people harbor a "dark side" and therefore must struggle to find the balance between light and dark, good and evil is not a new idea. Such a struggle is not only seen in literature and mythology; it also plays a central role in several psychoanalytic theories.

Freud, Jung, and the Psychology of Evil

Many psychologists have theorized about humankind's struggle between good and evil, but this dialectic tension plays the most central role in the theories of Freud and Jung. Sigmund Freud met the young psychiatrist Carl Jung in 1907 and the two became fast friends. Jung stated that he was immediately struck by Freud's remarkable intelligence, and Freud quickly began to view Jung as his most promising protégé and the eventual heir to the psychoanalysis school of thought. Given their close collaborations during their seven-year relationship, it is not surprising that Freud and Jung's theories share some basic similarities. Both theories place great emphasis on the unconscious, believing that it represents a powerful influence on individual behavior. Both also devote a substantial part of their theories to the explanation of why humans engage in harmful behaviors that hurt themselves and others. According to both theorists, humankind's greatest evil acts—war, murder, sexual assault—stem from impulses housed within the unconscious mind.

However, toward the end of their collaboration, the two theorists' ideas began to diverge. Jung started to reject several basic tenets of Freudian theory, and this created a rift between the two that eventually terminated their collaborative relationship. One area where Jung disagreed with Freud was the emphasis on sexual instincts. Freud believed that repressed sexual impulses serve as the primary motivational force in our lives, whereas Jung felt Freud placed too much emphasis on sexual motives. A second area of disagreement, one more germane to the analysis of Dexter, was in regard to their differing opinions about what the unconscious is and how it should be dealt with. To illustrate their diverging perspectives, imagine that the dark side of your unconscious is like a monster hiding in the shadows underneath your bed. Freud believed that the only way to rid humanity of its dark side was to throw open the curtains and expose the monster to the sunlight of our conscious mind. Only by forcing the dark side to become conscious will we able to banish our evil impulses. For this reason, Freud's therapy often relied on techniques that were designed to bore into the unconscious and extract repressed information, such as dream analysis or free association. Jung, on the other hand, felt that our dark side was just as much a part of our "authentic self" as the light side. Rather than banishing our inner monster, Jung felt we need to coax it out of its hiding place and invite it to join with the other elements of our psyche.

In sum, Freud perceived the unconscious as a reservoir of evil thoughts and motives. From this perspective, the human struggle is concerned with an attempt to dominate our dark side and eradicate its influence. Conversely, Jung believed the unconscious housed both good and bad aspects of our personality. Even though the unconscious can be a source of evil, Jung also believed it was the source for socially beneficial expression, including art and other creative endeavors. From this perspective, the human struggle is instead concerned with an attempt to coexist with our dark side.

Because Freud and Jung developed some of the most complex ideas regarding humankind's dark side, their theories provide an excellent basis for the psychological analysis of Dexter's struggles with his Dark Passenger, beginning with Jung's theory in regard to archetypes.

Jungian Psychology

According to Jung, a major component of the human psyche belongs to the collective unconscious—a storehouse of primordial knowledge, experiences, and images that are shared by all members of the human race. This volume of knowledge is unconscious, meaning that we do not have direct access to its contents. However, the collective unconscious still manages to find its way into our lives by indirectly guiding our behavior.

Jung believed that this indirect influence of the collective unconscious was most evident in a culture's art, imagery, myths, and stories. Some of Jung's ideas originated from his observation that the art and myths of various groups of people share surprising similarities, despite dramatic differences in culture and language. Jung labeled these templates "archetypes" and described them as "a kind of readiness to produce, over and over again, the same or similar mythical ideas."

When our human ancestors repeatedly endured the same experience, the emotional reaction to that experience was imprinted onto our collective unconscious and eventually an archetype was formed for that particular experience. Once formed, an archetype serves as a mythical tendency, a predisposition to respond to events in a particular way. And since these archetypes are universal, they exist in storytelling from all eras. For example, the classic "hero's journey" is seen across culture and time, from Homer's *Odyssey* to James Cameron's *Avatar*. Although each culture's specific myth is unique, most myths share a few basic character templates or archetypes.

Jung spent much of his professional life identifying and defining the various archetypes commonly seen in mythology, art, and dreams. Although there are likely an infinite number of archetypes, only a handful appear most frequently. When it comes to stories about the struggle between good and evil, three major archetypes are often present, and it is the relationships between these three characters that form the story's foundation. These characters are the Hero, the Shadow, and the Wise Old Man. For example, in the Star Wars series, the majority of the storyline focuses on Luke Skywalker (Hero), his nemesis Darth Vader (Shadow), and Luke's mentors Obi-Wan Kenobi and Yoda (Wise Old Men). And in the more recent Harry Potter series, the story focuses primarily on Harry (Hero), his nemesis Lord Voldemort (Shadow), and Harry's mentor Dumbledore (Wise Old Man). *Dexter* also employs this tripartite of archetypes, although the series puts a unique spin on the relationships between these characters, especially when it comes to the Shadow and the Hero.

THE SHADOW ARCHETYPE

The strongest archetype within the Dexter series is definitely the Shadow, so we will begin our Jungian analysis with this character. According to Jung, the Shadow represents those aspects of the self that are dark and that we try to deny. The Shadow is composed of all of our repressed motives and tendencies, our secret desires—those things we wish we could do but don't because we realize they are socially unacceptable. For this reason, the Shadow is the part of ourselves that we prefer not to recognize. And, according to Jung in *On the Psychology of the Unconscious*, no matter how "good" or "bad" you may be, everyone has a shadow-side:

> It is a frightening thought that man also has a shadow-side to him, consisting not just of little weaknesses and foibles, but of a positively demonic dynamism. The individual seldom knows anything of this; to him, as an individual, it is incredible that he should ever in any circumstances go beyond himself. But let these harmless creatures form a mass, and there emerges a raging monster; and each individual is only one tiny cell in the monster's body, so that for better or worse he must accompany it on its bloody rampages and even assist it to the utmost.

Jung often treats the Shadow as a fractured part of the self. It is an externalized entity that feels separate from our "authentic self," its needs and impulses often conflicting with our own personal needs. Interestingly, Dexter speaks of his Shadow side in much the same way. Whereas Jung referred to the Shadow as the "dark half" of personality, Dexter has, with great insight, called it his Dark Passenger. By using this particular label, Dexter is essentially externalizing his dark side. Even though Dexter feels his authentic self is driving the car, he also feels as if his dark side is always riding shotgun and at any moment may try to take over the steering wheel.

Unlike most TV show characters, Dexter Morgan has a fully formed Shadow. For Dexter, his Shadow is primarily comprised of his need to kill. Just as Jung describes in the above quote, when Dexter's Dark Passenger begins to get "hungry," he must find a way to feed it, and often that means accompanying and assisting the entity on its bloody rampages. In flashbacks, we see that Dexter attempted to repress this killer drive as a teenager, but ultimately he was unsuccessful. So Dexter is stuck with the challenge of finding a way to "feed the monster" without letting it ruin his life.

For most of us, the Shadow represents a small but power-ful part of our psyche, but for Dexter, the Shadow dominates his personality, at least when we first meet him. As Dexter said in the quote that opened this essay, he doesn't want to fight his Shadow because he feels it is all he has. However, what Dex-ter said next may give the audience hope. After describing the needs of his Dark Passenger, Dexter said, "Lately there are these moments when I feel connected to something else . . . someone. It's like the mask is slipping and things, people who never mat-tered before are suddenly starting to matter. It scares the hell out of me" ("An Inconvenient Lie"). This last comment suggests that the Shadow is losing some of its grip on Dexter and that other parts of his psyche are starting to emerge. He is becoming more than just his Shadow.

Dexter's struggle against his Shadow can also be seen in his connections with others—in particular his relationships with Rita, his wife, and Debra, his sister—and how these have evolved over the course of the series. In the first season, Dex-ter admitted that he started a relationship with Rita to create a cover. He purposefully selected a partner who was as damaged as he was, so that her relationship (and sexual) needs would be minimal. Similarly, Dexter struggled in the beginning of the series to truly feel an emotional connection with his sister Debra.

The problem for Dexter is that maintaining authentic relationships can, at any moment, threaten his ability to express his Dark Passenger. First, from a practical point of view, close relationships with others makes it harder for Dexter to hide his behaviors, and so they increase the likelihood that he will get caught. For example, when Dexter moved in with Rita, he had a very difficult time finding a safe place to hide the tools of his trade. Second, from an emotional point of view, these relationships make Dexter more vulnerable. His emotional connections with others create cracks in his armor that his enemies can (and eventually do) use against him.

Yet despite the added difficulty that comes with these relationships, Dexter continues to nurture his connections with others. This was most clearly seen in the evolution of his relationship with Rita across the first four seasons. Although Dexter started out by using Rita as a cover, as their relationship developed, it was clear that he slowly started to truly feel something akin to affection for her. Eventually, Dexter moved in with Rita and her children, and by the fourth season, he even started a family of his own with her. Similarly, when Dexter's sister Debra told him in the fourth season that she loved him, he replied, "I'm so thankful" ("The Getaway," 4-12). Dexter is slowly becoming whole, right before the audience's eyes.

But it is important to remember that Dexter is not the only one with a dark side. According to Jung, we all have a Shadow-side to our personality. One needs only to watch the opening credits of *Dexter* to see how our daily mundane tasks are rife with possibilities for brutality and violence. Dexter himself highlighted this fact in the very first episode of the show when he said, "Needless to say, I have some unusual habits, yet all these socially acceptable people can't wait to pick up hammers and smash their food to bits. Normal people are so hostile"

("Dexter," 1-1). And as reluctant as we may be to admit it, Dexter is correct in this statement. All of us have had times when we had a violent thought or wished we could harm another person—these represent our own Shadow selves. Thankfully, most of us do not act on our darkest impulses, but, according to Jung, it may be just as harmful to deny the existence of our Shadows.

Jung strongly believed that for a person to be mentally healthy, he or she must find a way to incorporate the Shadow into the whole psyche. If the individual simply tries to repress his dark side, the Shadow will find a way through the cracks in the psyche and often express itself in disturbing ways. As Jung stated, "Everyone carries a Shadow, and the less it is embodied in the individual's conscious life, the blacker and denser it is."

In addition to creating a fractured psyche, denying or repressing the Shadow can lead us to project our negative traits onto others. For example, a man who denies his own hostile thoughts may assume that those around him are hostile and out to get him. Therefore, according to Jung, a key part of the human experience is to find a way to deal with our Shadow in socially appropriate ways in order to limit its influence on our thoughts and lives.

This struggle to deal with the Shadow—a process sometimes referred to as a "Shadow Dance"—forms the basis for *Dexter*. The show's main premise asks: Can Dexter find a way to incorporate his Dark Passenger into his everyday life? Will he ever find a balance between the dark and light aspects of his self? That is, the show is really an exploration of Jung's idea of incorporating rather than denying the Shadow self.

Just as Dexter struggles to find a way to merge his Shadow with the rest of his life (e.g., moving his "tools" out of his apartment and into the shed in his new home's backyard), we too must find a way to accept and express our own Shadow side rather than deny it. Interestingly, this struggle to deal with our own Shadow is the very reason we enjoy watching *Dexter*.

Watching a show about a man who kills killers allows our own Shadow to essentially "come out and play" for a while. For one hour each week, we exercise our Shadow by allowing it to imagine the things we would do if we were in Dexter's shoes. Therefore, the audience enjoys *Dexter* because it gives them a socially acceptable way to feed their own Dark Passengers.

HERO ARCHETYPE

Any story with a villain must also have a hero. What makes Dexter so unique is that these two opposing personalities are housed within the same person. Although a portion of Dexter's psyche is devoted to his dark, murderous impulses, another part of his psyche wants to be good.

In one of Dexter's flashbacks, we saw how Harry, Dexter's father, taught a teenage Dexter how to use his murderous impulses for good by molding his Shadow into a vigilante. Harry told Dexter, "Okay, so we can't stop this. But maybe we can do something to channel it. Use it for good. There are people out there who do really bad things and the police can't catch them all" ("Dexter").

The Hero archetype forms the basis for nearly every mythology. The Hero's primary purpose is to overcome the monster of darkness, but in addition to this objective, the Hero archetype typically includes a number of other defining features. First, the Hero's birth usually involves "unusual circumstances." Second, as a child, the Hero often escapes from a murder attempt (e.g., myth of Zeus). Combined, these two traumatic experiences play an important role in the Hero's development and sense of purpose.

Both of these hero qualities could easily apply to Dexter. As the show progressed, Dexter discovered the circumstances surrounding his birth and childhood: Harry, Dexter's adopted father, was having an affair with Dexter's mother, a criminal informant named Laura. When the drug lords overseeing Laura found out about the affair and her role as a CI, they made an example of her by slaying her with a chainsaw in a shipping container while her two sons, Brian and Dexter, watched. The boys escaped the brutal attack, but were left to sit in the bloody container for several days until Harry recovered them. According to Harry, it is this traumatic experience that instilled in Dexter the need to kill.

In order for Dexter to be a true Hero, though, he must be pitted against a separate evil entity, the "monster of darkness" mentioned above, and this takes place in two ways. First, each episode usually features Dexter pursuing, catching, and killing a criminal who managed to escape the justice system. Second, and more integral to the series storyline, is the fact that a new adversarial character is introduced each season and Dexter must spend the entire season trying to dispose of him or her. In both cases, Dexter's victims represent a Shadow archetype, in the sense that they are an expression of the dark side of humanity. However, the "season nemesis" seems to represent the true opposing force to Dexter's Hero side. Importantly, this nemesis always seems to represent the darkest aspects of Dexter's psyche. These characters are Dexter's Shadow externalized and they remind us of what Dexter would be like if he did not keep his Dark Passenger in check.

When Dexter first meets these adversaries, he is usually intrigued and attracted to them because they share similar aspects of his personality. In this way, his initial attraction to them can be seen as a reflection of his temptation to fully embrace his own dark side. In season one, this character was Dexter's brother Brian, the Ice Truck Killer. At first, Dexter was intrigued and impressed with Brian's killing methods. For example, when Dexter saw how the killer drained the bodies of blood, he thought: "No blood. No sticky, hot, messy, awful blood . . . Why hadn't I thought of that? No blood. What a beautiful idea!" ("Dexter"). In season two, it was Lila, a woman he met at a Narcotics Anonymous meeting. Dexter immediately saw her as a kindred spirit and engaged in a sexual affair with her. In season three, it was Miguel Prado, a district attorney who served as Dexter's first true friend and protégé. And in season four, it was the Trinity Killer (i.e., Arthur), who initially served as a role model for Dexter on how to successfully integrate family life with the life of a killer.

Despite his initial attraction to these characters, each time Dexter eventually recognized their evil side and was compelled to dispose of them. Whereas Dexter attempts to rein in his Shadow, these nemesis characters represented what happens when the Shadow takes over completely. Therefore, when Dexter decided to kill them off, he was essentially choosing again and again to let his Hero side triumph over his Shadow side. In this way, Dexter is able to keep his Shadow in check and prevents it from completely taking over his own life. Thus, each time Dexter killed one of these adversaries, he symbolically killed off the darkest extensions of his Shadow side and reasserted the dominance of his Hero side.

WISE OLD MAN ARCHETYPE

A third major archetype represented in *Dexter* is that of the Wise Old Man. Typically, the Wise Old Man archetype is depicted in stories as an older male authority figure who offers guidance and advice to the story's young Hero. This character is distinguished for his wisdom, sound judgment, and moral qualities and often possesses knowledge that is necessary for the Hero's survival. Oftentimes, the Wise Old Man continues to offer advice even after death (e.g., Obi-Wan Kenobi and Yoda in Star Wars).

The ultimate purpose of this archetype is to induce self-reflection and insight in the Hero before he continues forward on his journey. For this reason, the appearance of the Wise Old

Man often serves as a warning that dangerous events loom on the horizon. This particular archetype can be seen in a wide variety of classic and modern myths, including Merlin in the Arthurian legend, Gandalf in the Lord of the Rings series, and even Jiminy Cricket in *Pinocchio*.

Within *Dexter*, the Wise Old Man archetype is clearly depicted in the character of Harry Morgan, Dexter's deceased adoptive father who dispenses paternal advice from beyond the grave. The audience was first introduced to Harry through a series of flashbacks that Dexter experienced during the first and second seasons. But starting in season three, Harry began appearing to Dexter in real time, possibly as a ghost or a figment of Dexter's imagination.

Because Harry was a highly respected police office, he was able to teach Dexter how to kill without getting caught. When Dexter was a teenager, Harry developed a simple but strict set of rules for Dexter to live by, and kill by. Referred to in the series as "The Code of Harry," these rules give Dexter guidance on how to stalk his prey, avoid capture, and blend in with normal society.

The two most important rules of the code—be sure the victim is a killer and don't get caught—have guided Dexter's behavior on several occasions. For example, in season four, Dexter considered but then rejected the idea of killing defense attorney Ellen Wolf after Prado said she should die because she repeatedly put guilty criminals back on the street. And in season two, when Sergeant James Doakes discovered that Dexter was the Bay Harbor Butcher, Dexter faced a unique dilemma in which the two rules of the code conflicted with each other. On the one hand, Dexter had an opportunity to uphold the second rule by killing off Doakes, but doing so would violate the first rule because Doakes was not a killer. Faced with this conflict, Dexter actually considered turning himself in to the police rather than break Harry's first rule and kill an innocent. Luckily for Dexter, Lila resolved the conflict by killing Doakes herself.

Because the Wise Old Man represents the Hero's moral compass, bad things usually happen when the Hero fails to heed this archetype's advice. For example, in *Star Wars: The Empire Strikes Back*, Luke Skywalker's friends are captured but he is warned by Obi-Wan and Yoda that it is a trap. Luke ignores their advice, travels to Cloud City, and is lured into a lightsaber duel with Darth Vader. Ultimately, Luke pays a steep price for his insolence when Vader cuts off his right hand in the fight.

A similar pattern can also be seen in *Dexter*. On the few occasions when Dexter has gone against Harry's advice, it has inevitably led to devastating results for Dexter. For example, in "The Getaway" (4-12), Dexter was trailing the Trinity Killer when he received a call from Rita. Harry warned Dexter not to take the call, but Dexter disregarded his advice and during the call accidentally side-swiped a vehicle. This in turn led to Dexter's arrest and, because he was in jail, Dexter missed his opportunity to finish off the Trinity Killer.

Dexter also ignored Harry's incessant warnings that he should not marry Rita and start a family because doing so would both put Dexter in danger of getting caught and put his family in danger of being harmed by those out to hurt Dexter. Dexter, of course, rejected this advice and paid the ultimate price with the death of Rita in the season four finale.

Freud's Id, Ego, and Superego

Other less-pronounced archetypes likely exist within *Dexter*, but the heart of Dexter's story clearly revolves around the three archetypes described: Shadow, Hero, and Wise Old Man. Interestingly, this trilogy of archetypes also maps onto Freud's conception of the psyche: the Id, Ego, and Superego.

According to Freud, the Id represents the most animalistic urges of human behavior. The Id acts in accordance with the hedonistic drive to seek out pleasure and avoid pain. Thus, it is the most amoral and selfish part of our psyche. As Freud put it, "It is the dark, inaccessible part of our personality . . . and most of [it] is of a negative character." Not only is the Id mostly negative, it also comprises the largest part of the human psyche. Textbooks often use the drawing of an iceberg to represent the Freudian psyche, with the iceberg tip pointing out of the water as a representation of the conscious part of self and the mammoth base of the iceberg that sits underwater as a representation of the unconscious part of self. And housed within this large unconscious are all of our most immoral, irrational, and violent urges (our Id). Notice how this take on humankind's dark side differs from the Jungian perspective. Whereas Jung treated humankind's dark side as an entity separate from the "core self," Freud perceived the dark side *as* our core self, in the sense that it makes up the majority of our personality.

The opposing force of the Id—the entity that keeps it in check—is the Superego. The Superego is the part of the human psyche that strives for perfection. It is comprised of our ideals, our goals, and our conscience. The Superego is the part of self that gives us a sense of right and wrong, the part that makes us feel guilty when we do something socially unacceptable.

Within the human psyche, the moral Superego is in constant battle against the selfish Id. For this reason, a referee is needed to balance out these two opposing forces, and this need is fulfilled by the Ego. According to Freud, the Ego is the part of the psyche that we are most consciously aware of. It is comprised of our intellectual, rational part of self and serves as a mediator between the Id, the Superego, and the external world. Its purpose is to strike a balance between our basic needs and our morals. The Ego must find a way to feed our primitive urges without bringing about complete social isolation and rejection.

So, if we were to imagine that classic cartoon image of a little devil on one shoulder of the person and a little angel on the other, the devil would be the Id, the angel would be the

Superego, and the person caught between them would be the Ego. Although the Ego does its best to serve both the Id and the Superego, in the end, Freud believed the Ego is typically more loyal to the Id. For instance, the Ego can employ defense mechanisms or use rationalization to justify the needs of the Id, and in doing so changes the perception of reality to fit the Id, rather than changing the Id to fit with reality. However, the Superego is always watching over the Ego and will often employ feelings of guilt or anxiety whenever the Ego goes too far in pleasing the Id.

Within the Dexter series, the Dark Passenger (Shadow) clearly fits the description of the Id. Since Harry serves as Dexter's moral compass, he fits the description of the Superego. When Harry appears to Dexter as an apparition and warns him to stick with the code, he is serving as an external manifestation of Dexter's Superego. Finally, the Hero side of Dexter—the part of Dexter that he strives to truly be—fits the description of the Ego. Just as the Ego must mediate between the Id and the Superego, so too must Dexter struggle to feed his Dark Passenger but also obey his father's moral code.

Ultimately, it is the psychic turmoil between the light and dark sides of the self that makes *Dexter* so fascinating and entertaining. Although most of us do not struggle with issues of the same magnitude as Dexter, we all have felt the tension between doing what we want to do—eating that high-calorie dessert, flirting with someone other than your spouse—and doing what is right—sticking to your diet, staying faithful to your partner.

The struggle we see Dexter play out on the television screen simply underscores the battle waged each day within our own psyche. For a short time, we are able to entertain that dark side that exists in each of us through Dexter's many trials. However, in the end, we ultimately hope that Dexter will win this battle, possibly in anticipation that we too will do the right things in life and not succumb to the temptations of our own "Dark Passenger."

Melissa Burkley, PhD, and **Edward Burkley, PhD,** are both assistant professors of social psychology at Oklahoma State University. Melissa Burkley's research focuses on stereotypes and prejudice and she also writes a blog for *Psychology Today* entitled The Social Thinker. Edward Burkley's research focuses on goals and motivation. When not watching *Dexter*, they enjoy photography, writing, and traveling.

You're rationalizing! You're in denial! You're intellectualizing! Those sorts of ready assessments of our friends and foes are so common-place that we may not even realize that they are part of the Freudian legacy. They are some of the better-known defense mechanisms, the tricks we play on ourselves when our anxieties and traumas become too much to bear in a raw and realistic way. Miami Metro is a steaming cauldron of psychological distortions. All of the people on the force, and everyone connected with them, get stirred up in the mix. But Dexter is the king of defense mechanisms. In his sparring with Doakes over whose sordid deeds are more justified, Dexter reigned supreme—at least in his own mind. Of course, we fans have our own defense mechanisms, too. Otherwise, how could we let ourselves cheer on a serial murderer with such gusto?

THE DARK DEFENDERS

Freudian Defense Mechanisms in the Minds of Miami Metro

WIND GOODFRIEND AND CHASE BARRICK

> "There are no secrets in life—just hidden truths, that lie beneath the surface."
>
> —Dexter, "Crocodile" (1-2)

Sigmund Freud is undeniably the most famous psychologist of all time. Many of Freud's theories are known for their controversial nature, such as the Oedipus complex (the idea that all young boys want to have sex with their mothers) or penis envy (that all girls wish desperately for a penis instead of their own inferior clitoris), concepts that are almost laughable today. These fringe ideas are not the reason Freud is so famous, however. His impact on psychology endures because the vast majority of his ideas laid the foundation for modern therapeutic techniques. One of the most bedrock notions within almost all therapy perspectives is the idea that we each have a hidden self, lying in wait to surprise us. This secret self lives in our unconscious mind, as the quote above suggests.

What is the purpose of hiding our own true natures, even from ourselves? Freud believed that when reality is too traumatic, too anxiety-provoking for our conscious minds to handle, our unconscious minds take over. We twist and distort reality as much as necessary so that we can keep pretending that everything is "just fine." Our unconscious mind plays these cognitive tricks on us all the time, so that we can fit in, go along with the crowd, avoid the crushing pressure of reality, and sleep at night. The term for these mental acrobatics is *defense mechanisms*. Within Dexter's world, defense mechanisms abound—in fact, Dexter has been using them since he was three years old, and likely could not function without them.

Denial

The most well-known defense mechanism is *denial*. Everyone is probably familiar with the old cliché for addicts: the first step is admitting you have a problem. Within denial, we refuse to admit (even to ourselves) that something negative or anxiety-provoking is really happening. If the problem doesn't exist, then it doesn't produce any difficulty. Denial may be the most ubiquitous defense mechanism in the minds of Miami Metro. Every person working there has been trained to notice clues pointing to someone's guilt, to follow paths leading to criminals. But in spite of their highly skilled training, almost none of them pick up on the fact that they are working alongside one of the most successful serial killers in the history of our nation—and that they are *friends* with him.

Denial can be seen more specifically in three people in Dexter's world. The most obvious example is Lieutenant Maria LaGuerta. LaGuerta has a lot to deal with in her precinct, including a boss who hates her, the constant sexual escapades of the cops and detectives who work under her, and a feeling of general loneliness and separation from everyone else in her life. The only person she always maintained a connection with was her past partner, Sergeant James Doakes. Unfortunately for LaGuerta, in season two Dexter framed Doakes to appear as the Bay Harbor Butcher. Although Doakes was actually innocent, all the evidence pointed to his guilt, a fact LaGuerta simply couldn't handle. She actually admitted to others that she was in denial about him being a mass murderer, because if her partner and friend was a killer, her entire concept of interpersonal trust would be shattered. Denial was probably the psychologically healthiest way for LaGuerta to deal with this situation, after Doakes died. She had to continue on, keep fighting criminals, keep leading her precinct; denial helped her do all of those things.

So in LaGuerta's case, denial was useful. However, denial is used by others within Miami Metro and their families and friends in ways which are much more destructive. Rita was a sweet woman who just wanted to find a man to love and respect her. However, she was in constant denial about the men in her life. She didn't even want to admit that she had a teenage marriage for a few short months. Her second husband, Paul, was an abusive heroin addict, a fact she had trouble admitting until after she found a replacement (Dexter). And although she didn't know it, Dexter was certainly not the man she thought he was. Rita's unconscious mind actually worked very hard to convince itself that everything about Dexter was comforting, safe, and good. Dexter knows the truth, however, and wondered if Rita was secretly attracted to evil men. In "Circle of Friends" (1-7), we saw her denial continue as Dexter asked about Paul:

> DEXTER: When'd you first notice it? This . . . darkness inside the guy you fell for?
>
> RITA: I always knew it was there . . . I guess I just didn't think I deserved better. 'Til I met you.
>
> DEXTER: I have a dark side, too.
>
> RITA: (laughs)
>
> DEXTER: What? I do.
>
> RITA: Somehow I doubt that. You have a good heart, Dexter. You're not like Paul. You don't hurt people.
>
> DEXTER: (pause) Innocent people. I don't hurt innocent people.

Rita just smiled, and laughed again. She wouldn't admit anything negative about him (at least not at this point in their relationship). In order to feel psychologically safe, Rita had to live in denial about anything scary in her partner.

A final example of denial can be seen in Dexter's sister Debra. Deb has spent her life trying to live up to her father's image as a legendary police detective, and therefore is on a quest to seek out killers. Her instincts are typically very good; she finds leads in cases time and time again. However, her biggest mistake came when she fell in love with the Ice Truck Killer (Brian, Dexter's brother). When Brian asked Deb why she never suspected him, Deb fell apart. Something about Brian drew her toward him; perhaps her unconscious mind simply wouldn't allow her to realize that she finally had found the killer she was always seeking—and that she had fallen for him.

Sublimation

A lesser-known defense mechanism is *sublimation*. To understand sublimation, think about a man who has too much aggression. Ideally, this man would beat people up wherever he goes. But society tells him that aggression is not an acceptable impulse. So, sublimation is when the unconscious mind finds a creative way of allowing socially unacceptable tendencies to come out in ways that are actually *praised* by others. This man could become a professional boxer or football player, making millions of dollars, probably getting to bed hot chicks, and certainly allowing his aggression to run free and play.

One fascinating (and extreme) example of sublimation can be seen in Dexter's season four adversary, the Trinity killer. For years, Trinity appeared to be a wonderful philanthropist as he traveled from city to city building homes for the homeless. His "Four Walls, One Heart" campaign brought him social praise (and the opportunity to kill people in all sorts of exciting new locations). But more directly, Trinity's projects provided concrete for him to sink kidnapped ten-year-old boys (still alive) within the foundation of the homes. (Indeed, his campaign title can be taken literally, as each of his homes has a human heart lying beneath it.) Clearly this urge is not socially acceptable, so he sublimated it: he found a way to satisfy his predilection for child murder in a way that would appear—to the outside world—praiseworthy.

Intellectualization

When reality is simply too emotionally terrible to handle, one way to deal with it is to use *intellectualization*. This defense mechanism strips away any emotionality and leaves the conscious mind only the logical, pragmatic, and objective view.

A profound example of intellectualization can be seen in Special Agent Frank Lundy, from the FBI. Lundy's entire career was built on finding and stopping serial killers. Part of this job was to witness repeated scenes of horror, and try to adopt the perspective of the murderers he sought. For many people, the sheer knowledge that dozens of serial killers are running around would be overwhelming. But Lundy remained perfectly calm and collected—he was logical, thoughtful, objective. This dispassionate mindset carried over into his relationship with Deb; Lundy told her that they weren't right for each other because he was twice her age. Again, he didn't allow his emotions to take over. He used logic to protect his heart just as he used it to protect his mind from the repeated analysis of horrific murders.

Lundy's use of intellectualization is another example of how defense mechanisms can often help us; though it almost got in the way of his relationship with Debra, it clearly worked well for him and propelled him to the top of his field. Lundy's ability to track killers may have eventually led to his death, but while he was alive, he was psychologically healthy, at least partially due to his use of defense mechanisms.

Identification

Perhaps one of the most obvious defense mechanisms used in Dexter's world is *identification*. When someone isn't sure of himself or herself, when that person has low self-esteem or needs the attention of others, he or she might "identify" with a powerful, successful other. Identification is when we model our own behavior on that other person's, to gain approval or success for ourselves. The cliché example of an object of identification is a parent; we emulate them and hope for an affirmation of our own worth.

For Deb, identification is the defense mechanism that has shaped the majority of her life. When Deb and Dexter were

growing up, their father Harry had to spend a lot of time training Dexter and teaching him the code. This was essential to
keep Dexter from allowing the Dark Passenger to take over,
but Deb saw it as father-son bonding, which left her out. Deb
desperately wanted attention, love, and acceptance from Harry.
When Harry and Dexter began regularly "hunting," Deb actually broke into Harry's gun cabinet and learned how to shoot.
She got pretty good at it, but when Harry found out, he only
yelled and punished her. In "Circle of Friends," Deb admitted
that she became a cop because she'd wanted more attention
from their father, and that she'd been jealous of his time with
Dexter. She also noted that the only time Harry had ever spent
with her alone was tucking her in at night. That was when he
would tell her stories about his cases at work, so she was drawn
to homicide as a way of getting closer him.

Unfortunately, Deb's identification with her father only
works as long as she views him as a distant hero. This became
a problem when Deb became sexually involved with Anton, her
confidential informant on a case. When Deb talked to Dexter
about whether Harry would have approved of Anton, Dexter let
her know that Harry had more in common with her than she
thought. After investigating her father's old files, she learned that
her sainted father Harry had his own demons; he had a series of
affairs with confidential informants (including, most controver-
sially, Dexter's biological mother). When Deb understood this,
her view of Harry changed, leaving her without a model to cling
to. Identification couldn't work as a defense mechanism if it
caused her trauma and anxiety instead of shielding her from it.

Deb does identify with another key person: Agent Lundy.
Lundy was older, and she even saw him as a father figure at
first, getting annoyed when he commented on her potty mouth.
Fairly quickly, however, Deb fell in love with Lundy. She even
called him a "god" when he questioned his own work on their
case; clearly she looked up to him as someone who could guide

her, give her attention, and love her in more than one way. All her hopes were pinned on him, which is why she was so upset when he left Miami after the Bay Harbor Butcher case ended, and why she was so broken by his death. Deb identifies with father figures because she needs someone to please. This general tendency occasionally leads her down the wrong path or makes her question her own judgment, but in general having the goal of being a successful detective and surrounding herself with like-minded others has had a positive effect.

Identifying with a parent to get positive attention is also seen in Christine, the daughter of the Trinity killer. Christine was never part of Trinity's "regular" family; she had always been left out, a secret. She explicitly told Trinity that she tried to get his acceptance by emulating him, and she even murdered Lundy and shot Deb to get this approval. When Trinity rejected her even after this supreme effort, Christine's mind simply couldn't handle it, and she committed suicide. In Christine's case this defense mechanism backfired, leading only to tragedy.

The Dark Defender: Dexter's Mind

The person at Miami Metro who has the most need of defense mechanisms is Dexter himself. He certainly has more unbridled complexity for his unconscious mind to rein in than most people; his entire life is based on his ability to convince himself that his actions are just, righteous, and morally acceptable. To achieve this feat, Dexter uses all of the protective methods described above, as well as additional ones we haven't yet discussed.

One mechanism used by Dexter that we don't see in any other character is *repression*. Freud believed that when we witness something so traumatic that it will break us, our memories are pushed so far into our unconscious mind that we don't even realize they exist. Instead, we simply have a blank spot in our personal biographies.

When Dexter was three, he and his brother witnessed their mother being murdered, saw her chopped into pieces with a chainsaw, and then were left in a freighter cargo box with no food, sitting in two inches of blood, for several days. This incident was so traumatic that Dexter blocked it from his memory for years. Unfortunately for him, his older brother Brian did not use repression, and became obsessed with helping Dexter recover this memory. Dexter didn't even know that he had a brother until Brian brought the memories back by re-creating them; when the memories surfaced, they brought back all the original anxiety associated with the event. Although the repression helped Dexter temporarily, it eventually backfired on him and put everyone in his life at risk.

Sublimation was used by the Trinity killer to make his socially unacceptable tendencies praiseworthy, but the king of this mechanism is Dexter himself. Dexter simply loves blood. Blood is beautiful to him, fascinating, poetic. His obsession with blood clearly stems from his childhood trauma, but Dexter knows that his fondness for blood is not socially acceptable. This is clear in every interaction he has within Miami Metro's police station, but was even more explicitly taught to him in the Code of Harry. So what can Dexter do? His unconscious solved this problem for him by steering him toward a career where he could sit in blood all day: a blood spatter expert for the police. He can know everything about blood and get paid for it: a perfect sublimation.

Like Lundy, who used intellectualization to stay objective in his search for serial killers in the FBI, Dexter often intellectualizes his own life, telling himself that he feels no emotions. Although we know this is not true (Dexter certainly feels anger toward people who threaten his family, and remorse when he makes mistakes), Dex has been taught to intellectualize his tendencies by his father (and note that Dexter's clinging to the "Code" with almost biblical devotion is also an example of identification). Harry encouraged Dexter to think about the evidence first before killing someone, and to avoid personal grudges or feelings of anger. While Dexter occasionally breaks this bylaw of the code, he realizes that letting emotions guide his choices is a slippery slope to avoid.

In "Truth Be Told" (1-11), Dexter thought about his newly recovered memories from childhood: "I've never had much use for the concept of Hell, but if Hell exists, I'm in it. The same images running through my head, over and over. I was there. I saw my mother's death. A buried memory, forgotten all these years. It climbed inside me that day, and it's been with me ever since. My Dark Passenger." Later in that same episode he consciously realized that he'd been using intellectualization: "No wonder I felt so disconnected my entire life. If I did have emotions, I'd have to feel . . . this." Although Dexter uses many defense mechanisms, he does occasionally have particularly good insight into his own psyche.

While all of the defense mechanisms described above are important to understanding how Dexter's psyche works, his most essential unconscious motivation is *rationalization*. Rationalization is used when we do something we know is wrong, but we come up with an excuse to justify it. For example, we may "fudge" a bit on our tax returns because we feel the government takes too much of our money. We might not pick up our dog's poop on the sidewalk if we tell ourselves our dog is small and thus the poop doesn't matter. Or we might kill dozens of people and tell ourselves that it's okay, as long as it follows the code.

Dexter is so caught up in rationalization that in "The Dark Defender" (2-5), he envisions himself as a superhero. This is where society grants killers permission: superheroes are defending the world against evil, fighting for truth and justice, saving innocent victims. These are all the lessons Dex wants to believe are true about himself, based on the Code of Harry. He's like

Batman: a dark figure, waiting in the shadows, who will avenge wrongs done to society by paying back the bad guys. He's saving future victims—so what he's doing is okay. Isn't it?

Dex started on the path of rationalization because of Harry's teachings. In "Popping Cherry" (1-3), we witnessed Dexter's "first time" (his first murder, not first sexual encounter). Harry had already taught him the code, including the telling lesson, "Killing will serve a purpose—otherwise it's just plain murder." Harry instructed Dexter to kill a nurse at the hospital who was giving him shots of poison along with his pain killers. Dexter seized on this chance to kill someone without feeling guilty: "The nurse was my first playmate. I'll always be grateful to her for opening up so many magnificent new doors for me." In that same episode, Dexter observed a young killer named Jeremy. Jeremy was convicted of killing someone four years ago, but Dexter granted him a pardon: "Jeremy didn't murder that boy four years ago. He was taking out the garbage—just like I do."

Dexter is accustomed to his own rationalization, but he knows that most people in his life wouldn't agree with the choices his unconscious has helped him to make. In "An Inconvenient Lie" (2-3), Dexter stood in the morgue surrounded by his Bay Harbor Butcher victims, while Lundy spoke to him about the case. Dexter tried to appear normal, saying what he thought Lundy would expect; he told Lundy that there's never any excuse for killing. To his surprise, Agent Lundy contradicted him, noting that the one good reason—the one justified reason—is to save an innocent life. This simple statement is the keystone to Dexter's entire world, the foundation of his entire system of justification. He honestly believes that by killing killers he's saving their future victims, and therefore his mission is a noble and fair one. And if Agent Lundy, a stand-up and moral man, also believed this, then Dexter himself becomes less culpable in his own mind. When Dexter was keeping Doakes prisoner in season two, they had several debates about whether

Dexter's actions were justified, and Dexter continually used rationalization to defend himself. Doakes asked Dexter why it's okay for Dexter to kill other murderers, and how Dexter could think that it's more "moral" than when Doakes is forced to shoot criminals on the job. Dexter argued that Doakes shoots people for a paycheck, whereas Dexter is doing it because it's the right thing to do. Doakes then tried to tell Dexter that a police officer killing on the job is just upholding laws like self-defense, but Dexter argued that the code is actually better because it requires a "higher standard of proof" than the law. Dexter even told Doakes that his code and brand of justice don't cost the city anything in taxes, so Dexter is a bargain! Clearly Dexter has thought out every excuse for his behavior, and he can twist any argument thrown at him.

Dexter's rationalization is a living thing, which can morph and expand as needed. In "Left Turn Ahead" (2-11), he told himself, "I'm sparing Rita and Deb by framing Doakes . . . Right?" In "Easy as Pie" (3-7), he convinced himself to kill an innocent person for the first time: his friend Camilla, who was dying of painful lung cancer. She'd asked him to do it, to help her die in the hospital. At first Dexter refused because killing an innocent is against the code, but it didn't take long for him to talk himself into it, using rationalization: "I'm doing a good thing, right? This . . . this is mercy."

Dexter's mental gymnastics keep expanding, so much that they start to run away without him. When he befriended assistant district attorney Miguel Prado, Dexter actually mentally debated whether he should murder a defense attorney at Prado's request because she was enabling the bad guys, even though she was just doing her job (the conclusion he eventually reached). Unfortunately for Dex, Prado killed her anyway. When Dexter discovered that Prado was running fast and loose with his code and had lied to him several times, Dex realized that the code is important for protection and became newly committed to it.

Although Dexter often stretches his ability to rationalize to the breaking point, he inevitably comes back to this defense mechanism as his home base, a safe place for his mind to live without anxiety. He can kill as many people as he wants, as long as his mind can continue to justify his actions.

How Will It End?

Freud believed that most defense mechanisms will eventually backfire, as we've seen in several examples above. So he recommended that, in therapy sessions, individuals identify their mechanisms, deal with the anxiety or trauma related to them, and move on in a healthy way. If you're using denial, you must admit it and deal with it. If you're using rationalization, you must realize you're doing so, stop doing it, and consequently stop doing the behavior you knew was wrong all along.

If Dexter took Freud's advice, what would happen? As mentioned above, he has a uniquely insightful view into his own unconscious mind. Dexter seems aware of most of his defense mechanisms. This was seen most clearly in the two occasions when Dexter contemplated suicide. Dexter's entire mental world is built around the concept that serial killers deserve to die. So the only logical conclusion would be that Dexter must, inevitably, kill himself.

In "Circle of Friends," Dexter felt an affinity to Jeremy, the young boy who was just starting to kill others. Jeremy appealed to Dexter because Jeremy was like himself—Jeremy said he was tired of pretending, tired of feeling nothing, tired of living only inside his own head. So Dexter decided to help Jeremy, just like Harry helped him. Dexter decided that Jeremy was just like him, and that Jeremy thus deserved some guidance and a mentor. Unfortunately, Dex's decision was too late—Jeremy killed himself. But what's most interesting was Dexter's first thought when he saw the suicide: "I guess I was wrong. Jeremy did hear my advice. He killed someone who deserved to die." But remember that Dexter liked Jeremy *because he saw him as another version of himself*: someone with no human emotions, someone with the need to kill others. The only logical, rational conclusion we can come to is that Dexter knows deep down that he, himself, deserves to die. He should make the same decision as Jeremy.

Dexter questions this path, though. In "There's Something About Harry" (2-10), Doakes told Dexter that his father had a secret, and Dexter eventually learned that Harry committed suicide. Why did Harry make this decision? Because he taught Dexter to kill but couldn't handle the reality of the "monster" he created. Harry walked in on Dexter chopping up a pimp, someone Harry had inadvertently pushed Dexter to kill. But Harry was stopped cold by the sight of his adopted son, casually covered in plastic and pimp blood, and he simply couldn't live with what he had created. After this revelation, Dexter decided that suicide is weak, "pathetic," because it meant leaving behind those who love you.

It seems that Dexter's choice to abandon suicide is clear, but that path has not really left his mind. In season four, Dexter became obsessed with catching Trinity. He actually found Trinity about to jump off a building to end everything, and he stopped this from happening. However, Dexter briefly wondered if Trinity was making the right decision: if suicide was the only way to end the cycle of violence and deal with his never-ending remorse. Dexter also wonders if this will eventually be his own decision.

What would Freud think about Dexter and his defense mechanisms? It could be argued that Freud would be proud of how well Dexter and his colleagues exemplify the various mechanisms Freud suggested. Some of them help, and some of them backfire, which Freud also suggested would happen. Freud would most certainly not agree with Dexter's justification for serial killings. But what about the big decision Dexter must eventually face: how to end everything? As audience members, most of us will recoil at the idea of Dexter ending his successful career as a vigilante. But why do we feel this way? It's likely that we loyal viewers are actually experiencing defense mechanisms ourselves. We are rooting for him, hoping he doesn't get caught, reveling in his joy when he chops up a bad guy. We're on Dexter's side. We must, therefore, be experiencing denial, identification, or, more likely, rationalization, right along with the characters of the show. We don't want *Dexter* to end, either through Dexter getting caught or through him ending his own life. In some ways, we want to *be* Dexter.

So, what would Freud say? Although suicide is not a socially acceptable choice, many people would be surprised to learn that Freud actually made this choice for himself. After years of living in fear from the Nazis (Freud was a Jew who lived in Austria almost his entire life) and living in pain from cancer of the mouth (all those cigars were needed to help cure his phallic fixations), Freud (with the help of his friend) took three doses of morphine to end it all. So when Dexter considers suicide, Freud would probably tell him that this choice is a noble one. At least, that's what Freud and Dexter can tell themselves, if their unconscious minds are creative.

Wind Goodfriend is an associate professor of psychology at Buena Vista University. She earned her PhD in social psychology in 2004 from Purdue University. In her final year of graduate school, Dr. Goodfriend received both the "Outstanding Teacher of the Year Award" and the "Outstanding Graduate Student of the Year Award" for her research. Since then, she has been nominated for and won several more research and teaching awards.

Chase Barrick is a student at Buena Vista University. He will graduate from Buena Vista University in 2010 with a bachelor of arts degree in psychology. He hopes to continue his education in the field of psychology as he attends graduate school.

Adult children from narcissistic families, Marisa Mauro tells us, fit a certain profile. They try too hard to please other people, they struggle with strong feelings of anger simmering just beneath the surface, they amass a collection of failed romances, they trust too little or disclose too much, and no level of success is ever enough. Deb? Sure. But Dexter? Dr. Mauro thinks so. She also believes that Harry was a narcissistic parent to both of his children. How could that be, when he devoted so much time to Dexter? Read on, and see what you think.

IT'S ALL
ABOUT HARRY

MARISA MAURO

Is the Morgan Family a Narcissistic Family?

A basic goal for most families is to raise healthy children who will one day become independent adults. In a healthy family, parents work to accomplish this task by assuming responsibility for their children's emotional and physical needs. Over time, parents gradually teach their children to be independent by allowing them to assume responsibility for meeting their own needs in a developmentally appropriate manner. Thus, the primary work of children is to learn to become independent adults. Along the way, children learn to identify and act on their feelings, wants, and needs.

In some families, however, that basic goal is skewed and the meeting of parental needs becomes of primary importance for the family. These families are called narcissistic families. The term, coined by therapists and authors Stephanie Donaldson-Pressman and Robert M. Pressman in their text *The Narcissistic*

Family, Diagnosis and Treatment, was derived from the mytho-logical legend of Narcissus and Echo. As the story goes, Narcis-sus loved himself to the exclusion of others. Echo loved him, but could not profess it; she had lost her own voice and was able only to parrot the words of others. Distraught, she followed Narcissus for some time, hoping to hear him speak affectionate words that she could finally say to him. Then one day it hap-pened. Admiring his reflection in a pool, Narcissus exclaimed to himself, "I love you!" Echo, elated, repeated the words, but they were lost on his inattentive ears. Eventually both died—Narcissus from the self-love that kept him attached to his reflec-tion, and Echo from unrequited affection.

The story, the authors relate, can be seen as a metaphor for the parent-child relationships observed in narcissistic families. The parents, like Narcissus, are too self-absorbed to anticipate, acknowledge, or react to the needs of their children. In turn, the children, like Echo, are forced to meet their own needs for love and attention by reacting to the whims of their parents. In this way, the children's emotional needs can go unattended and they are deprived of the opportunity to experience gradual independence and learn about themselves. Instead, they wait to see what their parents expect and then react, negatively or posi-tively, to those expectations. Consequently, the children become a reflection of their parents' expectations and are deprived of the opportunity to be themselves.

The tendency toward reacting and reflecting follows chil-dren of narcissistic families into adulthood, where they con-tinue to react to the needs and reflect the expectations of others rather than realizing and attending to their own. Even-tually these individuals become distressed by this situation and are likely to become angry. Most of the time their anger is not readily apparent. Instead it lies just below the surface, barely concealed by their tendency to please others. Occasionally, however, it breaks through, erupting sometimes even over trivial matters.

Dedicated *Dexter* fans might recognize these characteristics in their unlikely hero, blood spatter analyst and part-time serial killer Dexter Morgan, who even as an adult lives his life strictly by Harry's Code, and his detective sister Debra, who chose her father's career as her own. Could their personal struggles and wavering sense of self-identities be attributed to a narcissistic family of origin?

Personality and Behavioral Traits of Adult Children of Narcissistic Families

Adult children of narcissistic families tend to have a similar set of behavioral and personality traits, touched on above, that clue their therapists into their dysfunctional upbringing. These characteristics plague the individual's psychological and emotional well-being, interpersonal and romantic relationships, and work life. Psychologically, they are distressed by their own pervasive desire to please others, chronic need to seek external validation, and difficulty identifying their own feelings, wants, and needs. They are also likely to suffer from strong feelings of hidden anger. Depression, chronic dissatisfaction, indecisiveness, and poor self-confidence are also common. Interpersonally, these individuals traditionally display difficulty trusting others, a trait that is sometimes broken by periods of vulnerability and total self-disclosure brought on by the very real psychological need to be known and understood by another person. With regard to romantic relationships they face many obstacles and often have a history of failed romances. At work, they have difficulty recognizing and relishing their own achievements and are continuously seeking new ways to achieve and attain success. To some extent, Dexter and Debra both suffer from many of these maladies.

DEXTER MORGAN

Let us first take a look at Dexter, whose personality and behavior is wrought with evidence of a narcissistic upbringing. We tend to attribute most of his behaviors to sociopathy, but considering him as the adult child of a narcissistic family may provide an even better explanation.

Psychologically, Dexter is perhaps most strongly afflicted by his self-proclaimed inability to identify feelings, yet it is also quite clear that he suffers from problems identifying personal priorities, a tendency toward people pleasing, and even a need to gain the approval of others—particularly Harry. The latter need is so strong that Dexter is often visited by his dead father via flashbacks and waking dreams that provide a running commentary laced with praise or disapproval for his every action. Dexter's inclination toward people pleasing is related. When not attempting to satisfy Harry's need to rid the world of ruthless murderers, Dexter can be found responding to the needs of Deb, Rita, or work colleagues. He claims to be doing so to preserve his cover, but he really appears to act out of a sense of duty or obligation.

Perhaps both traits have evolved from Dexter's difficulty with identifying feelings. Though antisocial personality disorder, sociopathy, or possibly even psychopathy can sometimes explain such a problem, there is a better explanation in this case. Dexter does experience feelings—he just doesn't always know what to do with them. We can see that Dexter is easily confused by evidence of his own emotions and often does not know how to respond to those expressed by others. His relationship with Rita is most illustrative of this struggle. Dexter seemed almost blindsided at times during seasons three and four by the discovery of what appeared to be feelings for her and the children, though his emotional growth throughout the series was always visible to the viewer. Because of his easy confusion when it comes to feelings and tendency to follow the whims of others, Dexter also demonstrates difficulty responding to his wants and needs. This manifests most prevalently in his obvious inability to prioritize, especially during season four. Dexter ran himself ragged attempting to meet the needs of his Dark Passenger, Rita, the children, Deb, and work. When he finally came to terms with his true priority—family—during the season four finale, he painfully learned that he was too late.

Telltale signs of a dysfunctional upbringing are also evident in Dexter's relationships with others and in his work behavior. With regard to the former, Dexter exhibits romantic foibles common to adult children of narcissistic families. This includes a history of failed romances and a hot-and-cold relationship with Rita that was often plagued with issues of trust. Dexter's dysfunctional tendencies in interpersonal relationships also extend to friendships, of which he has had very few, if not just one: district attorney Miguel Prado. Within these relationships, Dexter has occasionally shown a tendency toward extremely unhealthy vulnerability, even disclosing his Dark Passenger to Doakes, Miguel, and Trinity. At work, both for the police department and for his Dark Passenger, Dexter displays characteristic dissatisfaction with his achievements, which can be assumed from his workaholic nature and constant search for more successes/victims.

DEBRA MORGAN

Deb, like her brother, possesses both the personality and behavioral tendencies typical to adult children of narcissistic families. Deb, in fact, appears to be an almost perfect case example. Psychologically, she seems to exhibit every trait identified above as common to adult survivors from these families. Like her brother, Deb obviously suffers from a strong desire to please others and seek external validation as a result of her own inability to identify and follow personal feelings, needs, and wants. Again, this seems to stem from a lifelong desire to please and gain the affection of her father Harry at the expense of learning her own needs. Deb also possesses a tendency toward anger that is closer to the surface than her brother. Although we know Dexter is angry (he does murder, after all), Dexter has trained himself to conceal his anger, whereas Deb shows hers frequently. Her swearing is our biggest clue to her anger, and it occurs often, with little provocation. In addition, Deb also has the misfortune of suffering from characteristic depression, chronic dissatisfaction, indecisiveness, and poor self-confidence. This is evidenced by frequent tearfulness, low mood, feelings of not being good enough, self-degradation, and constant consultation with Dexter.

These personal traits affect Deb's interpersonal relationships and work behavior. Like her psychological traits, Deb's tendencies in both arenas are consistent with individuals identified as having narcissistic family origins. Interpersonally, Deb lacks friendships, particularly with other women, and has an abundance of failed romantic relationships. In addition, she is easily hurt by her tendency to foolishly trust in others and responded, for a time in season two, by constructing a protective wall around herself. At work she has difficulty acknowledging her success and, in seeking new goals to attain, she works long hours to the detriment of her personal life. Even when she attains those goals, she never seems satisfied.

Elements of a Narcissistic Family System

Clearly Dexter and Deb show personality traits consistent with adult children of narcissistic families. To understand how this came to be we need to take a look back in time at the Morgan family. Through Dexter's flashbacks we can learn more about Harry's parenting style and its role in his children's personality development and psychological growth across time.

All narcissistic families, according to Donaldson-Pressman and Pressman, display three common elements, introduced briefly above. Perhaps most prominent initially is a skewed sense of responsibility, which reverses the caretaking roles of parents and children. This creates the second element, a behavioral pattern in which the children react and reflect parental needs. The cumulative effects of the first two elements produce the third: problems with intimacy that follow the children into adulthood.

SKEWED RESPONSIBILITY

Healthy families have parents that accept responsibility for meeting the needs of the children in a developmentally appropriate manner. Parents attend to needs that children are unable to meet on their own without help. As children grow more capable through age and psychological maturity parental responsibilities lessen. Thus, children are responsible for learning to gradually meet their own needs over time. Parents make sure that their own needs are met or get help from other adults to meet them.

Parents in narcissistic families invert this sense of responsibility over time. Children of narcissistic families are often well cared for in infancy as their needs are simple and meeting them produces a response that is reinforcing to the parents. When a hungry baby is fed or a wet child is changed his or her mood quickly brightens, which pleases the parent. These needs are easy to anticipate and psychologically simplistic. As children grow older, their emotional demands become more complex and disruptive as they seek to differentiate themselves from their parents. This process is upsetting to a self-centered parent who may have entwined his or her identity with that of the child. The parent begins to view the child as self-centered and disobedient and stops responding to the child's needs. In doing so, the parent also increases attempts to have the child meet his or her needs. The expectation is that the child will be an extension of the parent and thus will work to satisfy parental requirements. The child, in order to survive, does just that. It is the only way that a child in a narcissistic system can continue to gain the attention, acceptance, and approval of the parent.

This skewed sense of responsibility flows from a parent that is preoccupied with meeting his or her own needs. Any number of reasons may explain such a preoccupation, including addiction, immaturity, mental illness, job stress, and/or interpersonal problems, to name a few. The Morgan family appears to be particularly affected by Harry's job stress and, to a lesser extent, the features of his personality that are consistent with narcissism. Dexter's flashbacks reveal that his father was grandiose and believed himself to be almost god-like with respect to the administration of justice. Harry was intolerant to defeat, and took personally decisions made within the criminal justice system. His decision to train young Dexter as a vigilante and then instruct him to murder—first nurse Mary and then Juan Rinez, a pimp Harry was going after for murder—exemplified this. Overall, Harry's need was to be revered as a good cop—a sort of savior, even—that put all the bad guys away. Both Dexter and Deb were recruited by Harry to fulfill this need.

Of the two, Dexter was recruited in the most flagrant sense. Harry took a boy who began to demonstrate symptoms of conduct disorder (killing animals, lack of remorse), most likely as a result of his early traumatic experience, and made him into a vigilante. In doing so, Harry did not recognize that Dexter had needs that required attention (therapy, etc.). Instead, he saw Dexter as a problem. In the episode "See-Through" (2-4), Dexter had a flashback that revealed that Harry's wife, Doris, suspected something was amiss. She and Harry were seen arguing about sending young Dexter for psychological testing. Doris prevailed, but Harry thwarted her efforts by instructing Dexter to respond contrary to what he truly felt during the exam. Afterward, Dexter was released to his parents without a treatment plan and Harry congratulated his son for hiding the "monster" within him. Harry continued with his own type of therapy, and taught Dexter the code, which he believed was the only way to save Dexter. Though created in part to satisfy Harry's need to take care of the bad guys, the code did teach Dexter one way of keeping his urge to kill in line. In this way, perhaps the code was good for Dexter; it controlled his behavioral urges. Nevertheless, young Dexter's urges were culturally unacceptable and illegal, and they placed Dexter at risk of harming himself as well as others. In this same vein, the code failed to acknowledge Dexter's psychological needs. Besides learning the code, he learned not to trust or express his own feelings. He followed Harry's lead, making his father happy and proud. Harry gained a son to use as a means to his own ends.

Deb, albeit more subtly than her brother, was also recruited by the family to help pursue Harry's needs. Because Harry's need to be a good cop—and by extension, to make Dexter a good vigilante—did not include Deb, her job was to stay out of the way and make as few demands as possible. Harry seemed to view his only daughter as a bother or an obstacle, as time spent with her meant time spent away from Dexter's training. Through Dexter's flashbacks we see that Deb frequently attempted to get her need for attention met by inserting herself into activities that Harry and Dexter engaged in together, including hunting and visiting crime scenes. In "Return to Sender" (1-6), for example, we learned that young Deb once asked to go on a pheasant hunt with her father and brother. Desperate to be included, she even offered to stay in the car and study during the hunt. Harry declined her plea. Later in the episode Dexter recalled that soon thereafter Deb was caught shooting cans with Harry's gun. She was a good shot, but Harry punished her with grounding and said, "I'm disappointed in you, Debra." For a time, young Deb was confused by this mixed message, as she saw her brother gain Harry's approval for the same actions. But eventually Deb learned that her expected role in the family was that of supporting daughter

REACTIVE/REFLECTIVE

In healthy families children are allowed to embark on a path of self-discovery. Through this journey, they become independent, proactive individuals who are guided through life by the feelings, wants, and needs that they develop along the way. This is in contrast to children of narcissistic families who are not able to learn about themselves because they are consumed with anticipating the expectations and needs of their parents. Their own feelings and thoughts may even be buried and not part of their awareness, having gone unacknowledged for so long. As a result, their emotions and actions, rather than being driven by internal motivation, remain, like Echo's, dependent on others.

The element of skewed responsibility in the Morgan household laid the groundwork for Dexter and Deb to become reactive/reflexive individuals. As both were recruited in fulfillment of Harry's needs, neither was given an opportunity to grow independent of him. Instead, both brother and sister were consumed by thoughts of pleasing their father, waited to learn his expectations, and then reacted.

Harry recruited his adopted son to satisfy his need to catch bad guys, grooming Dexter to be a killer. He was able to do so in part because Dexter saw his father's yearning to put away criminals and his pain when they slipped through the cracks in the legal system, and was compelled to respond. In "There's Something About Harry" (2-10), Dexter had a flashback to Deb's birthday party years earlier when Harry received bad news about a case he was working on. Juan Rinez, a murderer he had been chasing (and the pimp Dexter later kills), was going to be set free. Harry, highly agitated, shattered a beer bottle and then, calming slightly, went to Dexter and said, "I did the right thing in training you. This just proves it." In reacting to Harry's need by participating in his training, Dexter got to enjoy spending time alone with his father and received a great deal of positive reinforcement for his actions. And for a time, Dexter became a perfect reflection of his father's expectations—a robotic serial killer with a certain sense of morality. Flashbacks of Harry in early episodes conveyed his sense of pride in his son.

Dexter began to change after Rita and the children entered his life. Rita expected him to produce his own feelings and judgments, which had long been buried underneath the code. Encouraged by her, Dexter began to shake off his narcissistic family upbringing and started down a path of self-discovery. In the process, Dexter learned that contrary to Harry's teachings, he could feel. Moreover, he wanted to feel for Rita and the children. This revelation and subsequent surge of emotion was shocking to Dexter and made him question all that he thought he knew about himself. His ensuing internal conflict was evident during a scene in "An Inconvenient Lie" (2-3) when Dexter stated:

> He's all I've got. Nothing else could love me. Not even, especially not me. Or is that just a lie the Dark Passenger tells me? Because lately, there are these moments where I feel connected to something else. Someone. It's like the mask is slipping and things, people that never mattered before are starting to matter. It scares the hell out of me.

These feelings spurred Dexter to re-evaluate his priorities and before long he was getting loose with the code. Threatening his newfound independence, a critical Harry began to appear in Dexter's visions, perhaps reflecting Dexter's unconscious worries about his own emotional growth.

Like Dexter, Deb is also a reflection of her father's needs. When Harry brushed off or harshly admonished her needs for attention and affection, she began to play a supportive role, anticipating and responding to her father's needs in the hope of gaining his approval and attention. She learned that it was safer to ignore her own feelings, hopes, and needs. Without them guiding her actions, Deb became a reactive and reflective young woman. This transformation can be seen in Dexter's flashback to Deb's birthday party mentioned above. Rather than getting upset that her father ruined her day and turned once again to Dexter, Deb simply left the little party in the living room and went to the kitchen to clean up Harry's broken beer bottle. In doing so, she successfully avoided the conflict and painful admonishments of the past.

Nevertheless, her inability to meet her father's primary need affected her deeply. This is evidenced most plainly in her many self-deprecating statements. For instance, Deb has referred to Dexter as "the superior Morgan," as in "Dex, Lies, and Videotape" (2-6) after she felt brushed aside by Lundy in favor of her brother during the Bay Harbor Butcher investigation. She continued her self-deprecating tirade later in the same episode, referring to herself as "the dipshit who slept with the Ice Truck Killer" and "the resident retard." Taken together, these statements point clearly to her unresolved issues of being the second-best child in the family. In reaction to this feeling of inadequacy, she has spent most of her life trying to prove Harry wrong. In season four Deb even admitted to becoming a cop in search of Harry's approval.

PROBLEMS WITH INTIMACY

The children of narcissistic families often have problems forming close or intimate relationships. Bonding is difficult for them because they have learned not to trust. Often this is due to the emotional unavailability of their parents but can also be due to more overt abuse. As a result, they learn to build protective walls around themselves, hiding their emotional needs and wants even from close friends and intimate partners. As noted earlier, this pattern is sometimes broken by periods of reckless vulnerability and self-disclosure initiated in almost desperate attempts to earn affection. As adults, they tend to suffer a string of failed romances and accompanying interpersonal pain.

Most *Dexter* devotees will agree that Harry was emotionally unavailable to both of his children, even though he certainly put in time with Dexter. This is most plain in Harry's failure to validate either child's feelings. As a child, Dexter was angry, a feeling that we know manifested in thoughts and sometimes actions of violence. Though we know that Harry acknowledged these thoughts and taught his son some coping strategies, he did not validate or explore their source, leaving Dexter emotionally isolated. The same can be said for Deb, who had a strong emotional need for love and reciprocal affection, but was rebuffed whenever she attempted to be included in activities with her father. In the end, neither child's emotional needs were met; Dexter was taught to conceal his true feelings while Deb was taught that hers were not important. The result was that both learned to hide their emotions. As adults in their thirties, neither have close friendships and both struggle romantically. Moreover, both engage in frighteningly injudicious disclosures and acts that create precarious breaks in their otherwise closed-off lives.

Dexter certainly suffers from a barrage of intimacy troubles that can be attributed to his narcissistic family upbringing. Issues of trust were at the forefront of his relationship with Rita. And although Dexter's secrets leave him more vulnerable than most, his failure to disclose them to her was consistent with a person who learned as a child to be emotionally guarded. At the very start of the series, we learned that Dexter was apprehensive of consummating his relationship with Rita. He feared that she would see that he was "empty inside" and leave him as other women had ("Dexter," 1-1). The pair was eventually successful in becoming intimate and Rita, to Dexter's surprise, was not put off. Perhaps even more telling of Dexter's problems with intimacy is all that he left unsaid to Rita. Not just his Dark Passenger but also his harrowing childhood, family history, and emotional struggles went undisclosed. These issues of trust appeared to Rita as signs of uncertainty. For a time, even Dexter seemed unconvinced by himself in the role of family man.

Dexter's reluctance to trust is sometimes broken by flagrant periods of total self-disclosure that do not end well. Both Miguel and Trinity, for example, were privy to Dexter's secrets for some time before their deaths. Each instance of vulnerability appeared spurred by Dexter's psychological need to be known completely by another person. His relationship with Miguel in season three was perhaps the most telling of this desire. The two developed a friendship and Dexter tested the relationship in "Sí Se Puede" (3-6) by telling Miguel about Clemson Galt, a white supremacist he had always wanted to kill. Miguel was unfazed and wished get in on the plan. Dexter was both surprised and delighted, and he began to teach Miguel the code, defending his decisions when admonishing visions of Harry warned him not to trust his new friend. This trust was broken when Dexter learned that Miguel had been fooling him and strayed from the code to murder Ellen Wolf, an innocent woman. Dexter seemed hurt, angry, and disappointed in himself. He rebuilt his metaphorical self-protective wall once more, not really showing himself again until season four.

Deb, too, suffers romantically and struggles with interpersonal trust issues. She has a history of failed relationships and bounces from one man to the next without much thought. One explanation for her behavior is that Deb is still desperately seeking a man's approval. The notable absence of close female relationships in her life may also hint at the emphasis she puts on obtaining the male approval she never received from Harry. Consistent with children of narcissistic families, Deb seems to define approval in terms of the attention and affection she receives from others. Evidence of her attention-seeking is found in her relationship with Brian (a.k.a., Rudy), the Ice Truck Killer, in season one, who showered her with affection and acceptance, as well as her relationship with Lundy, in seasons two and four, who praised her achievements. In addition, in season four she became uncomfortable with the more balanced relationship she had with Anton. With him there were conditions for acceptance, including honesty, availability, and commitment to him alone. Anton confronted Deb about her feelings toward Lundy and demanded a certain amount of her time and attention, even when that meant taking her away from work. Because this unsettled Deb, she was easily drawn away from the relationship and back to the comfort of Lundy.

In her relationships, Deb is much more trusting than Dexter, but like him her disclosures are sometimes careless. Deb frequently lets down her guard when members of the opposite sex express an appealing interest in her. Quick to initiate sexual relationships and fall in love, Deb often finds herself vulnerable to the wrong man.

Healing

Though they are fictional characters, Dexter and Deb Morgan seem to share a set of personal and behavioral patterns consistent with individuals raised in narcissistic family systems. A review of their upbringing supports this theory and suggests that Harry may have been too self-absorbed to adequately meet the needs of either. Although it is plausible that Harry may have genuinely tried to protect Dexter with the code, there is no similar explanation for Deb. In addition, even with the code to control Dexter's behavior, Harry failed to meet his son's emotional needs. Given this theory, we can develop further ideas about the characters and even use it to predict where they might go from here.

First, let me propose that this inquiry suggests possible solutions to other, more common questions about Dexter and his sister. For example, how did Dexter come to be a serial killer with a sense of morality? Using narcissistic family theory, we might ascertain that it is because he was molded into an extension of Harry himself. Also, we might wonder why Deb continues to choose the wrong men. This analysis offers that she might be doing so in ill-conceived attempts to seek the male affection she never earned from her father.

Second, we might settle some of the concerns about Harry's moral character. Early episodes had us convinced that he was the ideal father and super cop, but later episodes have made us question that, given the evidence of adultery, lack of compassion toward his daughter, and questionable cover-ups at work regarding Dexter's past. The narcissistic family model suggests that Harry's actions may not have been intentionally malicious, but instead caused by psychological immaturity as a parent and possible untreated narcissism.

Finally, the model shows us where Dexter and Deb can go from here. Healing and positive improvement can stem from the discovery that one's family of origin was not in fact perfect. This is the journey that Dexter and Deb embark upon throughout the series. As brother and sister gain a more realistic view of their childhoods, they begin to change, as if they are just beginning to discover their true identities. And in a sense they are. Once they accept the reality of their childhoods, survivors of narcissistic families move forward in their personal lives because they can finally learn about themselves.

Marisa Mauro, PsyD, is a psychologist in private practice
with a focus on forensics in Austin, Texas. She also works as a freelance
writer and regularly contributes to her blog, Take All Prisoners, on Psychol-
ogyToday.com. Previously, Dr. Mauro worked as a clinical psychologist at
the California Department of Corrections and Rehabilitation. Much of her
work there was focused on violent offenders, gang members, and inmates
serving life sentences. She has also taught as an adjunct professor and
conducted research on personality, academic success, career success,
eating disorders, and suicide.

Are these people diagnosable? If you ever wonder about that while watching the characters on Dexter, this essay is for you. Take Lila, for example. She can't possibly be "normal," can she? If not, which official clinical category would she fit? Was there a sense in which Rita was right when she pegged Dexter as an addict? Those are some of the questions Adi Jaffe confronts. Be careful, though—he may just convince you that you have a glimmer of some of these troublesome personality traits yourself!

THE KILLER
WITHIN

ADI JAFFE

There's something a little bit off about Dexter Morgan. While this may not seem to be an outlandish claim for a man whose primary recreational pastime is the abduction and dismemberment of some of society's least savory characters, it has nevertheless been at the core of the series bearing his first name from the very beginning. Dexter's disconnect from the societal norms that surround him, and the extraordinary amount of effort it takes for him to effectively pass for normal, to "keep the mask in place," make for the most interesting and complex moments in the show. We are fascinated by this portrait of a brilliant killer, infinitely more capable than we could ever be when it comes to brutally incapacitating a violent gang member, and yet on the verge of a complete breakdown when ordering a mocha latte. The cold indifference, relentless self-interest, and capacity for sadistic violence that make up Dexter's Dark Passenger capture our attention not because they are completely foreign to us, but because we have all known people with similar traits. This, luckily, is not to say that we all know a secret serial killer, though you might do well to avoid anyone who collects doll legs or has a homemade leather suit. Rather, the source of our uncomfortable familiarity with Dexter's antisocial behavior was made evident in the show's second season, when his then-girlfriend Rita made a fairly accurate, if incomplete, assessment of the mounting evidence: Dexter is an addict.

Dexter's response, a misleading admission that he is, indeed, an addict, is not far from truth—while drug addicts feel a need to consume a substance, he is gripped with an uncontrollable compulsion to commit murder. He even more closely resembles a behavioral addict, although their compulsion centers on typically acceptable activities, often as innocuous as eating, that they have simply taken too far. We find that addicts, like Dexter, often project an entirely false persona in the pursuit of disguising their true intentions and compulsions, as hiding behind a carefully constructed mask is essential to allow them to continue with the behavior that is often their biggest motivator. Indeed, addicts and their behavioral patterns tend to make us feel uneasy in much the same way that Dexter does. Most people derive their sense of self-reliance and safety from their ability to read and assess others, and addicts, like Dexter, make that work harder by constantly presenting a false outward "self." And while it is highly unlikely that our inability to properly assess the intentions of that old friend from high school will result in being chopped to pieces and left on center ice at the BankAtlantic Center, the likelihood of losing a car, wallet, or prescription bottle to a desperate addict is far higher.

Most of America's thirty million addicts have trouble "only" with alcohol (fifteen million) or marijuana (five million), the most commonly abused drugs in the United States. Some addicts fill themselves with powerful pills that flood their brains with feel-good chemicals like dopamine and opioids, while others rely on drug-filled syringes. Still more find themselves compulsively acting out behavioral addictions like gambling or sex. The American Psychological Association (APA) has even begun to review (albeit inconclusively) whether videogame addiction should be included in the 2012 DSM (the Diagnostic and Statistical Manual of Mental Disorders), a concept that draws a chuckle until you realize that compulsive video gaming has been responsible for some horrifying deaths across the world, including examples from China and South Korea of addicts playing for fifty-plus straight hours before going into severe cardiac arrest. There's no doubt that some of these addictions make us more uncomfortable than others, but all addicts share something in common—their compulsions (like Dexter's) have taken over and hijacked their ability to make decisions for themselves that better, rather than further destroy, their lives.

Although a series of vivid flashbacks to horrific childhood trauma has given us a wider view of the origins of Dexter's dark compulsions, addicts rarely give us a clear objective view of the demons that haunt them. While no doubt some addicts can point to a particular moment or event that initially drove their addiction (though that moment is unlikely to be on par with the chainsaw-based murder of a parent by Cuban drug dealers), plenty of addicts have no such obvious moment to look to, having instead been deeply emotionally affected by a moment or moments that might seem mundane or inconsequential to an outside observer. Indeed, the subjectivity of trauma, and the subsequent range of possible reactions from and affects on the afflicted, owes much to genetics and biology: factors as minute as variations in the length of the fourth type of the dopamine receptors in a brain can make a person more compulsive and more likely to become addicted, meaning that few addicts can adequately, or accurately, even begin to assess their own lives and choices.

However, we know a few things for certain about addicts, beginning with the unshakably strong connection between addiction and personality disorders that brought Dexter Morgan to a Narcotics Anonymous meeting in the first place. The DSM IV, also known as the APA's diagnostic "bible," defines personality disorders as "an enduring pattern of inner experience and behavior that deviates markedly from the expectations of the culture of the individual who exhibits it." Right off the bat, this evokes the "mask" of normalcy that we've so often heard Dexter describe. Dexter doesn't feel what others feel and though he recognizes that his experience is different, he can't seem to adjust. It's important to note the role that cultural norms play in the definition, as well—as is usual for psychiatrists and psychologists, "normal" is defined by the context of culture as opposed to an objective definition, an approach that puts a real emphasis on a person's ability to connect with, and relate to, what's happening around them. Also of importance is the indication that these thoughts and behaviors must be "an enduring pattern." Though we all have our moments of disagreement with social mores or expectations, and most of us can even think of at least one time when we have impulsively made a major transgression, this is still generally not enough to qualify as a disorder. Getting into a bar fight or streaking through your college graduation ceremony may not be particularly upstanding or dignified behaviors, but so long as they're not part of an overall pattern of reckless rule-breaking, they tend to fall well within the metric of momentary lapses in judgment and conduct we consider normal. A true personality disorder is a long-lasting problem that essentially pervades all aspects of a person's life in a way that interferes with their ability to function in society. This would seem to fit the serial killer, and the crack addict, with equal emphasis.

Although the specifics of his story might divide professional opinions on whether he fits the clinical definition of an addict, for the purposes of this essay it is safe to say that Dexter displays both addictive behavior and a personality disorder.

Whether personality disorders cause addiction or whether the addictive behavior brings about the development of these disorders seems to depend on the circumstance, but these two afflictions undoubtedly support one another, to the tune of a three times higher prevalence of personality disorders in addicts versus the general population. Similarly, in *Dexter*, Dexter is not the only addict with a personality disorder—or personality disorder sufferer with an addiction. Some of *Dexter*'s other characters give us a look at typical symptoms of three of the most widespread and significant entries in the DSM's "B Cluster" of personality disorders, defined as the "dramatic, emotional, or erratic" disorders. Known respectively as Antisocial, Borderline, and Narcissistic personality disorders, all three have been linked extensively with addiction, in addition to having been diagnosed extensively in killers, violent criminals, and even serial murderers.

Antisocial Personality Disorder

Looming largest amongst these disorders is probably *antisocial personality disorder*, also known as ASPD. The APA defines antisocial personality disorder as "a pervasive pattern of disregard for, and violation of, the rights of others that begins in childhood or early adolescence and continues into adulthood." In other words, those afflicted with ASPD, who are commonly referred to as sociopaths or psychopaths, have little to no ability to feel empathy. That inability to connect to others, and the compulsion to violate those rights, leads many people with ASPD directly into a life of crime. Those with ASPD are known to lie and steal, are highly impulsive, and have problems controlling their behavior and emotions. They are known to display superficial charm and an extreme sense of entitlement, and, as would seem obvious, often have serious and recurring problems with the law.

The clear parallel here is Dexter Morgan himself, an extremely intelligent and genial fellow with a triple-digit body count. From childhood, Dexter has had not only a disregard for the rights of others but a genuine compulsion to violate them in the form of murder. He admits to having no natural compassion for the people around him, a disregard that is mollified only through the strict moral code drilled into him by his adoptive father, a police officer who recognized the signs that his son might turn into a complete monster without guidance. The skills and self-control that Harry Morgan taught Dexter are meant to explain to us how it is that someone as twisted as Dexter can manage to maintain the elaborate veneer of normalcy that he does, while further emphasizing the superhuman amount of self-control that this requires. Although the mainstream success of the show clearly depends on no small amount of hedging on just how monstrous Dexter's killer behavior is (we have to root for him, after all), we are at least given a back story that suggests that his was a hard-earned self-discipline, something that separates him from those he hunts, whose lack of control, code, and follow-through earn them an earlier exit from their chosen profession, whether via handcuffs or the inside of a garbage bag.

Interestingly, those with ASPD likely rarely use drugs to overcome emotional difficulties, because, well, they feel little if anything. However, many of the same factors that make ordinary individuals likely to take drugs—namely impulsivity, high risk-taking, and environmental influences—are present at extreme levels in ASPD individuals due to their disregard for societal norms that are meant to keep those attributes in check. Research has shown such similarities can be traced to brain function in areas most associated with impulse control and emotional regulation.

Borderline Personality Disorder

In season two, Dexter found himself under the spell of his Narcotics Anonymous sponsor Lila, a charming and seductive artist who purported to understand the darkness within Dexter in a way that he thought impossible since Harry's death. While drawing ever closer to Lila, Dexter began to uncover more and more of her dangerous, erratic behavior, which seemed to be controlled by far more emotion than his own. In fact, Lila displayed classic symptoms of *borderline personality disorder*, a disorder characterized by extreme and highly variable moods.

People with BPD have chaotic and unstable interpersonal relationships, but unlike individuals with antisocial disorder, whose relationships suffer from lack of empathy, the relationship trouble for those with BPD stems primarily from the severe emotional roller-coaster experienced by anyone pursuing, or being pursued by, the BPD sufferer. Despite what are often the best of intentions, BPD sufferers subject those around them to their severe bouts of tension, anger, depression, and anxiety, which often shift radically and without warning. Prevailing wisdom seems to suggest that these emotions are triggered by perceived rejection or failure. As Lila pursued Dexter, first with an innocuous offer of NA sponsorship, then with a rapidly escalating series of seductions, rejections, and ultimately arsons, kidnappings, and murders, we witnessed dramatic swings in mood, self-image, and conduct that followed even the smallest disappointment or perceived threat of loss. In one memorable sequence, Dexter approached his parked car at work to find Lila, whom he had recently rejected as his sponsor, sitting inside. She opened the conversation with what sounded to be a calm, reasoned argument for a continuation of their relationship, but when Dexter firmly rejected this, she began to cycle wildly through a series of emotions, from anger to desperation to self-pity. Aside from the impulsiveness and recklessness she displayed, extremely common traits among borderline individuals, her own insecurity and hyper-sensitivity to rejection pegged her as a textbook BPD sufferer.

With regard to addiction, borderline personalities dwell among the many drug and behavior addicts with impulse control problems. People with BPD tend to approach drugs, as well as alcohol, sex, gambling, and other unsafe behaviors, with characteristic recklessness, particularly as this behavior often aids them in their manipulative and unbalanced relationships with others. BPD sufferers' behavioral issues generally arise from just how far outside of the normal boundaries of accepted behavior these people are willing to go in order to achieve what they want. This, in combination with their extreme, overly dramatic moods and split-second emotional reactivity, can result in uncontrollably volatile behavior. When Lila, impulsively motivated by a perception of emotional rejection from Dexter, had sex with Dexter's friend Angel and then drugged herself to make herself seem like the victim of an assault, it showed both her emotionally guided impulsivity and her aggressive willingness to do almost anything in the pursuit of her objective. (It also displayed aspects of *histrionic personality disorder*, a similar and somewhat overlapping attention-seeking disorder that involves the heavy and compulsive use of flirtation and seduction in order to receive validation, and is also correlated with addiction.)

For BPD patients, killing can be, like most everything else they do, an impulsive, fleeting reaction—an instant punishment for a slight or a quick reaction to an internal sense of being unappreciated, as when, later in the season, Lila's reckless behavior culminated in the attempted murder of Dexter and Rita's children.

Narcissistic Personality Disorder

Another personality disorder shared by addicts and killers alike is *narcissistic personality disorder*, which, according to the APA, is marked by "a pervasive pattern of grandiosity, need for admiration, and a lack of empathy." If this sounds like a combination of borderline and antisocial disorders, you're a quick learner. Named for Narcissus, the mythological Greek character who loved his image so much he drowned in a pond while watching his own reflection, narcissists care about themselves almost exclusively. While the antisocial individual derives no validation from their perception by the outside world (Dexter, for example, is only invested in his personal and professional reputation insofar as it keeps people from realizing that he is a serial killer), the narcissistic individual is eternally occupied with their adequacy, prestige, and the impression they leave on others.[1] Yet, unlike the similarly obsessive borderline personality, narcissists worry little about relationships with others and show a profound lack of empathy, because of their preoccupation with themselves. We see evidence of narcissism in well-heeled, handsome serial killers with power fantasies such as Ted Bundy, as well as in despotic and highly self-regarding dictators such as Saddam Hussein and Adolf Hitler. Drug abuse among narcissists is prevalent, with cocaine gaining at least some studies' mention as a particular drug of choice for this group (but, interestingly, not for individuals with borderline or antisocial personalities).

---

[1] When, upon seeing his vigilante killing spree represented heroically in a comic book, Dexter began having visions of himself as the "Dark Defender," a killer superhero who manages to save his own mother from being murdered, he was displaying a textbook narcissist fantasy although, based on his typical behavioral patterns, he himself would not be considered a typical narcissist.

Dexter gave us an excellent portrait of a narcissist who is both a traditional addict and a criminal in Rita's first husband, Paul Bennett, a man obsessed with remaining in control of the very family that he drove away through abusive violence and drug abuse. Paul viewed his family as an extension of himself, and his drive to possess them yet again was not motivated by a sense of fatherly responsibility or a need to make amends so much as a compulsion to forever be the focal point of his own saga, a self-obsession that could not coexist with the rejection that Dexter's relationship with Rita represented.

As we can see from the wide range of overlap in even these few examples, these disorders and their descriptions are imperfect classifications that attempt to categorize a wide range of behaviors that themselves stem from a wide range of physical and chemical specifics in the human brain. The relationship between addiction and personality disorder is just as complex. Although personality disorders often influence sufferers' drug use, even predisposing them to addiction, the relationship is reciprocal: chronic drug abuse can physically alter the brain in such a way as to perpetuate these symptoms.

When Dexter Morgan sat in the back of that stuffy church hall at the Narcotics Anonymous meeting, he was among people more similar to himself than he realized. Heavy drug abuse has been shown to damage the neurotransmitter function and areas of the brain that control, among other things, empathy, leading to antisocial and narcissistic tendencies, as well as the areas important to emotional regulation, which can bring about symptoms of borderline personality. Though it would be a rarity for any level of drug abuse to permanently change a relatively well-adjusted person into the Bay Harbor Butcher, the effect of drugs on the brain is profound enough that it is not uncommon to test a newly "clean" addict for the full range of mental-health disorders, not only because the tests are understandably unreliable when one is actively using drugs, but also because changes to the brain from drug use can be unpredictable and are often long-lasting.

There is one last thing that Dexter has in common with other addicts. While Dexter seems to have thus far kept his omnipresent mask in place, the show continues to push him toward a point beyond which maintaining the façade and giving in to his dark compulsions will prove mutually exclusive. He would not be the first addict to face such a choice. Just as the shattering of Dexter's double life would lead to condemnation, prison, and potentially worse, more traditional addicts often find that the conflict between their addictions and the rest of their lives sets them on a road that ends in personal, emotional, and physical destruction.

Not everyone has had to deal with the fallout of discovering that the charming stranger dating their adopted sister is actually their brother, fewer still that their brother is a serial killer, and even fewer on top of that have had the entire experience made all the more difficult because they themselves are also a serial killer. But plenty of people have discovered that their charming significant other is a liar, a cheater, or a drug addict, and plenty have lost money, health, friends, and safety at the hands of trusted people whose addictions and personalities made them unable to honor that trust. The difference between the addict, the killer, and the average Joe is a little closer than we like to think about. It's a matter of degrees, of different points on the spectrum of "normal" functioning. Most everyone's had moments of narcissism, and few of us have managed to avoid overreacting emotionally. Even fewer of us have never known the feeling of truly wanting something even though it was inappropriate. It can sometimes be difficult to know exactly when lines are crossed and *patterns* of behavior develop that make life difficult. However, by exaggerating these normally sordid and uncomfortable themes and setting them up in a bright, cartoony Miami where the cops are witty and beautiful and the serial killers seem to outnumber the general population, *Dexter* gives us a darkly humorous place to process our own experiences with addicts, sociopaths, and antisocial personalities, as well as those tendencies in ourselves. Though the crimes are larger than life, the underlying disorders and behaviors are dead on.

Adi Jaffe is wrapping up his final year at the top-ranked UCLA psychology doctoral program. He specializes in behavioral-neuroscience and assessment as they relate to addictions and addiction-related behaviors and has received several awards from organizations such as NIDA, APA, and more. Adi maintains one of the most comprehensive addiction sites on the web at www.AllAboutAddiction.com and writes for *Psychology Today*, TakePart, and other online and print publications. He's published numerous academic articles and has given dozens of presentations at national and international conferences.

How dare they! Writer David Barber-Callaghan and evolutionary psychologist Nigel Barber want us to take seriously the possibility that Dexter—our darling Dexter—is no better than Rita's ex, that mean, abusive, violent, drug-addled Paul. No, wait, I've understated their case. They think that Dexter is in some ways even more abusive toward Rita than Paul was. Can you imagine?

RITA'S ROCKY RELATIONSHIPS

Is Dexter Any Better Than Paul?

DAVID BARBER-CALLAGHAN AND NIGEL BARBER

A female acquaintance always pursues the "wrong type of guy," perpetually ending up in dysfunctional or abusive relationships. Against all odds, she finds one Mr. Wrong after another. Is she just unlucky? Hardly. *Dexter*'s Rita Bennett provides insight into the cyclical aspect of real-world abusive relationships. Over the course of the series, Rita moved from one abusive marriage with Paul Bennett—who nearly beat her to death—to another with Dexter Morgan.

Most viewers would consider Dexter a real step up from Paul as a partner for Rita, yet the two men share many abusive characteristics. Dexter is always careful to keep the violence of his Dark Passenger from Rita, but abuse doesn't have to mean physical violence. And in some ways, Dexter is as abusive as Paul—if not more so.

Abusive Relationships

What exactly constitutes an abusive relationship? Relationship abuse is shockingly common. According to the American Psychological Association, around one in three women in America will be victims of relationship abuse in their lifetime. According to police reports cited by the Center for Relationship Abuse Awareness, in heterosexual relationships the overwhelming majority of domestic violence—up to 95 percent—is perpetuated by men. However, his evidence is seriously biased because police have a preference for arresting (and charging) men, who are seen as more likely than women to cause serious harm. Surveys show American women are as likely to hit their husbands as vice versa, as noted in Phillip W. Cook's 1997 book *Abused Men*. Evolutionary psychologists nevertheless describe a worldwide pattern of violent possessiveness through which men seek to establish sexual control over women, a pattern responsible for most of the crimes of violence against women.[1] Rita's first marriage falls into this category.

Relationship abuse is not just violence, of course. The Center for Relationship Abuse Awareness defines it as a "pattern of abusive and coercive behaviors used to maintain power and control over a former or current intimate partner."[2] It is important to note that the goal of the abuser is not to harm the victim but rather to bend the victim's will to his control. Psychologists have identified three main categories of abuse: physical abuse, sexual abuse, and emotional abuse. Physical abuse refers to any intentional bodily harm, whereas sexual abuse can be any form of unwanted sexual attention and harassment as well as physical harm such as rape. Emotional abuse (also known as mental or psychological abuse) "occurs when one person controls

---

[1] Barber, Nigel, *The Science of Romance*, 2002.
[2] Center for Relationship Abuse. Center for Relationship Abuse Awareness, 2005.

information available to another person so as to manipulate that person's sense of reality."[3] The manifestation of this type of abuse can range from lying to manipulation to verbal abuse. All three of these forms of relationship abuse can cause lasting psychological harm.

These three types of relationship abuse were clearly portrayed in Rita's relationship with her husband Paul Bennett. For half of the first season, Paul was locked away in jail, but his influence remained tangible. As Dexter remarked, "In her own little way, [Rita is] as damaged as me" ("Dexter," 1-1). Dexter's sister, Debra, first met Rita during a domestic abuse call and later introduced her to Dexter, telling him, "Rita's ex-hubby, the crack addict, repeatedly raped her. Knocked her around. Ever since then, she's been completely uninterested in sex" ("Dexter"). The psychological damage from Paul's abuse was devastating and pervasive.

Rita's plight raised a familiar question. Why was she apparently so clueless about defending herself? Why, for instance, did she not alert the police that Paul had violated his restraining order, so that he would be put back in prison where he could not threaten her or her children? The short answer is that she was still suffering from the trauma of her marriage.

Rita's Post-Traumatic Stress

One of the worst consequences of physical and psychological victimization is post-traumatic stress disorder, and Rita was a textbook case. How was her post-traumatic stress established, and how did this explain her seemingly irrational approach to dealing with Paul after he was released from prison?

Post-traumatic stress disorder (PTSD) is a serious anxiety disorder resulting from psychological trauma. Such trauma

---

[3] Patricelli, Kathryn, "Types of Abuse," Mental Help.net, 2010.

must be severe. Precipitating events of PTSD include combat experience, abduction, violent rape, and other situations that involve threats of imminent death or loss of physical, sexual, or psychological integrity. Rita's experiences with Paul clearly qualified as capable of causing PTSD.

Her behavior, psychology, and reactions to others undeniably revealed symptoms of the PTSD she developed from years of enduring Paul's abuse. First, she suffered from an overwhelming and incapacitating fear of Paul, even when he was incarcerated. Rita relived the abuse as it replayed in her mind in a continuous loop. She felt that she was living in a nightmare. Gloomy, depressed, Rita seemed to find it difficult to experience pleasure of any kind. She was numb, alienated, detached, and found it difficult to relate to other people with the exception of her children. Notice how she did not appear to have any friends other than Dexter and how her relationship with Paul kept even Rita's mother at a distance.

One way to suppress flashbacks to the trauma is to attempt to screen out all stimuli associated with the event. That is one possible reason that Rita was initially not interested in sex with Dexter. Another may have been that she was incapable of feeling pleasure, which would explain why she initially chose to perform oral sex on Dexter rather than having intercourse ("Let's Give the Boy a Hand," 1-4). Rita perceived this as a major milestone on her road to emotional recovery. Her post-traumatic stress impacted more than just her sex life. The trauma was so difficult for Rita to manage that when one of Paul's former business associates stole her car as compensation for two ounces of owed blow, Rita refused to allow Dexter to file a police report. She said, "Paul's out of my life . . . I just want my past to go away" ("Popping Cherry," 1-3).

Early in the first season, Rita recovered to the point of asserting herself more with Paul, and took the dangerous step of demanding a divorce. But she was playing with fire, of course, and Paul was more than capable of devising ways to punish her for defying him.

The Ghost of Abuse Past

Halfway through the first season, Paul was released from jail due to overcrowding. The first thing he did was "ask" to go to his and Rita's daughter's birthday party. Rita confided in Dexter that she did not want Paul to attend, but also said that "even if [she] says no, he won't listen" ("Return to Sender," 1-6).

Relationship abuse deals fundamentally with issues of power and control. Though it's obvious that Paul is abusive, it's worth taking a closer look at the methods he uses to exert his power and control over Rita. The National Center on Domestic and Sexual Violence distinguishes eight clear categories of manipulation. They are (1) coercion and threats, (2) intimidation, (3) emotional abuse—which is more accurately called verbal abuse, (4) isolation, (5) minimizing, denying, and blaming, (6) using children, (7) economic abuse, and (8) male privilege. Though Paul relies on many of these different methods, the above quote from Rita illustrates male privilege: "making all the big decisions [and] acting like the 'master of the castle.'"[4] In Paul's previous interactions with Rita, he had not allowed her to make any of the decisions or had ignored the ones she did make. Rita is well aware of this, and later in the same episode told Dexter, "Even if I tell him not to come, he'll show up here eventually" ("Return to Sender"). Rita was accustomed to Paul exerting his control on their relationship. Rita also told Dexter, "He said if I left he would find us and use the kids" ("Return to Sender"), an example of an abuser's propensity to use coercion and threats as a method of control.

---

[4] "Power and Control Wheel," National Center on Domestic and Sexual Violence.

Though Rita managed to convince Paul to avoid Astor's party, in the next episode, he escalated their disagreement by picking the kids up from school one day and taking them to the carnival. He did this without prior warning or approval and in spite of the fact that Rita had full custody and that she had instructed the school's administration not to release the kids into Paul's care ("Circle of Friends," 1-7). This is an excellent example of "using children." The National Center on Domestic and Sexual Violence defines using children as "making [the victim] feel guilty about the children, using the children to relay messages, using visitation to harass her, [and] threatening to take the children away." Paul's day trip used his children to insinuate himself back into Rita's life and make her feel guilty about separating him from the kids. Additionally, Paul's actions carried the implicit threat that he could make the kids disappear at any time and that Rita was powerless to prevent him from doing so.

The next morning, Paul strolled into Rita's home during breakfast with a box of donuts. His casual attitude reflected the male privilege that he felt. When Rita started to tell Paul that he "can't do this anymore," he became angry, yelling, "What? What!? Help raise my kids?" ("Circle of Friends"). Each of his exclamations was accompanied by a forceful gesture. Not only was Paul using the children to his advantage, but he was also resorting to intimidation with his overt display of anger. He later tried some of the same tricks on Dexter while Dexter was babysitting the kids. Paul even went as far as taking a swing at Dexter only to stop short, inches from his face. (Dexter was somewhat less responsive to Paul's bullying.)

Though Dexter was tempted to see that Paul disappeared permanently, Rita took matters into her own hands by confronting Paul herself. Their argument over visitation rights to the children addressed the key issue in all relationship abuse: control. In asking Paul to sign the divorce papers, Rita said to Paul, "A judge put me in control. I'm in control now, and I have the power to make sure that you never see your children unless you do exactly as I tell you" ("Circle of Friends"). Rita was responding to Paul's abusive use of the children in kind by mirroring his devious manner of fighting. In the next episode, Rita remarked to Dexter, "I finally feel like I'm in control. I never felt that way with Paul" ("Shrink Wrap," 1-8).

Her attempts to seize control did not go over well with Paul, unsurprisingly. In the next few episodes, Paul reverted to his old ways and expressed his abusive traits more freely before Rita and Dexter left town for a weekend in order to follow up on the death of Dexter's biological father. The weekend trip meant that Paul would not be able to visit with the children, so Paul arrived at Rita's house full of bluster. Rita firmly vetoed the visitation, and Paul responded by smacking a cup off the table. Once again, Paul resorted to intimidation in hopes of controlling Rita. During the trip, Paul drunkenly called Rita and started describing all the fun he could have had taking his kids to the circus, trying to make her feel guilty.

After Rita returned home, Paul showed up and stumbled in while the kids were sleeping. Rita told him, "It's late, and you're drunk, and you can't keep coming by here unannounced." Paul replied, "You don't call the shots. Okay?" In turn Rita said, "Look, Paul, I want you to leave." Paul started shouting, "I don't give a fuck what you want. I want my fucking kids! . . . Those kids are going to remember who the head of this fucking family is" ("Father Knows Best," 1-9). In this discussion, Paul's anger revolved around his loss of control and he relied once again on the tactic of male privilege to try and regain his lost power.

Rita led Paul away from the kids' room, ending up in her bedroom instead. Paul threw her down on the bed and started to disrobe, and Rita only managed to escape by hitting Paul with a baseball bat she had stowed under her bed. Paul struck back by pressing charges for assault, turning Rita's life upside down in a petty legal act of retaliation. "I could drop the charges if you agree to unsupervised visitation," said Paul ("Seeing Red," 1-10), masterfully using threats and coercion once again to control Rita.

As far as Dexter was concerned, Paul was a serious problem. So Dexter solved it. After he framed Paul for violating his parole, Rita was theoretically free to lead a more normal life. But by removing him from the picture, Dexter was not giving Rita back control over her interactions with Paul. He was taking that control for himself, one of Dexter's first acts of emotional abuse. While Dexter appeared to save Rita from Paul's abuse, their relationship was, in fact, just another turn on the abuse carousel.

Dexter's Psychological Abuse

One of the most gripping aspects of *Dexter* is its psychological realism, made all the more remarkable by the highly unusual situations in which the protagonist finds himself. Dexter, of course, is a sociopath who lacks the capacity for feeling normal emotions of love and grief. Some of the most poignant moments in the series come when he grapples with visible displays of emotion in the other characters and tries to make sense of what they would be feeling. Emotionally stunted himself, he could not offer Rita a normal relationship. He amused himself by playing with the children and kept her at a distance, romantically speaking. When Dexter's deficient emotional system and Rita's fractured psyche were brought together, it was inevitable that their relationship would be psychologically abusive. Rita's experiences with Paul made her the perfect woman for Dexter, and not just because previous sexual abuse at Paul's hands made her initially uninterested in sex—something that was particularly attractive to a man who does not feel emotionally capable of making love. Rita's own emotional numbness made her an ideal candidate for Dexter's kind of psychological abuse.

Though on the outside Paul and Dexter appear to be dia-
metrically opposed, they share dark, troubled sides. As Dexter
commented in regard to Rita, "Her husband was a crackhead
and her boyfriend was a serial killer. It's kinda hard to not take
that personally" ("Return to Sender"). Though Dexter was never
physically abusive to Rita, his lies and manipulation added up
to emotional abuse. Dexter had an affair, continuously lied to
Rita, and murdered numerous people over the course of their
relationship. Worse, Rita had no idea what she was mixed up
with. At least with Paul, his abuse was easy to recognize. It's
harder to fight back against abuse you can't clearly identify.

Rita's first inkling of Dexter's darker side came from Paul,
who attempted to explain how he was framed. "He's not the
man you think he is," warned Paul ("Born Free," 1-12). But Rita
chose to ignore Paul's warnings and became even more involved
with Dexter. When she later confronted Dexter about Paul's
story, Dexter admitted that he impulsively struck Paul over the
head, then carried him to a nearby motel and injected him with
heroin. Rita asked Dexter where he got the heroin, and leapt to
the conclusion that Dexter was a junkie, just like Paul. Evasive
as ever, Dexter responded, "I have an addiction," and allowed
Rita to push him into a Narcotics Anonymous program he didn't
actually intend to complete ("Waiting to Exhale," 2-2).

He attended the NA meeting for five minutes, hoping to lie
his way out of the situation. Rita knew NA procedures from her
previous experience with Paul's addiction and caught Dexter in
his lie when she asked to see his newcomer's pin. "You're a terrible liar," she said. "I can't go through this again" ("An Inconvenient Lie," 2-3). Forced to follow through with the program,
Dexter committed to attending the meetings, where he encountered Lila, his sponsor.

As sponsors go, Lila was rather unconventional. For one of
their first therapeutic escapades, Dexter lied to Rita and went
to Naples, Florida, with Lila to track down one of his mother's

killers. Rita later discovered Dexter's deception and learned that Lila and Dexter "spent the night together in a hotel" ("Dex, Lies, and Videotape," 2-6). Rita assumed that Dexter was cheating on her with his attractive sponsor and yelled, "I thought that you were different than Paul, but you're the same. Actually you're worse. You made me trust you" ("Dex, Lies, and Videotape"). Perhaps here, Rita pointed out one of the biggest difference between Paul and Dexter's different brands of abuse. While dating Paul, Rita knew to expect his abusive behavior, but Dexter's abuses came as a surprise. Because of this shock value, Dexter's transgressions were more devastating.

Even when Dexter came clean about the trip to find his mother's killer, Rita was hurt by the fact that she was excluded from that important moment in Dexter's life. "You chose to include Lila, and not me," she said ("Dex, Lies, and Videotape"). To make matters worse, despite the fact that Dexter did not have sex with Lila during the trip to Naples, he slept with her after Rita found out about the trip. Rita was so hurt by this betrayal that she could not stand any further contact with Dexter and kicked him out of her place and her life.

Deb lectured Dexter about his behavior, asking him, "How could you do this to Rita, let alone her kids? You're like [Paul]" ("That Night, A Forest Grew," 2-7). He continued his fling with Lila knowing full well that he was damaging Rita's emotional well-being. If anything, his relationship with Lila taught him new methods of manipulation. Lila was a master of manipulation, willing to set fire to her own apartment to keep Dexter in a relationship with her, acting all teary-eyed after the fire and saying, "Promise me that you won't leave me, that you won't go anywhere" ("That Night, A Forest Grew").

Although Rita and Dexter broke up, the kids still felt a strong connection with him, and Cody left his toys in Dexter's satchel, forcing a visit. Dexter arrived in the morning with a box of donuts in one hand—much the same way Paul did halfway through the first season. Rita told Dexter, "Don't ever do it again. It's too hard on the kids, and it's too hard on me. It's Paul all over again" ("Morning Comes," 2-8). Dexter assumed Paul's role as the emotionally abusive father figure who, as far as Rita was aware, was also addicted to drugs.

Though Dexter was not physically abusive to Rita, he did show evidence of physical abuse in his relationship with Lila. When she broke into Rita's home, he started with threats, warning Lila, "Stay away from Rita. Stay away from me. Or you will see the monster" ("Morning Comes"). After another unpleasant encounter with Lila, Dexter became physically abusive, grabbing Lila forcibly by the shoulders and yelling at her. Dexter eventually did show Lila "the monster," murdering her.

Despite the pain caused her, Rita forgave Dexter and took him back, and in the next season became pregnant with his child. Rita understood Dexter's uncertainty about what to do, saying, "I don't want to force him into anything. That's kinda what happened with the ex-husband. Well, that and the fact that he [Paul] was a sociopath" ("Finding Freebo," 3-2). Rita had no idea of the savage irony that her words carried. After some initial doubts on Dexter's part, they got married. (In the process, Dexter learned that Rita was married for six months when she was sixteen ["Do You Take Dexter Morgan?" 3-12]. Although little was revealed about this marriage, its brevity suggests that it could have been the first in a series of abusive marriages.)

As Rita and Dexter grew closer, Dexter had to lie to her and manipulate her in order to perpetrate his killings, skipping dates with her in favor of grisly engagements with his victims. Dexter's repeated, poorly explained absences constituted serious psychological abuse. "I've been calling you for hours," Rita complained one morning ("Waiting to Exhale"). On another occasion, Dexter totaled his car and suffered a concussion while racing home from a kill. He passed it off as a minor accident.

"You lied to me, Dexter," said Rita. "I saw your car. It wasn't a fender bender—it was destroyed" ("Remains to be Seen," 4-2).

For, Rita, the most shocking discovery came a few days later when she discovered that Dexter had kept his old apartment the entire time that they had been married ("Dirty Harry," 4-5). Rita showed up at his place later that day and confronted Dexter, thinking that he was either using drugs again or having another affair. Dexter said, half aloud and half in narrative soliloquy, that he had "nothing to hide—except for the syringes, scalpels, and bone saw." Rita replied, "The most disturbing thing about your lying is that I'm beginning to see just how good you are at it" ("Dirty Harry").

Their dispute led to several rounds of couples therapy. In one of the sessions, Rita complained, "And when he does talk to me, it's lies all the time" ("If I Had a Hammer," 4-6). To make matters worse, Dexter got arrested for assaulting a policeman and became the second husband that Rita had to pick up from jail ("The Getaway," 4-12). To Rita, he seemed more and more like Paul in his abusive and deceptive tendencies. Their relationship remained tense until its tragic end, when she was murdered by the Trinity serial killer.

In her marriage to Paul, Rita lost control of the relationship due to his abusive tactics and felt powerless, as is true of any real-world battered wife. Her traumatic experiences caused post-traumatic stress disorder, and her subsequent emotional dysfunction rendered her an ideal candidate for Dexter's cold-hearted scheming. We may want to think that Dexter is better than Paul, or that he saved her from abuse. And it was true that Rita no longer bore any physical marks. But Dexter's manipulative, controlling ways proved to be just as damaging. The cycle repeats in fiction just as it so often does in the real world.

David Barber-Callaghan is a creative writing major at Vanderbilt University. His short stories and poems have been published in *Teen Ink* and elsewhere. Barber-Callaghan has long been involved with youth radio in Maine as a journalist, producer, engineer, and peer trainer, and his pieces have aired on national radio. He plays lead guitar in the band West End Detour. Summer finds him in Kamp Kohut, in Maine, where he serves as a counselor in radio communications.

Hailing from Ireland, **Nigel Barber** received his PhD in biopsychology from Hunter College, CUNY, and taught psychology at Bemidji State University and Birmingham Southern College. Using an innovative evolutionary approach to societal differences, Barber has authored over 50 academic publications. Books for general readers include *Why Parents Matter*, *The Science of Romance*, *Kindness in a Cruel World,* and *The Myth of Culture: Why We Need a Genuine Natural Science of Societies*. He lives in Alabama and blogs for PsychologyToday.com.

Admit it—you liked Lila more than Rita. You at least thought she was more intriguing. What was it about Rita that made her seem like such a nothing? Did you notice, though, how she grew into a more complex and psychologically interesting person over time? Why did she have to die, just as she was becoming less annoying? Tamara McClintock Greenberg proposes some brilliant answers to those questions that made me slap my head and ask, "Why didn't I think of that?"

DENIAL

AND RITA

Women, Power, and "Getting Caught"

TAMARA McCLINTOCK GREENBERG

*D*exter is a story of a serial killer with sociopathic tendencies (as he is not entirely void of feeling connected to others, as a true sociopath would be) whose main challenge is living in society while struggling to conceal both his destructive impulses and his acts of brutal murder. One of the "hooks" that draws us to and keeps us enmeshed in the series is the way we viewers are able to connect with Dexter Morgan. It keeps us watching and rooting, even for behaviors that most of us can't realistically identify with. Dexter's getting away with murder is something we become very invested in.

Though it might not seem obvious at first, Rita, Dexter's main love interest throughout most of the first four seasons, was also concerned with "getting away with it," at least in a psychological sense, as she often seemed to be trying to get away *from* something: her own aggressive impulses.

There is much that can be said about Rita. She, and her relationship with Dexter, sometimes seemed like just a prop to help Dexter hide behind the mask of normality that he wishes to portray. But the story of Rita herself was much more nuanced. We saw her develop from a battered woman to a confident wife and mother, all the while managing her own, though frequently repressed, anger at injustice. We saw her get mad, get even, and then emerge as a complicated woman who struggled with the traps and triumphs known to many women who are married and raising children. Even those viewers who thought of her as annoying cannot deny the significant changes she underwent. But Rita's success story is short-lived: at the end of season four, we learned that although Dexter has not yet gotten "caught," Rita did, with her untimely and gruesome murder.

Is Rita Really Unaware of the Dark Passenger? Her Motives

Rita, who was alternately whiny and naïve in the beginning of the series, developed into an assertive (some would say nagging) wife and mother over the first four seasons. While this description coaxed us into viewing Rita as a woman who had overcome considerable adversity and may have even caused us to feel sympathetic toward her, questions remained as to how much she was really in the dark about Dexter's actions. In fact, the juxtaposition of Dexter's aggression and Rita's denial of it are what made the dynamic between these two a fascinating aspect of the series. At times the couple seemed to have some aspect of connection, while at others merely seemed to be playing "house," with both of their characters appearing numb and only acting as if they were a family, as opposed to really being engaged in a more meaningful way.

In "Dexter" (1-1), Dexter remarked about Rita, "She's perfect because Rita is, in her own way, as damaged as me." Rita was introduced to us as having survived a violent relationship with her ex-husband Paul, a heroin addict. Her fantasy about Dexter was that she had found the "the one good truly decent man left on the planet" ("Crocodile," 1-2). Though Rita initially appeared weak and superficial, we saw glimpses of the woman she wanted to be and, in some aspects, would become. In the first season, she stole her neighbor's neglected dog and gave it to a needy family. In regard to her keeping her fruit trees in good health, she grinningly said, "I kill things" ("Popping Cherry," 1-3). Rita's clumsy, apologetic stance did seem to be masking a more hostile side, which perhaps made her more like Dexter than we initially thought.

And yet, it was easy to ignore her. Amid the other action in the first season, from the compelling Debra to the Ice Truck Killer, it was easy for Rita to fade into the background as we anticipated Dexter's next move. As the story of season one unfolded, with the identity of the Ice Truck Killer begging to be known and the horror of Dexter's childhood slowly being revealed, it was hard for Rita's story to compete in either excitement or pathos.

Perhaps we ignored Rita because Dexter did, too, using her only insofar as she supported his cover of normalcy. It wasn't until the second season that we learned more about Rita's own hostility and need for justice and her potential for destructiveness, as she became a major player in Paul's demise and gained both Dexter's attention and ours. When Rita found the shoe that substantiated Paul's claim that Dexter attacked him and shot him up with heroin, we saw glimpses of her darker side, as well as evidence that Rita understood how violent Dexter can be. Dexter did away with Paul (by sending him to jail) and Rita knew it, yet she protected Dexter. This suggested not only that Rita wanted to be rid of Paul, but also that the story of Dexter's true behavior may have substantiated her belief that, in him, she had found her savior: unlike Paul, Dexter would do anything to protect her and her children. But did she protect Dexter because she was in denial about him and was desperately clinging to her fantasy? Or was she relieved that she could vicariously stand up to Paul and have a hand in his demise?

Rita clearly thought Dexter was her knight in shining armor. But what did it mean that she chose a serial killer (albeit the Robin Hood of serial killers) to save her? Perhaps she was not as in the dark as she seemed. It was meaningful that she rarely questioned what Dexter was doing late at night; he always had an excuse such as "difficult case," or "new serial killer," and Rita accepted all explanations at face value and with minimal discussion. Yet Dexter is not a detective, but a blood spatter expert: late night forays are not often part of the job. Even when Rita did try to hold Dexter "accountable" it was with a story that was not really true, as when Rita convinced herself in season two that the true explanation behind his negligent and erratic behaviors was related to drug addiction. This story was one Rita knew well, and so it was likely easy to accept this narrative as opposed to doing the harder work of figuring out who Dexter really is. Another aspect of Dexter being a drug addict was that Rita had a new and clearly defined role as Dexter's savior, a role that let her feel powerful and valuable. She could then focus on the need to get and keep Dexter clean and sober, as she lovingly provided support.

I don't mean to suggest that Rita consciously knew Dexter is a serial killer. If Rita did know about Dexter's darkest behaviors, it was a knowledge that was deeply out of her awareness, allowing her to preserve her denial. But she knew enough about him that she should have realized that he is not as mild-mannered and harmless as he sometimes appears. Rita's denial of Dexter's violent drives served a dual purpose. By not knowing about him, she also did not have to know herself.

But Do We Like Her? Rita's Connection With Viewers

Despite the emerging complexities in the character of Rita, as well as the outstanding acting abilities of Julie Benz, in many ways, Rita was unlikable. Why? Rita's lack of self-awareness and denial of her own anger as well as other complex feelings make her difficult to connect with, especially when compared with the other strong women in the series (Debra, Lieutenant LaGuerta). Even the brief but powerful introduction of Lila, who briefly threatened Rita's turf as Dexter's confident but unstable sexual partner, is easier to understand, even if we couldn't relate to her wild and violent behaviors. Lila's manipulative and desperately clingy ways were revealed quickly and we understood her true motives and desires. In many ways, she was the *anti*-Rita. Though ultimately a villain, she was powerful and strong. She knew exactly what she wanted and would do anything to get it. In contrast, Rita seemed to "go along," and as long as events in her life corroborated her internal story that everything would be okay and that she had a protector, she seemed unusually chipper for a hard-working, single mom.

Rita did seem to be somewhat more forthright and honest about her feelings in season three. Rita displayed strength through her pregnancy, initially telling Dexter that she did not need him to be present in their baby's life. She told us, and Dexter, that she could go it alone, and did not want a marriage that wasn't sincere. However, when Dexter awkwardly mentioned (again) the apparent advantages of a marital merger to benefit their child, Rita—suffering from morning sickness—vomited in response. Her true feelings remained unclear. Was she really okay with not marrying Dexter? Or was she hoping that if she *appeared* strong, this would entice Dexter into chasing her? We didn't know, but more important, it was not clear that *Rita* knew.

It was in the ways that Rita didn't know herself that she was not quite as likable or as easy to connect with as the other women in the series. Most of the time, Rita denied her anger. A key exception to this was during her pregnancy, when Rita launched into angry tirades toward and in front of Dexter, her children, and her new friend, Silvia. In these moments, Rita was more likable, or at least more genuine. However, her denial was pervasive; she blamed these displays of aggression solely on "hormones," denying that they might have been reflective of true feelings. Yet, perhaps she had some awareness of something amiss when she said, "It's like I have this monster living inside of me and I don't know how to control it" ("The Damage a Man Can Do," 3-8). Of course, Rita might not have been talking about her vague awareness of her own aggression. Perhaps she was aware on some level that her child with Dexter may be equally as destructive as he is. But because Rita was so indirect and in the dark regarding her own feelings, and because she wanted so much to see things through rose-colored glasses, we couldn't know for sure.

Rita did not like to revisit past hurts. In the first three seasons of *Dexter* we saw her exhibit an impulse to move on quickly from every painful event that confronted her: Dexter's dishonesty, his relationship with Lila, his "addiction," his mysterious absence when she had abnormal bleeding during her pregnancy, and her secret and lie to Dexter about her first marriage. Rita's approach to life was to keep smiling, keep moving, and look ahead. And though I imagine that many of us can relate to the desire for everything to be okay, there was something quite unsatisfying about Rita's "head in the sand" approach. Though Rita's method of coping may have had some adaptive benefit, it left the viewer longing for more information. What was she really feeling? And who was Rita, really? What did she really want? Unfortunately, Rita's death prevented us from knowing the answers.

Rita, Women, and Aggression

Rita's history—spousal abuse, financial struggles, and the difficulties of being a single mother—is the kind of realistic but painful set of circumstances that we do not like to see on television. But as is often the case, how we respond to portrayals about women in popular culture media is complicated and contradictory; they reflect our own conflicting and internalized views of gender stereotypes. On the one hand, we like our female role models to be strong. For example, read any gossip magazine to see how we deny vulnerability in new mothers. We expect them to give birth, lose weight immediately, look gorgeous, and never mind sleep deprivation, the overwhelming demands of a newborn baby, or the depressive effects of postpartum hormones. On the other hand, women are not supposed to be too aggressive. The women in *Dexter* engage in aggressive behaviors only in ways that do not cause real harm. Debra Morgan gets away with being aggressive through her hilariously placed and graphic expletive comments when faced with any sort of frustration or vulnerability: she is good at speaking her mind when offended. But Debra's aggression is usually experienced as harmless. She blows up, spouts off, and things go back to normal. For example, when confronted by Batista about her undisclosed relationship with Anton, and how this might threaten her promotion to detective, Deborah fired back with a comment about how Batista met his girlfriend, one of their colleagues, while seeking a prostitute. But she then apologized, feeling guilty for her outburst. And perhaps Debra's aggression is not quite as unsettling because she never really finds happiness, meaning that we women never really envy her. We are constantly reminded of her vulnerability. Debra's love interests are evil, ineffective, or killed, and she is more often than not alone. In the end, we feel sorry for Debra, and whatever aggression she expresses is neutralized by sadness we feel for her circumstances.

In part, it is sociocultural ideas about women and aggression and what Rita's character pulled forth in us that made her difficult to connect with. Rita was in denial about Dexter's murderous impulses. However, as I have suggested, Rita might not have been as ignorant as she seemed. What did it mean that Rita might deny her own aggression by finding partners who seem to have no problem expressing theirs? One possibility is that Rita did not have to think about her own aggression, and its potential for destruction, as long as it was being acted out by those close to her (whether or not she was consciously aware of other's aggression). One can imagine Rita unconsciously believing that she is not the destructive one, he is. Indeed, aggression in others can serve this purpose for all of us—when others act out, it distracts us from our own troubling feelings.

Aggression is often suppressed in women. We women are not supposed to be aggressive and when we are it raises concerns, in ourselves and sometimes in others. Men are allowed to express these forceful instincts more freely. They can "kill," either literally (in war) or symbolically (in sports or in the boardroom), and as a culture, this is defined as more acceptable. I do not mean to relegate the difficulties in accepting aggression in women as issues that are present only in men, however. We women are often just as susceptible to feeling more at ease watching men engage in aggressive acts while expecting women to stand back and ignore their own impulses. By supporting Dexter, Rita was able to give expression to her own aggression through him.

Rita was not alone in this; most of us, male *and* female, are taught to avoid aggressive feelings and behavior. Aggression is ugly, and most of us want to avoid these messy, scary, and complicated feelings. We all split off our own truly aggressive impulses, so that we too can function. Dexter gets away with murder, and we need him to, so we can rest assured that someone is doing the dirty work for us. Dexter has to keep doing what he does, so we don't have to.

Final Analysis: Crime and Punishment

The issue of "getting caught" is central to *Dexter*. We viewers buy into Dexter's story and his rationale for his need for murder, and we want to see him get away with it. Why shouldn't we? After all, he is "taking out the trash," as it were, and Harry's Code does make sense to many of us, even if we couldn't truly imagine the pleasure that Dexter gets from torturing and killing his victims. The idea of getting caught or not getting caught, however, is complicated psychologically. Not getting caught for "crimes" has a deep resonance for many of us. In a paper in *Psychoanalytic Dialogues* in 2009, Adam Phillips describes quite vividly the psychological consequences of *not* getting punished for wrongdoing. When we are not punished, when we get away with it, no matter how minor the infraction, our perceived sins haunt us. (That is, at least, most of us. Dexter is unique and rare in that he does not seem to suffer psychologically [through guilt] from his crimes.) Perhaps Dexter's lack of punishment created a tension in the ongoing nature of the television series and some resolution was needed. But since Dexter is our hero, he can't get punished or caught, at least not yet. We need Dexter to live freely. But if punishment serves to restore some kind of homeostatic psychic function, as Adam Phillips suggests, then someone has to pay for Dexter's crimes. At the end of season four, that person was Rita.

Rita's murder raised all kinds of questions and observations. On some level it appeared that just as Rita became a more fully functioning and complex woman, she died. As one fan said to me, "Just when we were starting to like her, she gets killed." And while feminist ideas regarding killing off strong women are seductive, I am not sure that fills out the whole story here. It is true, Rita got stronger and then she died, but maybe this was a necessary sacrifice for the story. Personally, I am sad at the elimination of a great actress in this series, but if I am right about the psychological nature of *Dexter*—that someone *needs* to get caught and pay for Dexter's actions—I am glad that it was Rita and not Dexter.

Rita's death also serves another purpose: it reinforces our need for Dexter to be someone who not only can get away with it, but who seeks justice, even if it is in a perverse way. And narratively, having Harrison, Dexter's infant son, relive Dexter's own experience of being "born in blood" is compelling. It may also be that Dexter's character needs to be and is more interesting when alone.

Rita was not easy to connect with. As another viewer said to me, "Rita was getting annoying. I am glad they killed her off." But the question remains, was Rita annoying because she became stronger? Or was she annoying because of her entrenched need to deny aggression, and because of that, never seemed real to viewers? In the end, what matters most may be how her death contributed to Dexter's story. In life and on television, we all want to get away from destructive feelings. Dexter the man, and *Dexter*, the series, allows us—like Rita—that freedom.

Tamara McClintock Greenberg, PsyD, MS, is an associate clinical professor of psychiatry at the University of California, San Francisco. She is the author of *Psychodynamic Perspectives on Aging and Illness* and *The Psychological Impact of Acute and Chronic Illness*, and she currently writes for *Psychology Today* online and *The Huffington Post*. She teaches and speaks nationally on a wide variety of topics, including health psychology, the culture of Western medicine, psychotherapy, psychoanalytic psychology, and medical consultation. She is in private practice in San Francisco.

Dexter fans can easily identify the key characteristic that separates our hero from all those other serial murderers, who are just vile: Dexter aims to kill only those who deserve to die. Paul Wilson gives the issue a fresh and stunning twist. He puts Dexter and other serial killers together in one category, and considers them far less frightening than a category of normal people: those who fit no official clinical diagnosis yet calmly and systematically contribute to the death of thousands. There's more. Wilson argues that under similar circumstances, many of us would do the same thing. See what you think.

WHY PSYCHOPATHS LIKE DEXTER AREN'T REALLY ALL THAT BAD

PAUL WILSON

Psychopathic serial killers are ruthless executioners who stalk their prey and dispatch them, often by the most sadistic means. Their victims, by definition, number in the tens or, in extreme cases, even the hundreds. Dexter is a stellar example of the psychopathic serial killer. Like others of his ilk, he can be charming, insightful, and even soft and gentle at times. Similar to many killers with predatory inclinations, Dexter hides behind the respectable coat of family and work. But in common with his psychopathic brethren, he delights in ritualistically dissecting his victims and then keeping a trophy of his handiwork—in Dexter's case a small glass slide of their blood.

Despite their commonalities, Dexter does not quite fit entirely into the serial killer species. He is the Robin Hood of serial killers and is unlike some of the other villains in the show, motivated as they are by sexual thrills or desires to brutally dominate other human beings. The fictional psychopaths in the *Dexter* series have no aspirations to wipe the evil-doers off the planet. Dexter alone is cannibalistic in his pursuits he kills his own kind rather than seeking the marginalized or defenseless. These killers, who eventually ended up as Dexter's own victims, did not give a damn about the ideology of those they killed— only about their victims' physical attributes and how those characteristics fulfilled their murderers' dark and horrible fantasies.

What is different about Dexter is that he knows exactly who he is and what he has to do in life, because Harry equipped him with the mental tools necessary to control his urges. Most of the other serial killers, though their personalities are not as well-developed as Dexter's, certainly don't have his code of conduct. Take his long-lost brother Brian, for example, a guy without Dexter's sophistication or subtlety or, for that matter, sense of morality. Arthur Miller, too, had no code of honor, no mission to rid the world of undeserving killers. He murdered and murdered again and again because he enjoyed the dark mysterious pleasure of killing.

Despite the differences between Dexter and the other predatory violent psychopaths in the series, one key thing they have in common is that they generally know who they want as their victims—what age group, what physical or behavioral characteristics, what ethnicity. Sure, there may be the occasional psychopath (in the non-fictional realm) who kills anyone, regardless of their characteristics, but in my experience these people are rare. Psychopaths, almost by definition, are focused on achieving certain goals and are not persuaded by what others think or say.

Dexter and those portrayed in the series share one more fundamental feature. Narcissism—self-love if you like—is ingrained into their psyche. They don't play by the same rules as everybody else and they don't obey the expectations of others. They are the centers of their own universes, oblivious to the suffering they inflict; but this focus on self is distorted even further by their tendency toward grandiose ideas—feeling all-powerful and able to achieve everything they set their minds to—tinged with an overwhelming resentment of the world around them. Sadistic serial killers are not known to willingly obey the commands of others unless it serves their own self-centered pursuits.

Given their predilection to sadistic violence and their core of narcissism, you would think I would be diagnosing these psychopathic serial killers as the ultimate in "evil." But they aren't the ones I worry about when I go to sleep at night. I worry about those of us who are normal.

I don't mean people who just appear normal. After all, Harry showed Dexter how to hide his psychopathic tendencies and how to appear to be an ordinary person. Appearing "normal"—whatever normal may be—is undoubtedly part of the art of being a successful psychopath. (What Jeff Lindsay and the writers who developed the series have achieved, more than in perhaps any other fictional portrayal of psychopaths, is to create a character who blends the gory, clinical actions of a psychopath with the day-to-day activities of a normal person.) Like Dexter, Miller was a nondescript fellow who easily blended in with any crowd. He was a family man, church deacon, and community activist whose multiple activities conveniently disguised his violent and predatory nature, and which in turn masked an extremely violent serial killer responsible for at least sixty murders. No, it is the ordinary among us, or the potential that we all have to inflict carnage and physical violence on our fellow human beings, that bothers me more than the Dexters of this world.

Many so-called normal people show psychopathic tendencies on at least a few occasions during their lifetimes. Indeed,

I would go as far as to suggest that most of us have fantasized at least once about violently hurting, even killing, someone we dislike. Of course, unlike Dexter, we don't act out on these violent fantasies and, though Dexter might well call it hypocritical, we continue to both see ourselves and to be seen by others as normal law-abiding citizens. But this is not what concerns me.

There is a parallel group of killers, those involved in genocide, where the tally of victims usually numbers in the hundreds, thousands, or sometimes millions. Psychopaths, terrible as they are, are nowhere near as frightening as the war criminals and camp or prison commanders who exhibit no psychopathic traits but who conduct their killings as part of normal, everyday business.

There are many reasons for this appraisal but one of them is very personal. I have spent a great deal of time observing and contrasting both psychopaths like Dexter with people who commit major human rights abuses like genocide. Take, for example, a man by the name of Kaing Guek Eav, otherwise known as Duch, who I observed during the Cambodian genocide trials currently underway in Phnom Penh under the auspices of a joint U.N.-Cambodian government tribunal.

Some background to the tribunal is in order. During the reign of Pol Pot and the Khmer Rouge between 1975 and 1979, somewhere between two and three million people died as a result of mass murder, starvation, or disease. Although the numbers vary according to the expert consulted, the current Cambodian government puts the figure at three million.

Duch, who commanded a prison called Tuol Sleng, otherwise known as S-21, when Pol Pot was in power, presided over the deaths of anywhere between 12,000 and 14,000 men, women, and children. These people were incarcerated, horribly tortured, and finally executed. Only seven prisoners who entered the prison came out alive. Children were bayoneted, women had their babies cut from their wombs, and men were chained to the floor of their cells until they died of starvation or suffocated in their own excreta.

The torture was so gruesome and so prolonged that those who received it would eventually confess to anything that their torturers put to them. Peasants who had never been outside their villages in the backblocks of rural Cambodia would admit to being CIA agents trained in Washington to spy for the U.S.A. Others would agree with their tormentors' belief that they had plotted to murder Pol Pot or some of his inner cabinet when in reality they didn't have the faintest idea who Pol Pot or his inner cabinet were. Indeed, the victims of Duch's torturers would admit to almost anything just to stop the torture from continuing.

Some prisoners in S-21 would be tortured or executed simply because they wore clothes made in Europe, a sign of Western decadence, or just because they were teachers or professionals and not workers or peasants—considered the only people worthy of living in Pol Pot's new utopia. The Khmer Rouge regime determined that Cambodia was to become a pure communist paradise regardless of how many hundreds of thousands of people were exterminated in the process.

Most of those subjected to this horrible ritual of torture, confession, and then murder were of course not guilty of anything. But the confessions were dutifully recorded, their photographs taken before execution, and the files with their confessions and photos safely archived, a model of bureaucratic efficiency that would be the envy of many Western government departments.

Duch, as commander of S-21, presided over this terror and was proud of his skills in organizing such a complex operation as mass murder on such a grand scale. He was born in 1942 into a poor Cambodian family, but as a school pupil was soon noticed for his intelligence and his interest in scholarly activities. He was described as studious with a particular interest in mathematics but with no political inclinations. After graduating from school Duch taught mathematics at a college, and one of his pupils told an academic who studied Duch's life that he was renowned for "the precision of his lectures as if he were copying texts from his mind onto a board."

Despite his obsessive nature Duch was otherwise pretty ordinary in every sense of the word. He married, regularly left the S-21 prison every day and went back to his wife and family, and was apparently a good father. During his trial some of his former pupils gave evidence that he was a kindly man who often helped them with extra tuition or would offer assistance in other ways, as well.

If Dexter were ever to come to such a trial, we could imagine others testifying similarly to his character. He, too, has a family, works efficiently, and is accepted by his colleagues and the police as just a normal guy. The difference with Duch was that, rather than simply *appearing* normal, he really was normal without a trace of psychopathy or mental illness in him. We know this because Duch was subjected to quite a detailed psychiatric examination by two psychiatrists who were appointed by the International Tribunal to assess him.

What the psychiatrists noted in their assessment (and what I also observed when I sat in the courtroom watching Duch give his crisp and remarkably honest accounts of his time as commander of S-21) was that he was a very ordinary, almost mundane person. There was absolutely no sign of the psychopathic characteristics that we usually associate with serial killers or with other types of predators. Duch, for example, did not appear to have enjoyed the torture or the pain he or his colleagues inflicted on the inmates who had suffered so cruelly and for such prolonged periods of time. Yet, in contrast to Dexter, who masked his murderous behaviors behind his "normal" job, for Duch killing *was* his job.

Neither was there any great sexual satisfaction or a sense of power obtained from the taking of a human life. He was just doing his duty, a middle-manager in the Khmer Rouge genocidal regime, calmly ordering the deaths of thousands of people. Just like the vast majority of middle managers in a corporation or a government bureaucracy, Duch was trying to be as efficient as possible, carrying out his bosses' orders.

The psychiatrists who assessed him confidently ruled out psychopathy or sadism as motivating factors in his actions. They did note, though, that Duch was the sort of person who liked to conform to orders given by those he saw as his superiors and that he could be very angry toward those he saw as his enemies.

I agree with the observations of the court-appointed psychiatrists. Duch answered questions put to him by the judges and prosecutors with precision, using phrases like "based on my analysis" or "according to the documents." On the margins of files he had written notes like "did not confess" and in another "kill them all." He was business-like and ruthlessly efficient, if you like, but these attributes are hardly a sign of mental illness or any known personality disorder.

Of course, being precise, showing confidence, obeying authority, and even expressing anger toward those who you ideologically oppose are hardly confined to genocidal prison commanders or Rwandan machete-wielding Hutu mobs. Indeed, if anything people with these traits support the views of world-renowned psychologist Stanley Milgram. In his famous "obedience to authority" experiments, Milgram demonstrated how ordinary people obey commands leading to pain, even to death, given by those in authority. The psychologist's experiments found that university students and others were happy to administer electric shocks to volunteer subjects just because a white-coated professor told them to do so.

Duch was very much like that, too. Francois Bizot, French anthropologist and author of *The Gate*, and also one of the few to escape alive from S-21, was told by Duch that he did not especially like his job but that he was willing to do almost any-thing that his superiors asked of him in order to obtain their approval. Like other journalists or scholars who had witnessed or studied those engaged in genocide, Bizot believed that the crimes Duch carried out could have been carried out by thou-sands of others.

Duch is far from being an exception in terms of having strong conforming personality characteristics when others who have committed genocide are considered. Historian Zygmunt Bauman made a simple but devastatingly chilling observation in *Modernity and the Holocaust*. "The most frightening insight brought about by the Holocaust and what we learnt of its per-petrators," he noted, "was not the likelihood that this could be done to us but the idea that we could do it." As David Chan-dler, who wrote the definitive history of Duch in *Voices From S-21*, notes, "if the significance of S-21 (or the Holocaust for that matter) could be reduced to a single sentence Bauman's is the one."

Indeed, many of the senior Nazis who executed or impris-oned inmates had personalities not dissimilar to Duch. They were not monsters—just ordinary men, who thought they knew right from wrong. When Rudolf Hoess, commander of Auschwitz, was asked if he ever stole or enriched himself from inmates, he replied, "What sort of man do you think I am?" Like Duch, Hoess had his own sense of morality but a perverted one at that.

Admittedly both Duch and the Nazi commanders were hardly in "normal" situations, controlling as they did the lives of thousands of their captives during times of great conflict. And war and civil strife are unique environments that we know often increase the chances of occurrence of genocide and other human rights abuses. We can glimpse this potential in the after-math of crises like Hurricane Katrina, where business is not as usual and so people fill the void and make their own rules.

Milgram's subjects, who thought they had inflicted great pain on other student volunteers, were not under conditions of war. Yet they too were quite capable of inflicting enormous harm on others just because someone who they saw to be in a position of authority told them to do it. As Robert Jay Lifton, who wrote the *Nazi Doctors*, observed, "ordinary people can commit demonic acts." It is this feature, the so-called "banality of evil," that permeates most scholarly analyses of genocide.

Now let us return to Dexter and the other psychopaths in the series. Although Duch may have also focused on his mission of murder, he was unlike Dexter in one significant respect. Duch was infused with an ideological fervor and a desire to please Pol Pot—not only because he "followed orders" but also because he was, unlike in his early years, now filled with ideological zealotry, a burning desire to see the revolution succeed.

In contrast to Duch, Dexter has no one issuing him orders that he feels compelled to obey. He is very clear in his own mind about what he wants to do, and that is to kill people he believes deserve to be killed. It is true that he was well-socialized and trained by Harry, who helped him develop his own moral code. But he is too independent, too narcissistic, too much his own man, too focused on carrying out his mission a mission of only killing other psychopaths and killers to control. Even Harry would have found doing so impossible had he lived to change his mind about how he had trained his son. Sure Dexter is obsessed about killing, but this is a personal quest and not an ideological crusade. It is about him and his needs much more than it is about the people he kills.

Indeed, it is hard to imagine Dexter (or most other psychopaths) "hating" anybody. Hate, after all, is a strong emotion, and psychopaths are generally lacking in emotion. They are cold, calculating, goal-directed, and obsessed with pursuing their own gratifications. They have neither the temperament nor the desire to wallow in the hysteria that engulfs a mob determined to hack to death or stone or shoot those they wish to exterminate. Nor do they want to pursue a systematic policy of executing the ideological enemies of their group, because they do not identify with any group. Psychopaths are, in their own minds, well above the mob or, for that matter, functionaries like Duch or the Nazi commander Rudolph Hoess.

The same cannot be said about those whom we think are "normal" according to what we know about those who commit genocide. Duch was "normal" and followed orders because he blindly, or consciously, elected to believe in the Khmer Rouge and what they believed in. He was normal, too, in the sense that he dutifully followed orders he believed were necessary for the group's safety. Not only did he follow orders, but he dispensed the carrying out of his murderous plans to his band of deputies and foot soldiers. His behaviors were also normalized in the sense that he was chairman of the board at S-21. His work allowed him to belong. It made him part of society, not separate from it.

As for Dexter—is it conceivable that he would join in a deliberate campaign of massacre with a coterie of like-minded brethren or underlings? Dexter may well have liked seeing the blood drain out of his victims, but unlike those who signed up to the Cambodian strategy he does not want to kill just anyone. He enjoyed being able to share the kill with Miguel Prado, but as soon as Prado asked Dexter to help kill targets who did not fit Dexter's criteria (with the rationale that, if Dexter was his friend, he would kill them because Prado wanted him to), Dexter instead ended their partnership. Dexter's targets were special victims, ones who had clearly carried out horrific crimes, carefully selected, targeted, and then eliminated, just as the victims of most psychopaths are. His narcissism prevents him from working long-term with others.

Just this year we have seen what "normal" people can do when it comes to genocide. In Nigeria, at the beginning of March, 550 people were slaughtered in three villages. Some recounted to journalists how they killed families of Christians with machetes, knives, and cutlasses in a brutal act of sectarian retribution. The operation had been planned at least several days before by a local group hell-bent on death and destruction. One of the killers proudly told a reporter how he had set his victims' house on fire so that they would run outside. Then he killed two women and one man, first by beating them senseless with a stick and then stabbing them with a short knife.

It is difficult to embrace the scenario of being born in Nigeria or Nazi Germany or Cambodia or Rwanda or Sudan, and more difficult still to wonder if we, too, would have engaged in the mass murder that has occurred in those places. Perhaps some of us would not, have but I suspect most of us might have succumbed to the mob. Or contemplate the situation of being ordered to kill Jews in concentration camps like Belsen or Birkenau or Cambodians in a Khmer Rouge prison and ponder if it is possible to resist. Again, perhaps some of us would have, but many of us, normal as we are, would not.

Dexter and most other psychopaths, I would suggest, would be the category of persons least likely to engage in genocide. Maybe that is why when I go to bed at night I don't worry so much about the Dexters of this world. I worry instead about the rest of us.

Professor Paul Wilson is a criminologist and forensic psychologist at Bond University, Gold Coast, Australia. He is the author or co-author of over thirty books dealing with crime, forensics, and justice issues. Paul gives evidence in court, works on miscarriages of justice cases, and recently was appointed on the expert witness list to the International Criminal Court based in The Hague. His recent writings focus on wrongful convictions and persons involved in genocide.

How do they do it? How do the writers of Dexter *get millions of ordinary, non-murderous viewers to root for a killer? Then, once the episode is over and those everyday people start to look at themselves instead of the screen, how do they make sense of what just happened? How do they reconcile the people they believe themselves to be with the people who, just moments before, were cheering on a serial murderer?* Dexter *is an extraordinary show, but the psychological processes that guide us as we watch are stunningly ordinary.*

FASTER, DEXTER!

KILL! KILL!

MATTHEW E. JACOVINA, MATTHEW A. BEZDEK, JEFFREY E. FOY, WILLIAM G. WENZEL, AND RICHARD J. GERRIG

When *Dexter* premiered in 2006, millions of viewers found themselves in the unusual role of rooting for a serial killer to dispatch his victims. When reruns began airing on broadcast television, the advocacy group Parents Television Council condemned the show because it "compels viewers to empathize with a serial killer, to root for him to prevail, to hope he doesn't get discovered."[1] We believe that each of these claims is true for many viewers—which is exactly why they continue to watch. But how is *Dexter* able to convert so many otherwise law-abiding citizens into knowing accomplices

---

[1] Stelter, B., "Ahead of Dexter's Broadcast Debut, Critics Slam CBS for 'Celebrating Murder,'" 2008. http://mediadecoder.blogs.nytimes.com/2008/02/15/critics-slam-cbs-for-celebrating-murder/

to a psychopath's killing spree? We suggest that *Dexter* exploits viewers' ordinary psychological processes to yield extraordinary enthusiasm for Dexter's murderous exploits.

Rooting for Dexter in the Moment

People who watch *Dexter* often confess to experiencing a shiver of delight when he lands another victim: as an episode unfolds, viewers feel themselves applauding Dexter's continued success as a murderer. To be sure, people like to see bad guys get punished.[2] However, this general tendency does not sufficiently explain why people support Dexter's particular methods. We suggest that people support Dexter because the unfolding story draws them into his narrative world. When people are transported to narrative worlds, they often respond as if they were participants in the events.[3] In fact, one of the great pleasures of narrative experiences is to get drawn into the story in a way that allows this type of active participation. Through participation, viewers become absorbed in the world of *Dexter* and root for him to murder.[4] For many viewers, the rooting is almost literal: they will hear their inner voice generating what we call *participatory responses* that represent statements of how they wish Dexter to behave.

Let's consider a specific example. In the episode "Remains to Be Seen" (4-2), Dexter was recovering from a car accident. When Dexter's wife, Rita, hurried to visit him in the hospital,

---

[2] Sunstein, C. R., "Moral heuristics," *Behavioral and Brain Sciences*, Vol. 28, 2005.
[3] Gerrig, R. J. and M. E. Jacovina, "Reader participation in the experience of narrative," in B. H. Ross (Ed.), *The Psychology of Learning and Motivation*, Vol. 51, 2009.
[4] Allbritton, D. W. and R. J. Gerrig, "Participatory responses in prose understanding," *Journal of Memory and Language*, Vol. 30, 1991; see also Polichak, J. W., & R. J. Gerrig, "'Get up and win!': Participatory responses to narratives" in *Narrative Impact: Social and Cognitive Foundations*, 2002.

Dexter was preparing to leave. He lied to Rita about the severity of the situation, and said he had been cleared to go. Most *Dexter* viewers will likely find these events familiar from their own real-world experiences: on some occasions, those viewers may have downplayed the severity of an illness or injury so that others would not worry; on other occasions, they may have come to understand that they were on the receiving end when others understated their pain or discomfort. These real-world memories create a context for viewers to offer Dexter mental advice. They might hear themselves think, "Don't get Rita worried!" or, "Your lie won't work!" Viewers don't need to expend any particular effort to formulate these responses. The content of the narrative automatically evokes viewers' memories. Those memories, in turn, give rise to these instances of mental advice. Viewers' own life experiences enable them to encode participatory responses that often take the form of mental advice. Viewers think, "Your lie won't work!" in response to Dexter for exactly the same reasons, and with much the same ardor, as they would in comparable real-life situations.

Because Dexter is the main character, he is frequently the recipient of this mental advice. Viewers root for Dexter in the moment, as an episode unfolds, regularly embracing his goals. According to research on participatory responses, readers and viewers regularly root in favor of characters' goals.[5] Thus, viewers' automatic responses to *Dexter* parallel their responses to other stories (even though they would not support Dexter's goals in the real world). Consider a scene in "Finding Freebo" (3-2), in which Dexter killed the murderous Freebo by jabbing a knife into his neck. This kill was not business as usual for Dex-

---

[5] Rapp, D. N and R. J. Gerrig, "Readers' reality-driven and plot-driven analyses in narrative comprehension," *Memory & Cognition*, Vol. 30, 2002; Rapp, D. N. and R. J. Gerrig, "Predilections for narrative outcomes: The impact of story contexts and reader preferences," *Journal of Memory and Language*, Vol. 54, 2006.

ter: assistant district attorney Miguel Prado sat in his car out-side the place where Freebo had been staying. Miguel had been hunting Freebo because of his supposed part in the death of Miguel's brother, Oscar. It was unclear how Miguel would react to learning that Dexter had just killed Freebo. Before Dexter had finished disposing of his victim's body, Miguel searched through the house and then exited toward the detached garage in which Dexter had set up his kill room. Viewers were privy to Miguel's impending arrival before Dexter. As a result, many fans—familiar with the experience of trying not to be caught doing something they shouldn't be—probably found themselves feeling anxious and mentally or literally shouting, "Hurry up!" or, "Hide the body!"

Research on narratives has provided evidence that the par-ticular content of participatory responses affects how a story is processed. As a narrative unfolds, readers and viewers develop preferences for specific outcomes—the desire for the outcome is what drives their participatory responses. What is also notable about these preferences is that when outcomes match people's preferences, they find those outcomes easier to absorb than out-comes that do not match those preferences.[6] What makes the experience of *Dexter* unusual, of course, is that viewers appear to develop preferences in favor of outcomes that they should find reprehensible. As a result, even implausible outcomes—so long as they match viewers' preferences—become easier to accept in a story. This phenomenon might help explain why Dexter's mirac-ulous ability to avoid getting caught is readily accepted by many viewers. For example, at the end of season four, Dexter was with Trinity's family when the police raided their home. After hiding briefly, Dexter then joined the police search of the scene. Pre-sumably, Trinity's family did not report to the police that a man named Kyle Butler (Dexter's fake name) disappeared seconds

---

[6] Ibid.

before the raid began. Had they made this report, there likely would have been a frantic search for a man matching Dexter's description, after which Dexter may have come under heavy suspicion. The fact that none of these events transpired seems unlikely. But because most viewers were probably rooting for Dexter to escape suspicion, these viewers should have been less likely to question the plausibility of Dexter's stealthy evasion.

This does not mean that viewers always agree with everything Dexter does, however. Narrative researchers have also provided evidence that people participate in characters' decisions, providing judgments with respect to the wisdom of particular decisions. Readers more readily accept story outcomes that are consistent with the decisions they mentally advised the character to make.[7] Throughout the series, Dexter has to make important decisions about whom to kill, when to kill them, and how to complete the job. At the time of these decisions, viewers are able to offer their own advice. Rooting for Dexter ultimately means wanting a good outcome for him, but sometimes this means rooting against Dexter's decisions in the moment. By participating in Dexter's decisions, regardless of whether or not viewers agree with any particular decision, they become more invested in the outcome of the choices he makes. They are attending to each of Dexter's goals as if they were their own.

Perhaps one of the most poignant decisions Dexter had to make (and viewers had to participate in) was when the serial killer Trinity attempted suicide by leaping from the roof of an unfinished building, and Dexter caught his arm. Viewers probably weighed Dexter's options, just as he did. In fact, viewers were likely divided about the decision they preferred. Some may have offered the mental advice, "Let him die!" whereas others thought, "Save him!" (presumably so that Dexter could

---

[7] Jacovina, M. E. and R. J. Gerrig, "How readers experience characters' decisions," *Memory & Cognition*, in press.

later kill Trinity in a more satisfying way). The scene offered a perfect context in which viewers' individual participatory responses to Dexter's decision would determine how they experienced the future outcome of that decision. Viewers who root against Dexter's decision to save Trinity are not suddenly turning on Dexter: They are, in the moment, rooting against his decision because they feel it will not be to his benefit in the long term. In the last episode of season four, "The Getaway" (4-12), viewers discovered what was, ultimately, the most significant consequence of Dexter's decision to let Trinity live. During the final scene, viewers were struck with a sense of horror when Dexter opened the bathroom door and found his wife Rita soaking in a bathtub full of blood, while his newborn son sat in a pool of blood on the tile floor next to her. Viewers who urged Dexter to let Trinity complete his suicide probably felt a sense of, "I told you something terrible would happen! I knew it!" Viewers who supported Dexter's decision to let Trinity live may have felt an added sense of guilt for having urged Dexter to make the decision that led to the dreadful outcome. In that way, viewers' reactions to this horrific scene accrue added complexity as a consequence of their earlier responses to Dexter's decision.

In the moment, most viewers want Dexter to succeed—they quite literally want Dexter to get away with murder. Moreover, most viewers' automatic preference will be for Dexter to be successful in all the roles of his life, including being a step-dad and husband. Still, we emphasize that viewers' preferences arise from their own life experiences. Thus, not all viewers will have the same participatory responses. This section has described what we believe to be a *typical* response to watching *Dexter* in the moment. But what happens when each episode ends, and viewers begin to engage in reflection upon the fact that they've been rooting for a serial killer?

Reflecting on a Serial Killer

Let's suppose that, in the moment, most viewers' preferences are in favor of Dexter's particular form of justice. Is this stance morally acceptable? If we asked viewers whether it would be right for them to murder, even if they had strong reason to believe the person they were murdering was a serial killer, chances are they would respond that murder is usually wrong. Viewers would undoubtedly vary in how strongly they react to the question, but generally viewers have not been inspired by Dexter to go out and hunt down serial killers in the real world. Within the moral and aesthetic world of *Dexter*, viewers enjoy rooting for a murderer. However, Dexter's world is different from the viewers' world. When viewers are prompted to step back from the world of *Dexter*, they may readily acknowledge that Dexter is not acting morally. Of course, this analysis requires the type of careful reflection that isn't often possible in the heat of the moment. In fact, moral judgments are very much affected by the mental resources people have available as they make them.[8] When people are absorbed in an activity, they have fewer mental resources left over to engage in other activities. While watching Dexter, viewers are participating in the action of the show—giving mental advice, making judgments on characters' decisions—leaving fewer cognitive resources available for stepping back and evaluating the morality of the show. Thus, one interesting consequence of *Dexter* viewership is that people have to reconcile what they want (as evidenced by their responses in the moment) with what they believe they should let themselves want (upon reflection). In our experience, even after reflection,

---

[8] Greene, J. D., S. A. Morelli, K. Lowenberg, L. E. Nystrom, and J. D. Cohen, "Cognitive load selectively interferes with utilitarian moral judgment," *Cognition*, Vol. 107, 2008.

many viewers are able to continue to root for Dexter. How could this be the case?

We suspect that the shift from participation to reflection often results in a state that psychologists have labeled *cognitive dissonance*.[9] Cognitive dissonance occurs when people hold two conflicting ideas simultaneously. In a classic study of cognitive dissonance, participants first engaged in an unpleasant activity for an hour.[10] Afterward, the experimenter asked participants to tell another student that the experiment was fun and exciting in exchange for a monetary reward. When the participants complied, they were in a state of cognitive dissonance: they had experienced a boring task, but they had publicly claimed that the task was exciting with little justification (i.e., only a trivial reward). To alleviate this dissonance, participants in this condition changed their beliefs. In a follow-up interview, the participants who received only one dollar for misleading their peer rated the task as being more enjoyable than participants who received twenty dollars (the large reward provided enough justification so that a "white" lie caused little dissonance), and control participants who were not asked to mislead a peer at all (and thus did not experience dissonance).

This classic study demonstrates that when people experience cognitive dissonance, they often seek to reconcile the conflict by changing their beliefs. In the study, the obvious way in which participants could eliminate the dissonance was to report that they had enjoyed the (actually quite dull) task—to convince themselves that the task they had experienced was pleasant, and thus what they told the other students wasn't a lie. In more complex circumstances, people may reduce dissonance in any number of ways. Consider how people justify

---

[9] Festinger, L., *A Theory of Cognitive Dissonance,* 1957.
[10] Festinger, L. and J. M. Carlsmith, "Cognitive consequences of forced compliance," *Journal of Abnormal and Social Psychology,* Vol. 58, 1959.

smoking cigarettes in the face of evidence that the practice is deadly: they may anchor on their small number of daily cigarettes or an otherwise healthful life style to minimize their discomfort. People reason, "Smoking may be bad, but it isn't bad *for me.*"

Dexter provides an abundance of means by which viewers can reconcile their dissonance to conclude, in a sense, that serial killing isn't that bad *for Dexter.* To begin, there's Harry's Code. In the series, Dexter follows the rules that his father laid out to kill only serial killers who have escaped justice. For Dexter, this serves as a guideline to decrease his chances of getting caught by the police. By choosing to kill killers instead of innocent members of society, Dexter limits the possibility that his murders will be investigated in great detail. The presence of Harry's Code implies that Dexter's drive to kill arises from a noble sense of justice. But in fact, Dexter describes his killing as being a means to satisfy his Dark Passenger, or the deep-seated need to kill. Yet, for viewers, Harry's Code provides a means to justify rooting for a serial killer. Viewers can relish the righteous retribution when Dexter kills killers who have slipped through the cracks of the justice system. Furthermore, Dexter dispatches his victims in a highly sanitized fashion and is never lewd with them. In fact, in "Dex Takes a Holiday" (4-4), his victim, Zoey Kruger, who was wrapped in cellophane, asked if Dexter was going to rape her. Dexter laughed as if the question was ludicrous, and reassured her that, "No one is raping anyone!" (He then killed her.) Dexter's victims and methods provide viewers with an acceptable level of morality for them to root for Dexter to kill, even though Dexter himself does not share the viewer's lofty moral justifications. In addition, viewers may feel safe that if they were to meet Dexter in real life, they would have nothing to worry about as long as they themselves are not killers.

Several other factors also make it possible to reduce the dissonance of rooting for Dexter. Family and work complicate

Dexter's priorities. On the one hand, Dexter might feel he should spend time with the kids or fulfill his professional duties as blood spatter specialist, attending to each of those needs while keeping up "normal" appearances. On the other hand, his overarching goal is always about making his next kill. The nuances related to each of Dexter's priorities and the tension created by his having to manage them all simultaneously allow viewers to find nuances in their own responses to Dexter.

Dexter's relationships do more than complicate Dexter's life; they also make him a more sympathetic character, and add suspense to the show by putting Dexter in awkward positions as he tries to juggle his family, his job, and staying true to Harry's Code. When people sympathize with a character, they experience more suspense and prefer positive outcomes for the character.[11] His interactions with Rita in particular provide a specific means for viewers to identify with his character. Viewers in relationships have probably shared experiences similar to Dexter's, in which he wants to make his partner happy but is unsure of what to say to achieve that goal. Even though viewers don't share the cause of Dexter's frustration (i.e., an antisocial lack of emotions and a desire to avoid getting caught as a murderer), they can still identify with the situation and develop sympathy for Dexter. Because viewers sympathize with Dexter, they will support him and hope that he succeeds.

These are not the only options for Dexter viewers who seek to alleviate cognitive dissonance. Recall the demonstration that dissonance reduction often results in belief change: participants reported a dull task to have been (somewhat) enjoyable. Similarly, frequent *Dexter* viewers may lose access to aspects of the program that strike more casual viewers as problematic.

---

[11] Jose, P. E. and W. F. Brewer, "Development of story liking: Character identification, suspense, and outcome resolution," *Developmental Psychology*, Vol. 20, 1984.

Research in psychology suggests that people are more likely to remember information that is consistent with a particular choice (such as choosing to support Dexter's behavior) and may even distort information that is inconsistent with that choice.[12] Suppose *Dexter* viewers selectively remember information that is consistent with their choice (such as the fact that Dexter's actions stop serial killers). This memory bias should help make dissonant information inaccessible. Thus, the bias will reduce both viewers' cognitive dissonance and the possibility that they will feel regret about their choice. These same viewers might further reduce dissonance and regret by distorting memories about Dexter that are inconsistent with their support for him (viewers may conveniently gloss over the fact that Dexter kills to sate his thirst for murder). The net result should be that viewers find Dexter even more sympathetic. They may cease to experience dissonance between their responses to Dexter and real-world moral values they hold dear.

Of course, this dissonance-free state can endure only until *Dexter* provides new complications. In season four, Dexter killed Jonathan Farrow, a photographer who Dexter believed was a murderer. Viewers later find out that Jonathan Farrow was not a murderer and are once again faced with a conflict. In the past, has Dexter ever accidentally killed somebody else who was not a murderer? Will he do it again in the future? Does Dexter feel remorse?

The opening monologue of "Road Kill" (4-8) revealed that Dexter was experiencing a conflict about Farrow that mirrored the dissonance of the viewer, drawing a direct connection between Dexter and the viewer. Dexter tried to justify the murder by saying that accidents happen to everybody and that his victim was a bad person anyway. But in the end, Dexter

---

[12] Mather, M., E. Shafir, and M. K. Johnson, "Misremembrance of options past: Source monitoring and choice," *Psychological Science*, Vol. 11, 2000.

still appeared to feel guilty about having wrongfully murdered Farrow. Throughout the rest of the episode, viewers are given multiple opportunities to relate to and feel sympathy for Dexter. While Dexter was on a trip with Trinity, Dexter's neighbor Elliot flirted with Rita over a drink. During this flirtation, viewers probably felt upset that Dexter's family life was being threatened (even though, if viewers considered the big picture, it would be clear that Rita was probably better off being with Elliot, who is not a serial killer). During Dexter's trip, as we noted earlier, Trinity decided to commit suicide but was prevented from doing so by Dexter, who planned to kill him later on his own terms. As he witnessed Trinity's suicide attempt, Dexter wondered to himself if he'd also attempt suicide in the future because of his crimes, further revealing his own sense of guilt. By the end of the episode, Dexter admitted that he felt remorse and that he *might* be human instead of a monster, though he was still hesitant to actually call himself human. The viewer, who had been experiencing a conflict over Dexter's actions, was given the opportunity to once again see him as a sympathetic character. We cannot say exactly how viewers will reflect on this complex tangle of information. Our only certainty is that dissonance is a source of motivation—and viewers will, therefore, feel internal pressure to reconcile their real-world moral values with the sense that Dexter is, somehow, a hero.

Why would viewers choose to watch *Dexter* when it frequently requires them to experience and resolve dissonance? Dissonance is accompanied by a strong state of arousal.[13] Although this state is often an unpleasant experience, within the context of a narrative, it may actually be pleasurable. Unlike the participants in most cognitive dissonance studies, *Dexter* viewers are

---

[13] Zanna, M. P. and J. Cooper, "Dissonance and the pill: An attribution approach to studying the arousal properties of dissonance," *Journal of Personality and Social Psychology*, Vol. 29, 1974.

choosing to watch *Dexter* for entertainment. When people read for entertainment, higher levels of arousal are related to higher levels of enjoyment.[14] We assume that this pattern extends to viewers' experience of *Dexter*: Dissonance should lead to greater arousal and, as a consequence, greater enjoyment. We suggest that *Dexter* viewers take pleasure in the dissonance it provokes!

We have suggested that readers quite naturally get caught up in stories. They develop and then mentally express strong preferences for characters to achieve their goals. As each episode of *Dexter* unfolds, viewers actively participate in ways that often support Dexter's agenda. When viewers reflect upon their experiences, they might experience cognitive dissonance. However, the complexities of *Dexter's* unfolding story arcs provide fertile grounds for dissonance reduction while, at the same time, periodically calling attention to the contradiction between viewers' support for Dexter and their ordinary moral values. In "Dex Takes a Holiday," Dexter slyly reminded his victim that he "knows something about creating a narrative . . ." Although he is not speaking for the writers directly to the audience, he might as well have been.

When viewers root for Dexter, it may seem reprehensible because he is a murderer. However, the mental processes involved in rooting for Dexter are the same as those involved in processing most any story. Television series frequently cause dissonance by challenging viewers' perspectives on morally suspect behaviors such as adultery—and prompting viewers to identify with the characters committing these behaviors. However, the type of boundaries that *Dexter* crosses, and the high

---

[14] Nell, V., "The psychology of reading for pleasure: Needs and gratifications," *Reading Research Quarterly*, Vol. 23, 1988.

degree to which the show prompts viewers to identify with Dexter, makes *Dexter* a particularly compelling experience for viewers. Few shows have successfully gotten viewers to identify with a murderer! In that sense *Dexter* provides information to psychologists about how far viewers' sympathies can be stretched. Still, so long as viewers do not consider picking up Dexter's hobbies, they should feel free to indulge their own temporary "Dark Passenger" and root for Dexter to successfully collect his next trophy.

Matthew E. Jacovina, Matthew A. Bezdek, Jeffrey E. Foy, and William G. Wenzel are all graduate students at Stony Brook University where they conduct research under the direction of **Richard J. Gerrig**. Gerrig is a professor of psychology in the Experimental/Cognitive program. The laboratory's primary research focuses on readers' experiences of narrative worlds. The group considers both the basic cognitive psychological processes that enable readers to understand discourse and the broader consequences of readers' experiences of being transported to narrative worlds.

Even if you were faced with the most horrendous killers, you probably could not saw them apart in the dispassionate way that Dexter does. That's one of the characteristics that separates Dex from us ordinary folks, right? But what if you were a surgeon—wouldn't you have to learn to cut calmly into human flesh, day after day? What if, as part of your job, you had to remotely pilot unmanned predator drones into areas that could include civilians? Can we place some of these situations into morally or legally justified piles, or are there no neat piles? Are we all capable of wounding others without feeling pain ourselves? These are troubling thoughts to ponder, but hey, you're a Dexter *fan—you can take it!*

BEING

DEXTER MORGAN

CHRISTOPHER RYAN

> We had fed the heart on fantasies,
> The heart's grown brutal from the fare.
>
> —William Butler Yeats,
> "Meditations in Time of Civil War"

I've watched every episode of all four seasons of *Dexter*, but I've yet to tire of the opening title sequence, which won an Emmy in 2007.[1] Like the excellent title sequence of HBO's *Deadwood*, it's all about the beauty lurking within the disgusting, the horror coiled among the commonplace. (You can refresh yourself on it online; just search "Dexter: Morning Routine" on

---

[1] Rumor has it that this sequence will be changed for the fifth season.

YouTube. Check out *Deadwood*'s opening sequence while you're at it.)

The camera opens with a macro close-up of a mosquito, preparing to stab its proboscis into human skin. Dexter comes into focus—we see the mosquito is on his arm—and preemptively swats the bug. Self-defense. Thus, the very first thing viewers see is a "just murder." Already, in the first instants of the opening credits, we are behind Dexter's eyes, absorbed in his perspective.

What a perfect victim for drawing us to Dexter's side. Show me a person who doesn't take some pleasure in killing mosquitoes and I'll show you someone who hasn't spent much time in the tropics. I'm not much of an avenger myself, but I've passed many steamy nights in cheap guesthouse rooms from Bangkok to Belize stalking the little bastards, finding a kind of grim joy in every fresh bloodstain I left on those damp walls. Unlike most insects, whose offense is just a by-product of them going about their business, mosquitoes are coming after us, coming for our blood, while we sleep in the malarial night. Exterminate the brutes I say.

Then the music starts. One critic described it perfectly as "spicy Latin in flavor and creepy Gothic in sensibility . . . like the *Addams Family* theme played by a Mexican Day of the Dead band . . ."[2] The melody transmits an uneasy blend of warning and welcome.

The rest of the sequence takes us through Dexter's morning routine—though in his case, we might call it his morning "ritual," in that his obsessive compulsion for control allows for very little variation. He shaves (against the grain, of course); he cooks and chews his meaty, bleeding breakfast—complete with runny yolks and bright red ketchup splats on the plate (or is that Tabasco?); his juice is blood orange (the close focus makes

---

[2] http://blogs.suntimes.com/scanners/2007/10/dexter_putting_it_together.html

the pulp look like particularly nasty roadkill); the dental floss drawn taught around his finger visibly cuts off blood flow, while the lacing of his boots echoes the strangulation.

The sequence ends with Dexter staring straight into our eyes for an overlong moment, as if a confidence has been shared—a gift that might just seal our fate. Then, the locking of a door and a neighborly nod to us as he heads off for work.[3]

Beginning with these powerful images, both *Dexter* the program and Dexter the character challenge us to join in, if we dare, for a journey along the razor's edge separating the cleansing execution of moral justice from the sticky evil that oozes from unfeeling killing—and, frankly, from the unfeeling *depiction* of killing.[4]

Dexter is all about cold blood, inside and out. His day job is to decipher the messages violence leaves behind—gory hieroglyphs splattered on walls or pooling significantly on the carpet. His painstakingly catalogued trophies from his own kills, clinical blood samples on glass microscope slides, are secreted away in an air conditioner. What could be more cold-blooded than that?

Since we are privy to Dexter's darkest secrets, we know what nobody else does: this killer's ruthlessness is leavened by a limited range of feelings, unlike the stereotypical sociopath, who fakes everything. He feels real affection (for his sister, for Rita and her kids, for Angel) and respect (for FBI Special Agent

---

[3] Unshaven. How the hell did that happen? Could this really be just a screw-up by the creative team that spent hundreds of hours putting together this two-minute masterpiece of visual narrative? Or is it a sly suggestion that even the most rehearsed, picked-over, edited, highly controlled process can still contain a missed detail, an incriminating oversight that may one day lead the FBI to your door?

[4] The subtle celebration of justified murder can have tragic real-world consequences. Several self-proclaimed *Dexter*-based copycat murderers have come before the courts already. Who knows how many more never mentioned the program in their interrogations, or have yet to be caught?

Lundy, for Arthur), if not love. He yearns for male connection (with his brother, with Miguel, with Arthur). He wants so desperately to share his experience that one suspects much of the pleasure he takes in his pre-murder conversations with his victims is just this: he can confide in them in their last moments—they'll take his secret to their watery grave, and soon. He can finally, briefly share the truth about who he *really* is. But of course, these feelings that bring him closest to his humanity represent the greatest threat to his performance and continued success in fulfilling his "heroic" destiny: ridding the world of those who brutalize the innocent.

And we do want him to fulfill this destiny, don't we? Part of the genius of the program is that by sharing Dexter's secret life with us in all its surface normalcy and profound justifications, we are emotionally—and even intellectually—aligned with this cold-blooded killer's view of the world. Miami *is* a safer place because of what he's doing—even if an innocent person occasionally gets offed in the process. Knowing what we do, both about the criminal underworld and about Dexter's traumatic past, we accept his perverse hungers as the price of justice, cheering him on as he battles "real" evil.

Tragically orphaned as a young boy, he was raised by kind-hearted adults who tried, often unsuccessfully, to understand the strange child he was. Gradually, it dawned on him, too, that he was different from everyone else and somehow disconnected from the source of his deepest, essential identity. But with his pain and isolation came unique abilities. His life would be all about learning to use these abilities to defend common, decent folk against those who would do them harm or, failing that, to seek revenge against those who already had harmed the innocent.

This is Dexter's story, of course, but it's a biography shared by Superman, Batman, and Spider-Man: the holy trinity of American superheroes.

Spider-Man has his webs, Superman his flight, and Batman his high-tech know-how. What's Dexter's superhero ability? Discipline. Obsessive and absolute, the "Dark Defender" must live by Harry's Code, because he knows that any deviation from the strict moral code Harry taught him can only result in disaster—for himself and the innocent civilians he loves, in his own reptilian way.

Dexter's well-intentioned cultivation of a disciplined numbness to others' pain isn't unique—or even unusual. A surgeon cuts into living human bodies, week after week, until she feels nothing at all anymore. It's just work. It's not a person under her scalpel so much as an object, a thorax, a liver. If she felt the trauma and horror most of us would feel at slicing into a living human being, she would be useless in the O.R. and lives that could have been saved would be lost. An essential part of a surgeon's psychological structure and training involves the cultivation of this ability to *not* feel what "normal" people feel deeply and immediately. Ask any doctor about that first experience with cadavers in medical school. She'll tell you about the joking, the nicknames the students give the bodies, the rituals needed to cultivate functional numbness.

In their 2007 book about post-traumatic stress disorder in veterans of recent wars, *Haunted by Combat*, psychologists Daryl S. Paulson and Stanley Krippner describe PTSD as "a condition that results from experiencing (or witnessing) life-threatening events that extend beyond one's coping capacity, emotional resources, and/or existential world view." Many first-year medical students work hard to extend their coping capacities and worldview in order to accommodate the presence of the dying and the dead. Adults have a fighting chance of finding their way through these sorts of traumas with their psyches intact—maybe even strengthened by their experience.[5] A child like Dexter was, locked in the bloody container with his mother's body for days, would have no such capacities or existential worldview to help him overcome such an experience. But the developing consciousness demands integration, so Dexter embraced his horrific experience, making the blood, the death, and the resulting numbness core parts of his being. Like a physician or nurse, Dexter has found a way to help alleviate others' pain by leveraging his own inability to feel it.

Should Dexter ever get caught and face trial, his defense attorney might consider arguing that his client was like a well-intentioned surgeon operating on the social body of Miami, removing malignant tumors, cutting away infected tissue, clearing blocked arteries. Yes, pain was involved, and sometimes unintended death as well. But even the best surgeons lose patients sometimes, and overall, Dexter's is a positive effect on society, right?

No? Why not? Do you object to the illegality of his dark campaign? Do you hold that we need strict, transparent rules regulating those who have the power and authority to kill? Or are you perhaps unwilling to accept the sacrifice of an occasional innocent bystander in this generally righteous process? If you're waiting for the police to catch the murderers first, remember that by definition "serial killers" keep getting away with it. The police have had their chances. If Dexter doesn't stop these monsters, who will? And when?

---

[5] But many don't. A recent study by the Veterans Administration found that there are an average of 950 suicide attempts *each month* by veterans who are receiving treatment from the VA. The same study found that eighteen veterans kill themselves every day in the United States. http://www.navytimes.com/news/2010/04/military_veterans_suicide_042210w

It's not just surgeons and soldiers who turn not-feeling to their professional advantage. We all do, in one way or another. In the mid-1980s, I twice hitchhiked from my preppy college in upstate New York to Alaska, looking for adventure and work in salmon canneries to finance the trip. I found both. The first summer, I got hired at Kenai Packers, the best place for that sort of work in Kenai. Unfortunately, I was assigned to the worst position in the whole place: slime-monkeys, they called us. At the time, I was, I cringe to admit, an over-sensitive, pedantic, vegetarian poetry student (who else carries a copy of D. H. Lawrence's collected verse while hitchhiking through the Yukon?).

A couple of weeks before, I'd found myself unable to bash a salmon's head against the rocks when we'd caught one while camping along a remote river. But after half an hour on that slime-line, gutting, beheading, and slicing fins from fish after fish as they came down the conveyor belt, all feeling had gone—from my frozen fingers to my overwhelmed conscience. I went on gutting fish eighteen hours a day, seven days a week, until there were no more fish to gut. By then (about six weeks later), any random jumble of shapes (a sleeping bag crumpled in the tent, the folds of someone's sweater, clouds converging in the sky) looked like fish guts to me. Whatever was beautiful and sacred in a salmon was lost to me, forever. (No sushi for me!)

But there's nothing *evil* in that, is there? They're just fish, after all. Similarly, people working in slaughterhouses mechanistically ripping the guts out of pigs, cows, chickens, and lambs occasionally remind themselves that these are—or were—"just" animals. And laboratory workers smearing shampoo into kittens' eyes or studying how much social isolation it takes to kill infant primates no doubt murmur the same self-justifying mantra as they search for sleep at night.

Evil is like pornography: impossible to define, but we know it when we see it. Don't we?

———

A recent text[6] on forensic psychology outlines four motivational systems that inspire serial killers:

1. *Visionary* killers have just lost it. They're convinced God, Satan, the neighbor's dog, or The Beatles are telling them to kill, and really, who's gonna argue with The Beatles?
2. *Hedonistic* types get off on the killing, normally in one of three ways:
   * lust (the torture excites them sexually),
   * thrill (they do it for the adrenaline rush), and
   * comfort (they do it for the money).
3. *Power/control* types are drawn by the ability to flick the switch from life to death.
4. And lastly, we have Dexter's motivational type: *mission-oriented*. Mission-oriented killers see themselves as making the world a better place by eliminating certain types of people: prostitutes, blacks, savages, heathens, homosexuals, Catholics, Jews, Armenians, Hutus, Tutsis, infidels, terrorists . . . the enemy.

What is Dexter's mission, then? To eliminate those "who deserve it." His Code is designed to prevent mistakes, much as the legal system is designed to avoid the execution of innocent convicts. But our legal system is as fallible as Harry's Code. The Innocence Project, a legal organization using DNA testing to uncover wrongful convictions, has exonerated 252 people since

———

[6] Bartol, C. R. and A. M. Bartol, *Introduction to Forensic Psychology: Research and Application*, 2008.

1989. On average, these innocent men spent thirteen years in prison. Seventeen of them were on death row.[7]

"Mistakes," as they say, "were made."

But a few hundred innocent men in prison is nothing compared to the so-called "collateral damage" we willingly accept in what we persist in calling "war," though war is rarely formally declared any more these days.

In *Blackwater*, his explosive exposé of one of the mercenary armies employed by the United States in Iraq, journalist Jeremy Scahill documents the deaths of scores of innocent Iraqi civilians at the hands of trigger-happy thugs for hire. But these represent just a tiny fraction of the overall civilian death toll in the latest Iraq war and occupation by U.S. forces, totaling well over 95,000.[8]

And the beat goes on. Drone attacks, coordinated by Blackwater employees (now renamed "Xe"), the Air Force, and the CIA have killed scores, if not hundreds, more innocent civilians in Afghanistan and Pakistan, a country with which the U.S. is not even at war. Today, as I write this, *The New York Times* is reporting that, "American troops raked a large passenger bus with gunfire near Kandahar . . . killing and wounding civilians . . ." Let's face it: we're more than willing to accept the sacrifice of innocent civilians in pursuit of our mission.

And what is our mission? Just like Dexter's, it is to eliminate those who seem to "deserve it."

———————

"But Dexter is a criminal," some will say. Yes, I suppose he is. But a deeper look suggests that we live in an era in which the relevant legal lines are drawn in shifting sand. For example, what is the legal status of the drone attacks in Pakistan and Yemen I

———————

[7] www.innocenceproject.org
[8] http://www.iraqbodycount.org

mentioned above? We are not at war with these countries formally. These governments have not officially allowed or invited these attacks. In recent testimony before Congress, David Glazier, a former Navy officer and current law professor, argued that the CIA's drone pilots are "liable to prosecution . . . for any injuries, deaths or property damage they cause." Additionally, Glazier argued that "these CIA officers as well as any higher-level government officials who have authorized or directed their attacks are committing war crimes."[9] U.S. drone and missile attacks taking place on foreign territory are illegal acts of aggression and every victim—innocent or not—has been murdered without trial by Americans.

I'm just saying.

The Iraqi government expelled Blackwater from the country because of the widespread illegality of their actions there, as documented by Scahill and others. Under the Bush administration, hundreds of men and boys as young as twelve were illegally detained, flown to third countries for interrogation (often including torture), and then warehoused at Guantanamo Bay, Cuba, with no legal basis ever having been established for any of this. Colonel Lawrence Wilkerson, who served as chief of staff to Secretary of State Colin Powell during the Bush administration, has recently stated that top White House officials knew full well that most of those being held at Guantanamo were innocent of any crime. Referring to Vice President Cheney, Wilkerson wrote, "He had absolutely no concern that the vast majority of Guantánamo detainees were innocent . . . If hundreds of innocent individuals had to suffer in order to detain a handful of hardcore terrorists, so be it."[10]

---

[9] http://www.wired.com/dangerroom/2010/04/drone-pilots-could-be-tried-for-war-crimes-law-prof-says

[10] http://www.timesonline.co.uk/tol/news/world/us_and_americas/article7092435.ece

Even Dexter, a serial killer, holds himself to a higher moral standard than that.

Lest you think I'm being politically partisan, let's not forget to mention that President Obama has reportedly signed off on plans to assassinate an American citizen living in Yemen, without due process of any kind.[11] This is far from an aberration in current American activities around the world. Independent journalist and constitutional scholar Glenn Greenwald has documented the many ways in which the Obama administration has simply continued many of the blatantly illegal practices begun under the previous administration, even as attempts to investigate or prosecute those who authorized them in the first place are obstructed by Obama appointees.[12] Sorry to harsh your buzz, but we *are* talking about murder, after all.

I've never made it through an entire episode of *24*. A few minutes of Jack Bauer's sneering snarl is enough to break my resolve. Everyone breaks eventually, you know. The unabashed celebration of torturing foreign "terrorists" feels too much like brainwashing to me. One of the show's co-creators, Cyrus Nowrasteh, whose father was an advisor to the torture-happy Shah of Iran,[13] explained the show's Cheney-esque rationale to Jane Mayer of *The New Yorker*: "Every American wishes we had someone out

---

[11] http://www.nytimes.com/2010/04/07/world/middleeast/07yemen.html?scp=5&sq=yemen%20assassinate&st=cse

[12] http://www.salon.com/news/opinion/glenn_greenwald/index.html

[13] The Shah was installed by the CIA in 1953 after Iran's first democratically elected government was overthrown in "Operation Ajax." The Shah's U.S. trained secret police, the SAVAK, were notorious for their brutal torture of citizens, which propelled the Islamic Revolution of 1979, which propelled the rise of Islamic fundamentalism in the Middle East, which fueled anti-American sentiment, and so on, all the way back around to *24*.

there quietly taking care of business," he said. "It's a deep, dark ugly world out there . . . It would be nice to have a secret government that can get the answers and take care of business—even kill people. Jack Bauer fulfills that fantasy."

But of course, this isn't a "fantasy" so much as an irrational, yet emotionally satisfying, justification for a reality that was, until very recently, considered criminal by all "civilized" nations. In this, as in so many other parts of American life, the televised fantasy prepares the public to accept radical reconfigurations of reality. Mayer points out that before the attacks of September 11, "fewer than four acts of torture appeared on prime-time television each year," but that, "now there are more than a hundred." Perhaps even more significant is the fact that pre-9/11, the torturers were almost always the bad guys. But these days, it's the "good guys" who are pulling out fingernails.[14]

Ubiquitous Fox commentator and right-wing radio host Laura Ingraham cites the popularity of 24 as indicating political assent to America's discarding of decades of international law prohibiting torture, noting that, "[People] love Jack Bauer. In my mind, that's as close to a national referendum that it's O.K. to use tough tactics against high-level al Qaeda operatives as we're going to get." Personally, she said, she found it "soothing to see Jack Bauer torture these terrorists."

What sort of person finds it "soothing" to watch someone being tortured?

If Americans are using their TV remotes to cast virtual votes assenting to the torture of suspected terrorists, that's not the only sort of remote action we're taking. This year, for the first time ever, the Air Force is buying more unmanned drone aircraft than conventional fighters and bombers. Many of the drones flying over Afghanistan, Pakistan, Yemen, and Somalia

---

[14] http://www.newyorker.com/reporting/2007/02/19/070219fa_fact_mayer?currentPage=all#ixzz0lAnmCd6h

are piloted by men sitting in front of computer screens at Creech Air Force base, about halfway between Las Vegas and Death Valley. One of these men, Lt. Col. Gough, described his bifurcated life to journalist Lara Logan: "To go and work and do bad things to bad people . . . and then when I go home and I go to church and try to be a productive member of society, those don't necessarily mesh well."[15]

No, they don't. Unless you're a psychopath, of course. And even then, it can be tricky. Dexter has often found it difficult to juggle picking the kids up at school, remembering to get diapers on the way home from work, and disposing of the body he only had time to partially dismember the night before. There just aren't enough hours in the day!

––––––––

In summation, I'm afraid I don't have any grand conclusions to offer. I'm not going to be able to wrap this up neatly, like one of Dexter's tightly packaged victims. All I know is that the numbness to others' pain, the anti-empathy that allows Dexter to dispassionately kill people—that *condemns* Dexter to kill other people—is something we all share, to an increasing degree. It's a numbness that spreads in us as we progressively disengage from tangible life and death in favor of the virtual. It's not just an issue for those of us guiding drones over distant deserts. Killing and torturing "bad guys"—even when we're not sure we've got the right ones—is becoming, somehow, ever more soothing to us all.

––––––––

[15] http://www.cbsnews.com/stories/2009/05/08/60minutes/main5001439.shtml ?tag=contentMain;contentBody

Christopher Ryan, PhD, is a psychologist. He is co-author (with Cacilda Jethá, MD) of *Sex at Dawn: The Prehistoric Origins of Modern Sexuality* (sexatdawn.com). He blogs at *Psychology Today* (blogs.psychologytoday.com/blog/sex-dawn) and at Huffington Post (huffingtonpost.com/christopher-ryan).

The Psychology of The Simpsons
D'oh
EDITED BY ALAN BROWN, PHD, AND CHRIS LOGAN

Psychologists turn their attention to "The Simpsons," one of America's most popular and beloved shows, in these essays that explore the function and dysfunctions of the show's characters.

9781932100709 • TRADE PAPERBACK • $17.95 US/$19.95 CAN • MARCH 2006

The Psychology of Harry Potter
An Unauthorized Examination of the Boy Who Lived
EDITED BY NEIL MULHOLLAND, PHD

Harry Potter has provided a portal to the wizarding world for millions of readers, but an examination of Harry, his friends and his enemies will take us on yet another journey: through the Muggle (and wizard!) mind.

9781932100884 • TRADE PAPERBACK • $17.95 US/$19.95 CAN • MAY 2007

The Psychology of Survivor
Leading Psychologists Take an Unauthorized Look at the Most Elaborate Psychological Experiment Ever Conducted ... Survivor!
EDITED BY RICHARD J. GERRIG, PHD

From situational ethics to tribal loyalties, from stress and body image to loneliness and family structures, *The Psychology of Survivor* is a broad look at cutting-edge psychological issues viewed through the lens of "Survivor."

9781933771052 • TRADE PAPERBACK • $17.95 US/$19.95 CAN • AUGUST 2007

The Psychology of Joss Whedon
An Unauthorized Exploration of Buffy, Angel and Firefly
EDITED BY JOY DAVIDSON, PHD

Revisit the worlds of Joss Whedon ... with trained psychologists at your side. What are the psychological effects of constantly fighting for your life? Why is neuroscience the Whedonverse's most terrifying villain? How can watching Joss' shows help you take on your own psychological issues?

9781933771250 • TRADE PAPERBACK • $17.95 US/$19.95 CAN • DECEMBER 2007

The Psychology of Superheroes
An Unauthorized Exploration
EDITED BY ROBIN S. ROSENBERG, PHD

In *The Psychology of Superheroes*, almost two dozen psychologists get into the heads of today's most popular and intriguing superheroes.

9781933771311 • TRADE PAPERBACK • $17.95 US/$19.95 CAN • MARCH 2008